PHILOSOPHY AND EDUCATION
An Introduction

PHILOSOPHY
AND
EDUCATION

An Introduction

by

LOUIS ARNAUD REID, M.A., Ph.D., D.Litt.

*Formerly Professor of Philosophy of Education
in the University of London*

HEINEMANN

LONDON

Heinemann Educational Books Ltd

LONDON EDINBURGH MELBOURNE AUCKLAND TORONTO
SINGAPORE HONG KONG KUALA LUMPUR
NAIROBI IBADAN JOHANNESBURG
LUSAKA NEW DELHI

ISBN 0 435 80750 1

© LOUIS ARNAUD REID 1962
First published 1962
Reprinted 1962, 1964, 1965,
1966, 1968, 1971, 1974

Published by
Heinemann Educational Books Ltd
48 Charles Street, London W1X 8AH
Printed Offset Litho and bound in Great Britain by
Cox & Wyman Ltd, London, Fakenham and Reading

Contents

PART TWO

Acknowledgement

I wish to acknowledge, with grateful thanks, the help of a number of my colleagues in my revisions of this book. My wife has read the whole more than once, and has helped me greatly with positive suggestions as well as with criticisms. Mr A. C. F. Beales, Mr K. Neuberg and Professor Niblett have all read me with sympathy and critical acumen, and Mr P. H. Hirst has read the proofs. I have made many cuts and have rewritten many passages after pondering their wise advice. Again, as I indicate in the Introductory Note, the book has been hammered out over a number of years during which there has been constant discussion with teachers of experience studying education at an advanced level. It is impossible to estimate all that has been gained by me through these various exchanges; I only know that the gain has been great, and that I want here to acknowledge my debts.

L. A. R., 1962.

To my students
of sixty nations

Introductory Note

This book is addressed to students of education of all kinds and at all stages—whether they be in training, or studying at an advanced level, or are continuing students who are themselves lecturers in departments of education or training colleges.

The term 'philosophy of education' (or indeed the term 'philosophy' itself) has, in popular use, the vaguest and loosest of meanings. At one extreme, it suggests almost any string of generalities or platitudes. Anyone, it seems, who makes broad statements about education, is 'philosophising', and everyone has his own 'philosophy'. This use is, of course, poles apart from that of the professionally trained philosopher, who means by 'philosophy' (at least) a long and difficult discipline of analytical and perhaps constructive logical thinking. One of the radical troubles about educational thinking—in England at any rate—is that philosophical ways of questioning have so little impact (practically none) upon the ordinary university student, and therefore upon students who later become teachers and perhaps lecturers in education. Teachers and lecturers in education have not for the most part—through no fault of their own—even an elementary philosophical equipment to help them ask, much less to answer, the basic philosophical questions about education in any ordered way; they have to make do as best they can with what they have got.

This has affected philosophical writing about education in England. Apart from one or two textbooks, introductions, collections of essays, almost nothing about education has been written by professional philosophers in England for many years. Further, the danger is that when philosophers do write about education, they tend to look at it as spectators from the outside. For example, the American Yearbook of Education, *Modern Philosophies and Education*[1] consists of a series of essays by professional philosophers who work out the implications for education of various 'philosophies'—realism, idealism, etc. This has a somewhat artificial air. If one believes (as I do and shall try to

---

[1] The Fifty-fourth Yearbook of the National Society for the Study of Education, Part I. Ed. Nelson B. Henry (University of Chicago Press, 1955).

illustrate) that the philosophical thinking about education which is relevant for teachers must arise from intellectual challenges within the experience of education and teaching themselves, then there must be a constant coming and going between educational experience and philosophical thinking about it. This thinking may be rough and ready; it does not issue in smooth self-contained finished philosophical doctrine, but it is at least alive and challenging, a going concern which is continually giving rise to further thoughtful questioning. I do not of course mean that the philosopher who writes about education is without philosophical presuppositions. He has a point of view, his own method of approach, and he does try to relate the questions which arise out of educational experience to the framework of his general philosophy. But his daily learning through educational experience (which includes, most importantly, what he is learning all the time from listening carefully to the conversations of his teaching colleagues) is a healthy empirical corrective to too-vague generalization. Much of the time, philosophical thinking about education has to detach itself, in order to gain perspective and objectivity, from the scene of action in the classroom; philosophy of education must often discuss philosophy rather than education specifically. But its *raison d'être*, its justification, finally lies in its relevance, in its illumination of the questions which arise out of educational practice.

This book is not a textbook—if that means a brief comprehensive survey of a whole field. It is an introduction, through discussion of a few questions basic to philosophy of education. It is meant to show by example certain ways of asking questions, and ways of attempting to give reasoned answers to them. It offers, incidentally, some tentative answers; it presents unashamedly a point of view as well as a method.

The questions have been selected (at least in Part I) in the course of teaching philosophy of education, both to students in 'training' for the teaching profession and to older teachers, some of long experience. (Here I acknowledge with deep gratitude the continually increasing debt which I owe to the shared experience of these teachers, in private and group conversations.) They are questions which arise, in different forms, again and again, and answers to them seem to be presuppositions in all other thinking about education.

There is a certain logical order in the arrangement, which I shall now outline in the rest of this Note.

If philosophy of education is to justify its inclusion as a subject in a short professional course for intending teachers, it must (as I have said), be relevant to education and teaching. But is philosophy relevant? Does it help? This can be, and is, denied for a number of reasons, one of which is a contemporary view of philosophy which holds that it is not the business of philosophy to deal normatively with questions about life, man, moral standards—and, by implication, about these and similar questions as they arise in the context of education. If we are to proceed at all, therefore, we have to begin by asking what philosophy is, its purposes and scope, whether there is a *prima facie* case for its relevance to education. This is discussed in Part I, Chapter I.

Next (Chapter II), education is a purposive activity, the direction and shape of which are determined by human beliefs. Some of these beliefs are quite deep-seated—e.g. about the nature of man (and therefore of children), about religion, about learning and knowing. But implied in all of these and most important of all are judgments of *value*, of what it is good, or not good, to do in education, of what is important, or unimportant. If the teacher is to approach his work intelligently, he ought to be as aware as possible of the assumptions he is making and of the effects which they may have upon what he does. If not, he is a blind leader. Particularly he ought to be aware of his 'values', which of them he sets above others, and why. These considerations inevitably lead to questions about standards, about the key-ideas by which men rule their lives and their educational policies, the ideas which shape and form everything else. How does one think of these things? Are they just a matter of personal or social feeling? How far can they be justified rationally? Are our basic educational purposes defensible upon a basis of reason? How does one make right decisions in particular circumstances? (Chapters III, IV, V).

The last question has a relevance to education. Classroom situations vary; they are very individual; the teacher has to be taking practical decisions all the time. What bearing can the above apparently remote academic considerations have upon the practical daily work of the teacher? Is this general thinking really at all relevant to down-to-earth doing? This is a very difficult and important question—and a very topical one, since criticism of the theoretical studies of teachers in training is persistent.

Chapter VI, therefore, scrutinizes the idea of the 'application' of theory to practice in education, and finds that it is a much subtler idea than is implied by many of the scurrilous attacks on 'useless' professional training which spill over the pages of educational newspapers. The question about 'applicability' is not simple, and the answer is not simple: but this does not imply that there is not an answer. Thinking about education may do something to a person which subtly modifies his vision and perspective, changing and illuminating his action as a teacher.

Chapters VII and VIII deal with the personal self and its freedom. Educational writers, at any rate in England and America, continually stress the importance of the growth and development of persons and of their freedom. This raises the difficult question of the nature of a person and of the ways in which persons can be said to be free or determined.

Part II continues the inquiry but with stress on perhaps more directly practical matters. Chapter IX deals with the idea of discipline, with a discussion of incentives (competition, rewards) and sanctions. The idea of punishment and its various motives are treated at some length. Chapter X analyses the idea of 'teaching'—an idea which certainly contains much more than the would-be teacher is aware of to begin with.

Chapters XI and XII contain a discussion of the need (especially in the teacher himself as an influence on his pupils) for development of what may be called 'depth' of experience and understanding in a world increasingly depersonalized by mass-conditioning, in which the roots of being get choked up. Can this need in any way be related to the educational curriculum, to approaches to the main fields of educational study, to the ways in which 'subjects' and pupils are taught? What educational values are to be found in the study of the sciences and humanities? What of the education of the imagination, of the sense of mystery and wonder? How important is the awareness of the dimension of 'depth' to the teacher who is to *educate* (in the sense of 'nourish') his pupils?

Chapter XIII is an inquiry into the proper aims for the professional education of teachers—a burning contemporary question and one of permanent importance.

PART ONE

PART ONE

CHAPTER I

'Philosophy'

1. Philosophy as a Guide: Popular and Traditional Views

A subject can be properly understood only by those who have worked and lived in it—whether the subject be history, or a science, or anything else. This is true of 'philosophy' and 'education'. It is very clearly true of philosophy. What philosophy is, certainly should be best known to those who are steeped in it: one can rightly expect a more competent answer from a professional than from an amateur. On the other hand, the exposition of 'philosophy' faces peculiar difficulties. If an expert is writing for experts about biology or chemistry or history, he can (in spite of some disputes) fairly safely assume a generally agreed field, a subject matter, and can make agreed assumptions about the methods used in the investigation of the subject matter. But there is no universally agreed field, or subject matter or method, in philosophy. The nature and function of philosophy is itself a kind of philosophical problem—over which there has always been controversy, from the days of the differences between Socrates and Anaxagoras, or between Plato and Aristotle. Since this is so, since the difficulty is philosophical, there is a peculiar difficulty in starting off. Before one begins to talk of the 'philosophy' of anything, one ought to say what philosophy is. This itself implies philosophy, which in turn entails a prior discussion. And so on.

This is not necessarily a vicious circle. Perhaps it is a benign one. But it is a circle nevertheless, and the only thing one can do is to plunge in, hoping that what cannot be clear all at once will become clear in the going. What then, in this spirit, can we say of philosophy?

There are a number of quite definite popular ideas of what philosophy is and what the philosopher ought to do and be. It

3

is often said that a great need of the present time is that people
should have 'a philosophy of life'. Philosophy ought not to be
simply the prerogative of a few professionals; it is needed as a
guide for the ordinary man in his everyday life. We live, it is
said, in a bewildered age. Scientific and technical knowledge is
enormously increased: but we have lost our way. Life lacks
meaning and purpose: it ought to have direction and integration.
The philosopher is the one person who can tell us what this is.
Purpose and integration ought to be provided by the philosopher,
since there is no one else to provide them. The scientist is concerned, it is said, with defined and limited questions, whilst
the technologist is concerned with the techniques of application;
in these things there are many purposes, but no underlying
Purpose. Man's chief end has been obscured. And it is contended
that this is a particularly urgent problem, since the rising genera-
tion, depressed by the apparent meaninglessness of life, is moved
by the impulse of the moment, or in despair turns to destruc-
tiveness. It is believed that the philosopher, like the poet, should
see life steadily and see it whole: in the obsession with particular
questions we have lost the sense of proportion in life as a whole.
All this can, of course, be extended and applied to philosophy of
education. If we are to educate sensibly, it is argued, we must
above all things do it with a sense of direction and proportion;
and to have this is to have 'philosophy'. Philosophy is love of
wisdom; the philosopher is the lover of wisdom, and it is 'wisdom'
that we need.

These opinions, as I shall indicate in a moment, are often
repudiated quite strongly by some contemporary philosophers.
But before going on to describe their reactions and the views of
the nature of philosophy with which they would replace such
opinions, it ought to be said that there is quite good historical
precedent for these popular views. In pre-Socratic times the
philosopher was the 'wise man'—sometimes he was a kind of
oracle. Heracleitus was reputed for his 'dark sayings'. The philosopher was conceived as a man who had a deeper insight into the
reality beyond appearance. Although Socrates himself claimed no
wisdom beyond the wisdom which knows its own ignorance, yet he
did claim that the way to practical excellence was the way of
knowledge, and the knowledge of the philosopher as distinct from
those 'opinions' which were taught by the contemporary sophists.

For Plato, again, it was necessary that the statesmen who ruled should be deeply versed in philosophy if they were to rule the state wisely. How can the statesman know what particular acts are best if he has not spent years in seeking to know the 'Form of the Good'? It is impossible for him to be practical in the best sense if he has not, in retreat, contemplated philosophy. Aristotle, again, though he believed in the superiority of the 'speculative' to the practical life, yet regarded as an important function of philosophy its practical usefulness. His works, the *Ethics* and *Politics*, were propadeutics to the work of practical statesmanship; his *Poetics* were instructions to the poet and dramatist. Not only the *Rhetoric*, but even the *Logic*, was a preparation for effective public speaking. But the idea of the philosopher as 'guide, philosopher and friend' perhaps most directly derives from the Stoic and Epicurean 'sages', guides to the art of living. In the Middle Ages, philosophic reason was the handmaid to religion and theology was the guide of life. In the Renaissance, humanistic reason took on fresh forms of guidance. From the seventeenth century, philosophy developed new interests and new methods, but throughout this variety there remained a substantial tradition of speculative reason as a guide to religious, moral and political living. Finally, if we consult the 1957 *Year Book of Education* [1] we find that this idea of 'philosophy' as in some way a practical is still accepted over a large area of the world.

2. CONTEMPORARY CRITICISMS OF THESE

But there has been a strong, sometimes a violent repudiation of the popular and the traditional view. Some of it started with the logical positivist revolution in Vienna between the wars, and it was continued by later linguistic analysts. Professor O'Connor [2] writes: 'In the past, both philosophers and their critics made the mistake of assuming that philosophy was a kind of superior science that could be expected to answer difficult and important questions about human life and man's place and prospects in the universe. In particular, philosophers tried to answer questions of the following kinds: Is there a God and, if so, what if anything can we learn by reason about His nature? Do human beings

[1] Ed. J. A. Lauwerys and G. Z. F. Bereday (Evans Bros.).
[2] *An Introduction to the Philosophy of Education*, pp. 1–4 (Routledge, 1957).

survive their death? Are we free to choose our own courses of action or are human actions events in a causal series over which we can have no control? By what standards are we to judge human actions as right or wrong? How are these standards themselves to be justified?' O'Connor believes that it is a mistake to assume that philosophy 'is a sort of superior and profounder science whose findings would give the answers to questions like these'. He speaks contemptuously of views voiced by the Roman Catholic philosopher Jacques Maritain, that all philosophical thinking begins with questions like, 'What are we?' 'Where are we?' [1] He says that these questions are regarded as characteristically philosophical by many laymen because they seem to have 'a ring of profundity in them'. They sound impressive; but they are, he thinks and goes on to argue, rather bogus. The extreme and most popularized version of the modern revolt against 'metaphysics' was Ayer's exposition of the logical positivism [2] which repudiated most of the important questions and answers of the past as 'nonsense'.

The term 'nonsense' had a technical meaning, confusion of which with the popular use gave it an undeserved emotional overtone. Logical Positivists were concerned with the problem of the *meaning* of language, and with the test of meaningfulness. The meaning of a statement, they contended, can only be discovered by asking how it can be verified. Of meaningful statements, it was said, there are two kinds, analytical statements and empirical ones. Analytical statements are necessary and certain because their validity depends solely on the definitions of the symbols they contain. But they give us no information about the world of experience. On the other hand, empirical statements do give us such information, and they can be confirmed or falsified by sense experience—through observation and experiment.

Now 'metaphysical statements' do purport to give us information about things. Traditional statements about God, the soul, freewill did profess to tell us about the nature of existence. Therefore they cannot be classed as merely analytic. Nor are they empirical, in that they cannot be subjected to ordinary experimental tests of sense experience. No scientific experiment can be devised which will verify, or falsify, the statement that God exists.

[1] For fuller discussion, see below, pp. 22–30.
[2] *Language, Truth and Logic* (First Ed., 1936) (Gollancz).

Since statements like this cannot be 'verified', and we have (it is said) no procedure by which we can set about verifying them, we can discover no meaning in them. They are not true; they are not false; they are meaningless, or in a technical sense, 'non-sense'. The use of this word did not quite mean that everyone who discussed metaphysics in the past was a fool or a charlatan—although the tone of voice in which it was sometimes said might seem to suggest that people who continued to be interested in metaphysics were in this class.

But the dismissal of metaphysical statements because they are not verifiable in sense experience seems arbitrary, and soon came to be seen as arbitrary and even self-contradictory (since the principle of verification is not itself verifiable in sense experience). Many modifications and refinements were introduced in reply, and the common contemporary repudiation of the afore-mentioned claims of philosophy is based, *inter alia*, upon a much subtler and deeper criticism of the use of language. It is quite true that many of the affirmations of philosophy, of religion, and also of ethics (e.g. the statement that lying is *wrong*) do not fall into either of the two classes, 'analytic' and 'empirical': but may there not be many other significant uses of language besides these two? Was it not a mistake to limit the scope of philosophy by a hasty assumption about the logic of language? Is it not better to broaden the possible scope of philosophy by making an open investigation into the rich variety of language?

3. LANGUAGE AND THOUGHT

This is in fact what happened, and the initiation of the outlook is substantially due to the work and influence of Wittgenstein, much concerned in his earlier life with the work of Bertrand Russell, though soon reacting against it.[1]

[1] The literature of the subject is very extensive. Much of it is to be found in articles in *Analysis, Mind, Philosophy, The Philosophical Quarterly, Proceedings of the Aristotelian Society*. Ayer's book has been mentioned: useful introductory books are:—

   G. J. Warnock: *English Philosophy since 1900* (Home University Library, 1958).

   G. Ryle, etc.: *The Revolution in Philosophy* (Macmillan, 1947)

   A. G. N. Flew (ed.): *Logic and Language*, First and Second Series (Blackwell, 1952 and 1953). (*Continued overleaf*)

Russell, a distinguished logician and mathematician, was influenced by logic and mathematics and by the English tradition of philosophy deriving from Locke. This tradition has been markedly analytic. Russell had a passion for the kind of clarity which comes from the analysis of a complex whole into its ultimate elements or components. We are confronted in our experience with complexities about which we are confused. The aim of philosophical analysis is to remove the confusion by showing the elements of which the complex is made up.

It is impossible in an introductory chapter of this kind to expound Russell's views and the reactions against them. Suffice it to say that Russell believed that the complex world which we experience can be broken down into simple, irreducible 'atomic' facts, and that corresponding to these there can be formed 'atomic' propositions. Starting afresh from these we can go on to make a number of combinations. Using the simple 'atomic' materials we can range widely, constructing propositional complexes ('molecular' propositions) out of the simple elements. There was thought to be an ideal logically perfect language of this kind concealed behind the muddles of ordinary language. It was the proper business of the philosopher to reveal the true logical language underneath the muddles.

Wittgenstein, who came to England from Vienna, became at one time Russell's pupil at Cambridge, and was deeply involved in the implications of 'logical atomism'. His notable book *Tractatus Logico-Philosophicus*,[1] was published soon after World War I. Of his collection of notes, *Philosophical Investigations*,[2] published posthumously, is a wide-ranging, though unsystematic, critical inquiry into language and its uses.

Wittgenstein gradually came to see that the theory of a logically perfect language was not so much a discovery of the true nature of language, as a sort of *a priori* metaphysical invention. This discovery startled him into deep thought about the illusions, the superstitions, the 'bewitchments' (to use his own term)

A. G. N. Flew (ed.): *Essays in Conceptual Analysis* (Macmillan, 1956)

J. Hospers: *An Introduction to Philosophical Analysis* (Routledge, 1956)

There are many references in these books of original works which the interested student will naturally take up. Chapters II and III of O'Connor's book, *An Introduction to the Philosophy of Education*, are useful.

[1] Routledge, 1922.   [2] Blackwell, 1953.

from which philosophers suffer and led him in reaction from the logician's archetypal dream to a passionate concern with the many varieties of language as it is actually used. *One* account of language will not do; there are an unlimited number of uses of language. Language is like a tool-box containing many tools used for many purposes. One must not start with the logician's prejudices about simplification, but must look at language in all its variety and live with it and in it. Using a language, he said, is part of our natural history, as much part of it as 'walking, eating, drinking, playing'.[1]

The convert tends to develop an extreme reaction against his former 'blindness' or 'bewitchment'. Wittgenstein, when it was revealed to him how a mistaken idea of language could lead to philosophical confusion, strongly tended to believe that linguistic confusion was the prime source of all philosophical muddle. It is often said, in criticism of contemporary philosophers, that they are too exclusively, even finally, preoccupied with the study of language for its own sake. Whether this is or is not an exaggerated generalization, it is not true of Wittgenstein himself. Warnock sums it up admirably: 'Is it necessary here to add that Wittgenstein of course does *not* suggest that philosophical problems are all "about language"? Of course they are not; they are about knowledge, memory, truth, space and time, perception, and innumerable other things. What he suggests is that, though thus not *about* language, they spring *from* language; they show themselves in distorted uses of language; they reveal confusion as to the uses of language; they are to be solved (or removed) by our coming to see and to employ our language properly. It would make no difference of substance here if one referred, instead of to "language", to "concepts". This may sound more important; but the problems were never thought to be *trivial*.' [2]

4. PHILOSOPHY AS 'VISION'

Philosophy, then, on this view is not about language, but it springs at least in part from language. But what is the 'philosophy' which springs from language? Philosophy arises not from ignorance of facts—which could be corrected by common-sense experience or science. It arises from a sense of bafflement about

---

[1] *Philosophical Investigations*, par. 25.   [2] *Op. cit.*, p. 89.

what is perfectly familiar but which we cannot, as it were, see clearly or straight. Wittgenstein compares it to seeing the pieces of a puzzle but not knowing how to fit the picture together. But *is* this all? Surely not. Surely philosophy must have some more positive function. This question is discussed, with great honesty, charm and penetration, by Dr F. Waismann in a paper in the volume *Contemporary British Philosophy*.[1] Because his exposition is an admirable preliminary to philosophy of education I propose to refer to it at some length.

Dr Waismann begins very much along Wittgensteinian lines. He points out that philosophy as it is practised today is very unlike science; it has no strict proofs; no theorems and no questions that can be finally decided 'yes' or 'no'. There are plenty of arguments, as we know, but no 'proof' in the sense of a mathematical or scientific proof. It is not, as we shall see, that philosophy tries to provide theorems or proofs and fails to do so. Something quite different is its aim. The questions of philosophy, as Wittgenstein had said, do not arise from ignorance of facts, but from confusion about what is in one way perfectly familiar.[2] 'What gives rise to it is nothing recondite and rare but precisely those things which stare us in the face; memory, motion, general ideas. . . . In looking at such questions, it seems as if the mind's eye were growing dim and as if everything, even that which ought to be absolutely clear, was becoming oddly puzzling and unlike its usual self.' And when we have worried about a philosophical problem to some effect we find that it 'is not solved: it *dis*solves'.[3] And a most important question arises. 'In what does the "dissolving" consist? In making the meaning of the words used in putting the question so clear to ourselves that we are released from the spell it casts on us.' Confusion is removed by carefully calling to mind the use of language. Philosophy advances not by adding new propositions to its list, but by 'transforming the whole intellectual scene and, as a consequence of this, by reducing the number of questions which befog and bedevil us. Philosophy so construed is one of the great liberating forces.' [4]

But this is only the beginning. Waismann goes far beyond Wittgenstein and writes, characteristically, as follows: 'What,

[1] Ed. H. D. Lewis (Allen & Unwin, 1956). [2] Waismann, *op. cit.*, p. 449.
[3] *Op. cit.*, p. 458. [4] *Op. cit.*, pp. 460–461.

only criticism and no meat? The philosopher a fog-dispeller? If that were all he was capable of I would be sorry for him and leave him to his devices. Fortunately, this is not so. . . .'[1] The aim of philosophy is not *only* 'to show the fly the way out of the fly-bottle', leaving him exactly where he started (as Wittgenstein in one of his epigrams had suggested). The pursuit of the questions of philosophy is the search for more profound understanding. 'The question is the first groping step of the mind in its journeyings that lead towards new horizons.'[2] The philosopher is distinguished for his passion of questioning, and as a questioner he cannot be clear all the time. The demand for clarity at *every* point has indeed been one of the paralysing obsessions of contemporary philosophy. 'No great discoverer has acted in accordance with the motto, "Everything that can be said can be said clearly" (Wittgenstein). And some of the greatest discoveries have even emerged from a sort of primordial fog. (Something to be said for the fog. For my part, I've always suspected that clarity is the last refuge of those who have nothing to say).'[3]

The function of the analyses of philosophy, including the study of language, is to enable us to *see* in a new way. Being now aware of linguistic and other analogies which were misleading him, the philosopher sees things in a strange new light. This emphasis upon 'seeing' is of the first importance. (It is a very old idea indeed; some of the most important metaphors of Plato are of light flooding in upon the scene, enabling the philosopher to 'see' things in a different proportion). 'What matters to the philosopher is more like changing his outlook than proving to him some theorem; or more like increasing his insight. Insight cannot be lodged in a theorem, and this is the deeper reason why the deductive method is doomed to fail: insight cannot be demonstrated by proof.'[4]

5. PROOF IN PHILOSOPHY

What Waismann has to say about proof in philosophy he says very clearly and emphatically: and it is very important. Philosophy uses arguments, but never finally settles questions by compelling or irrefutable argument such as one can have in

[1] *Op. cit.*, p. 461.   [2] *Op. cit.*, p. 464.
[3] *Op. cit.*, pp. 464–465.   [4] *Op. cit.*, p. 469.

mathematics or even in scientific verification. 'No philosopher has ever proved anything. The whole claim is spurious.'[1]

Arguments in philosophy do not irrefutably prove or demonstrate, but are important in helping us to see afresh. How do arguments help? Dr Waismann uses brilliantly the analogy of the barrister and the judge to illuminate his contention. The philosopher does not strictly prove. What he does 'is something else. *He builds up a case.* First, he makes you see all the weaknesses, disadvantages, short-comings of a position; he brings to light inconsistencies in it or points out how unnatural some of the ideas underlying the whole theory are by pushing them to their farthest consequences; and this he does with the strongest weapons in his arsenal, reduction to absurdity and infinite regress. On the other hand, he offers you a new way of looking at things not exposed to those objections. In other words, he submits to you, like a barrister, all the facts of his case, and you are in the position of the judge. You look at them carefully, go into the details, weigh the pros and cons and arrive at a verdict. But in arriving at a verdict you are not following a deductive highway, any more than a judge in the High Court does. Coming to a decision, though a rational process, is very unlike drawing conclusions from given premises, just as it is very unlike doing sums. A judge has to judge, we say, implying that he has to use discernment in contrast to applying, machine-like, a set of mechanical rules. There are no computing machines for doing the judge's work nor could there be any—a trivial yet significant fact. When the judge reaches a decision this may be, and in fact often is, a rational result, yet not one obtained by deduction; it does not simply follow from such-and-such: what is required is insight, judgment.   Now in arriving at a verdict, you are like a judge in this, that you are not carrying out a number of formal logical steps: you have to use discernment, e.g. to descry the pivotal point. Considerations such as these make us see what is already apparent in the use of "rational", that this term has a wider range of application than can be established deductively. To say that an argument can be rational and yet not deductive is not a sort of contradiction as it would inevitably be in the opposite case, namely, of saying that a deductive argument need not be rational'.[2]

This, he contends, alters the whole picture. The philosopher

---

[1] *Op. cit.*, p. 471.   [2] *Op. cit.*, pp. 480–481.

may see an important truth and yet be unable to demonstrate it by formal proof; this does nothing to detract from its rationality. We are taken to the central purpose of philosophy, namely *seeing* freshly. The seeing is the seeing of a man-in-the-whole-living-enterprise-of-his-thinking, and this can never be adequately translated into propositions, though propositions are necessary all the time. In Waismann's words, 'a philosophy is there to be lived out. What goes into the word dies, what goes into the work lives'.[1]

6. 'METAPHYSICS'

This liberal view of philosophy as fresh vision, or as a case built up in rational, though not scientific ways, as accepting a flexible view of the nature and use of language, is an answer to the over-violent repudiation of 'metaphysics' (or speculative philosophy) so evident some years ago. Professor O'Connor, for example, wrote: 'Most would agree that the traditional philosophers promised more than they were able to deliver and that their claims to interpret the universe on a grand scale must be rejected for just the same reason that the claims of alchemists, astrologers or magicians are now rejected. The reason is the simple fundamental one that the results of any sort of inquiry are acceptable in so far as they are publicly testable, reliable and coherent with the rest of public knowledge. Traditional metaphysics, like astrology and alchemy, cannot meet these requirements'.[2]

[1] *Op. cit.*, p. 490 *sq.*
[2] *An Introduction to the Philosophy of Education*, p. 17.
I refer to Professor O'Connor frequently because he is, alas, one of the very few professional philosophers in England to write a book on philosophy of education, and because his book is likely to be read by students of education. But it is to be regretted that, in spite of his defence of reason (see pp. 23–28 *op. cit.*) he here and elsewhere uses rhetorical devices, rather than reason, in order to persuade. Observe, for example, the *innuendo* here. Alchemists, astrologists, magicians do not scientifically verify their statements. Metaphysics does not 'verify' its statements. Quite true. But what is it hoped that the casual reader will conclude? That 'metaphysics' is about on a par with astrology (and not only in respect of non-verifiability). Astrology, alchemy— bah! *Therefore*, Metaphysics—bah! Surely the writer should think it obligatory at least to indicate the *differences* between astrology (etc.) and metaphysics? The reader should therefore take this book—in at least its earlier parts helpful—with a watchful eye.

But the validity of all this depends on what one means by 'publicly testable, reliable and coherent with the rest of public knowledge'. There is more than one view of what it may mean.

Philosophy of education, to which this is an introduction, is not necessarily, and certainly not all, 'metaphysical' if by metaphysics one means speculative constructions about matter, life, mind, God, the relation of body and mind, the status of sense-perception and its relation to the external world. Nevertheless philosophy, once it starts, has no stopping-place. Although the focus of attention in philosophy of education may be upon the foreground questions which arise out of the thought and practice of education itself, the treatment of these focal problems inevitably entails assumptions about knowledge, the nature of man, the status of moral and other values, the nature of the world, whether divinely ordained or otherwise. A book, even a large one, on philosophy of education cannot possibly enter into detailed discussion of all the philosophy there is. Nevertheless it cannot avoid looking into these larger questions from time to time, as we shall do in this short book—and it is important for the student of education not to let himself be inhibited by arbitrary notices 'No Road' posted across ancient rights of way. Questions of education do press upon ultimate questions, including metaphysical ones. And even if philosophy of education cannot *itself* explore all the arguments fully, it will be a legitimate part of its work, as we shall see, to examine what the implications for education will be *if* such and such a philosophical position is adopted.

'Metaphysics' is not, we agree, a demonstrable science. But, in addition to the law-court-like conduct of its affairs expounded by Waismann, philosophy has various ways of rationally testing its statements. The statements of philosophy have constantly to to be tested against the claims of 'experience' in a wider sense than is used in science—moral experience, the experience of personal relations, aesthetic and religious experience. It is true that all these forms of 'experience' are personal and in a sense private. But they are not merely so; we can converse about all of them, and make considerable progress in understanding by doing so. In all these forms of experience there is a *given*, involuntary aspect, which we are compelled to accept as given, and to conform ourselves to, whether we like it or not. Moral and religious experience as well as sense-experience seem to contain elements which impinge upon us in a way which we cannot entirely resist or control. It is again true that all our thinkings are human constructions, and that there are alternative constructions. Yet these constructions are not *simply* arbitrary or haphazard; they are at least attempts to give rational accounts of a nature of things beyond us which has its own obstinate independence. Philosophy does possess its tests of greater or lesser approximation to truth —the familiar tests of coherence or consistency, of comprehensiveness (does e.g. this philosophical theory sufficiently account for all the *different* kinds of evidence of experience? Does it, for instance, dismiss ethical or religious claims as merely subjective illusions?). And there is the important question, Does this philosophical view give new illumination, yield new insights? Is it fruitful? And so on. In serious philosophy one does not simply pick one's fancy.

Dr A. C. Ewing has put it very positively in his essay in *Contemporary British Philosophy*. He maintains that although metaphysics does not discover new 'facts' in the same sense as the sciences do, yet by the use of reason it is able to make genuine discoveries which go beyond empirical facts. Roundly rejecting the Logical Positivist 'proof' that metaphysics is impossible, he argues that even the anti-metaphysicians are inevitably making assertions about the external world and about minds other than their own, and that there are no *general* principles which can be laid down to limit the metaphysician. Although it may not be possible, in the old sense, to 'prove', for example, the existence of God, it is possible to put forward good arguments for theism. And as one scientific theory is to be preferred to another not only on grounds of practical convenience, but on grounds of coherence and comprehensiveness, so (as I have already suggested) philosophers are entitled to use these criteria in metaphysics. Moreover, although there are and always will be disagreements in philosophy, there is every reason to think, if one looks at the history of philosophical controversy, that philosophy progresses towards truth through a kind of dialectical supplementation of one point of view by another. 'As the pendulum swings now to one side, now to the other, the various contributions will be successfully improved.' [1]

[1] *Contemporary British Philosophy*, p. 149.

For all these reasons I hope that the reader may feel able to approach those questions of philosophy which bear upon education with an open mind.

In this introductory chapter I began by briefly reviewing popular and traditional views of philosophy—as wisdom, as seeing life steadily and seeing it whole, as a guide for living. . . . I then referred to contemporary attacks on these views. The attacks—to some extent justified—arose out of a too limited view of the use of language, verification and the kind of rational justification to be expected of philosophical statements. More flexible accounts of the use of language and of rational justification re-open the paths—temporarily and arbitrarily closed—to basic thinking on the great traditional questions of philosophy. The student of education is not necessarily interested in all of these, but it is important that he should be able to approach those which are relevant to his study, without unnecessary inhibitions.

CHAPTER II

Philosophy and Educational Assumptions

1. PRELIMINARY QUESTIONS

Philosophy of Education in the most general sense is the application of philosophy and the methods of philosophy to problems of *education*. What 'education' should mean we shall inquire in the course of this book. Provisionally it can be said that education is a purposive activity towards ends which are (rightly or wrongly) deemed to be good. One can, of course, speak of 'education' as something which just happens to a person. *Experientia docet.* Travel, we say, is a good 'education'. And the word could be used of deliberate attempts to attain 'bad' ends, e.g., 'educating' young people to like dangerous drugs. But these are special uses: in the main we shall have in mind 'education' as directed intentionally by agents (parents, schoolteachers, university dons . . .) for the 'good' of other people, the pupils—though it is of course quite possible that educator and pupil may be united in person: one may educate oneself. This is not meant to be a precise or complete definition of education, which ought to take account of physical and social and cultural influences, often unconsciously absorbed. But on the whole, to attempt to educate is to do something intentional and purposive, and towards what is believed to be good. This good is complex, containing many aims, such as the acquisition of skills, the passing on of the cultures and traditions of a society, the development of critical minds, the development of character and personality along the 'right' lines, and so on.

Some ends or aims of education are universally agreed upon; others are more controversial, though amenable to discussion. About some aims there seem to be irreconcilable differences. A scientific humanist, for example, sincerely believes that religious education is a mistake (except perhaps in so far as it is information about a cultural tradition). The Christian believes it to be essential, with equal sincerity. Communists indoctrinate Communism: most of us disapprove of this. And so on. One of the most important things which philosophy of education has to do is to dig up and bring out into the light for critical examination the assumptions (some of which are concealed or at least taken for granted) which are made about education. It is important too to discover whether or how far conflicting claims can be *rationally* discussed, and even rationally altered. Or, putting it in terms of our general discussion of philosophy, how far can philosophy applied to educational matters help us to deeper insights and better practice by the display of assumptions, the examination of the language and concepts employed in educational discourse, the thinking of educational ideas together in relation to one another, as well as to major ideas about man, his values, his universe. In other words, how far can analysis, criticism, ethical thinking, theory of knowledge, metaphysics, help the educationist to put his thought and work into better and truer perspective?

In this chapter I should like to develop this general question further and to ask two distinct yet related questions. They are: What generally ought philosophy (or the philosopher) of education to aim at doing? [1] and, What ought a *teacher* of philosophy of education, specifically addressing students, to aim at doing? [2] The two questions, although they overlap, are not the same. It may be part of the duty of a teacher of philosophy of education to do something which is not itself philosophy at all, or part of the direct business of philosophy. Education and teaching is a very practical business which when done well is done in a certain spirit and manner and with a certain inspiration. It may very well be that the philosophical teacher of teachers has an obligation to do something more than teach them philosophy. But it is important to distinguish this from the first question, which is, 'What ought philosophy of education as an intellectual enterprise to be considering and aiming to do?' This of course can only be *adequately* answered by complete and exhaustive treatment of philosophy of education. The following only represent some issues of outstanding importance.

[1] Section 2.   [2] Section 3.

2. Four Questions

Philosophy of education should, I think, show the implications for education of one's assumptions about four different kinds of things: (i) beliefs about the ends or purposes of education—or more generally beliefs about 'values'; (ii) beliefs or disbeliefs about religion, some of them 'metaphysical'; (iii) other metaphysical beliefs; and (iv) beliefs about the nature of knowing.

Quite clearly these beliefs are not mutually exclusive. One's ideas about educational values may well include religious beliefs. Again, as suggested, one's metaphysical assumptions may be of a religious as well as of a secular or a neutral kind. And, although ideas about knowing may seem at first sight to be in a different class from the others, they may easily be affected by them. The pragmatist or instrumentalist theory of knowledge, which has had so much influence upon methods of teaching, is a view which believes that knowing is essentially a practical activity, that one knows in doing (or even that doing *is* knowing). This being so, it is inseparable from the ends or values which we desire when we *do*. Again, a 'realistic' theory of knowledge, one form of which maintains that knowledge is a sort of reflection of things as they are, naturally presupposes a metaphysical assumption, that the world has a definite fixed structure already there to be known—a view which is sometimes denied by the pragmatists or instrumentalists. Perhaps these distinctions may seem to be arid and unreal; I shall try to specify them a little more by illustrations, which will take up nearly all of the rest of this chapter.

I should like to make two things clear. First, the illustrations are only illustrations. In this chapter I shall mainly raise the questions, discussing them briefly but *not* in detail. A few selected ones will, however, be discussed in later chapters.

Secondly, 'philosophical assumption' is ambiguous. It might mean (a) *anybody's* assumptions on some fundamental issue—assumptions which *ought* to be examined philosophically according to methods of well-tried philosophy. Or it might mean (b) the assumptions of philosophers which they do in fact make part and parcel of their systematic philosophical thinking. It is the first sense (a) that I intend here by the 'philosophical' assumptions behind education. Ordinary people—not philosophers—make many assumptions. Teachers do. I am arguing that some of these assumptions *ought* to be considered philosophically, and by the people who are teachers and not professional philosophers. In effect, my use of 'philosophical assumptions' here and now can be interpreted as 'assumptions potentially or implicitly philosophical', or as 'assumptions which *ought* to be considered in a philosophical way'.

(*i*) *Beliefs about values.* These are of the most obvious importance in educational thought and practice. 'Obvious', however, is a relative term. What may come to be seen as obvious after reflection, may have to be discovered through very hard mental work, work which has to be carried out sometimes against strong emotional resistance. But let us first take examples which seem obviously at first sight to affect education.

The values of political totalitarianism have very direct and marked effects upon education. Nazi ideas, for instance, were directly implemented in teaching about freedom, truth, justice. Freedom for the individual person to grow—which we regard as so important—did not exist; truth became subservient to propaganda, justice became identified with the interests of political power. Again, in states where military values are extolled (as in ancient Sparta or pre-war Japan) the virtues instilled from childhood are those of obedience to rule, self-sacrifice, the subordination of oneself to the state. Humility here is at a discount (except in a very restricted sense); the Christian virtues of gentleness and love are regarded with contempt. To come nearer home; in our own competitive society, these last-mentioned values are in fact lowly rated, however much they may be given lip-service. Again, the content of the curriculum is strongly influenced by values of practical success and utility: it is, for example, taken for granted in many schools that 'the arts' are luxuries to be sacrificed as soon as serious preparation for examinations begins.

The effect of such values as these upon education is obvious enough. But there are some educational values which we take for granted at first sight as desirable, and which take on a different 'look' when we force ourselves to reflect upon them. It is usually assumed, for example, that any teacher worth his salt wants to be an 'efficient' teacher, that we all know what this means, and that practical teachers can leave 'theorizing' about it to those who have nothing better to do—perhaps to those who 'can't teach'.

It is of course true in one sense—self-evident, tautological—that a teacher wants to be 'efficient'. What is not so self-evident as it seems is the meaning or intention of efficiency. Efficiency for what? Common answers would be, 'in keeping discipline', in teaching children so that they 'know their stuff', the test being the inspection and the examination; the teacher who gets 'good results' is the teacher marked out for promotion. Much of this is unexceptionable as far as it goes, but it is often little realized by the teacher entirely preoccupied with the foreground what a short way it takes us in ensuring that the children are being educated. They are 'receiving a good education'; how far are they really becoming *educated*? Examinations have their real importance, but obviously many of the things which are of vital importance in a person's growth are not examinable in this way. Everyone knows, on a moment's reflection, that a teacher can get 'good results'—or at any rate can improve 'results'—by cramming and slave-driving, or that the appearance of 'good discipline' can be obtained by repressive means. What is not obvious, what requires extensive thinking, is the long-term meaning of 'efficiency' in teaching and education, the meaning of 'discipline', of 'knowing', of 'growing', of 'teaching' itself, of 'education'. . . . Or, more correctly, what requires really deep consideration, is, 'What conceptions of these are educationally important?' If education is a purposive activity of the utmost importance for the welfare and growth of young human beings, the most careful of critical and constructive thought about ultimate purposes of education is surely necessary, and in particular necessary for those who are teaching from day to day or who in any way organize education.

This would seem to be plain enough; yet the fact is that some of those who seem to wish teaching to be regarded as a profession are constantly belittling the 'theoretical' side of the professional education of teachers and in particular their initiation into philosophical thinking about education. The objectors (or some of them) seem to think that the training of the teacher should consist solely or mainly of apprenticeship in a school under an experienced teacher. Of course, as everyone knows, there is a skill and art and craft of teaching which has to be learned in practice, and is well learned under initial guidance. To insist on the concentrated attention of the teacher to teaching is right and needs no defence. But to say that this is *all* (or nearly all) that is needed is nothing less than dereliction of responsibility to teachers and to children. The professional education of the teacher is certainly not, as we shall see, merely an exercise in intellectual thinking. As certainly it is not the mere learning of a craft. If it is true that intellectual exercises *can* be irrelevant to the practical work of education, it is equally true that the very practice of teaching *can* be irrelevant to education in any important sense. (In other words, there is efficient teaching which is not educative, or is miseducative.) If which this practice is directed to the wrong ends, or without the understanding which this serious enterprise demands, then *everything* can go wrong. Apart from this extreme, we all know that practical preoccupation necessarily involves attention to the immediate situation. This preoccupation, if it is exclusive—if the teacher has never had, nor will have, systematic guidance in thinking of the fundamental, long-term aims and values of education—inevitably produces myopia, which, we know from experience, is often lamented by deprived teachers who suffer from it. Not thinking alone, not practice alone, but the illumination of practice by thinking, and the assimilation into the teacher's being of his deeper understanding of education so that his practice is directed and transformed—here is a major aim of professional teacher education.

This is not a digression, but a reinforcement of the contention that philosophical reflection about the *values* of education is itself important for the practice of education.

(*ii*) *Beliefs about Religion.* We said (page 19) that the four kinds of assumptions which affect education overlap with one another. Clearly, beliefs and disbeliefs about religion are also beliefs about values. But they go beyond them into 'metaphysics' and are worth looking at for their own sakes.

We in this country assume in our talk of education (not always necessarily in our practice) what may be broadly called a 'humanist' outlook. By 'humanism' here I mean simply an attitude which is marked by a care and concern for human beings as persons. A humanist in this sense believes that the welfare, betterment, fullness of life, true happiness of human persons (including, of course, children) is a matter of prime concern. This kind of thing is continually advocated in writings on education, as it undoubtedly affects much of our practice of it. In Great Britain perhaps we tend to take this for granted, forgetting that in many parts of the world concern for the individual human person is anything but a *sine qua non*. And even in our own circles, the near-idolatry of competitive success in examinations, in careers, in commerce, or the increase everywhere of the use of irrational techniques of persuasion, are by implication anti-human. Still, it is fair to say that our outlook in education is strongly tempered by humanism and that the great majority of teachers in this country are ready to agree and co-operate about human ends in education. Nevertheless, there are deep differences between kinds of humanism which amount in the end to deep differences about religion. It is worth while looking broadly at the effects upon educational outlook and practice which may be occasioned by these differences about basic assumptions. I shall speak in this context of the contrast between two sorts of humanism which have to be called, for want of better words, 'secular humanism' (of which 'scientific' humanism is one kind) and 'religious humanism' (of which 'Christian' humanism is one kind).

It is easy to misunderstand this distinction in several ways: and it is certainly easy to over-simplify. In the first place the terms 'secular' and 'religious' are used here as purely descriptive and not as evaluative. Furthermore, the terms are being used, for purposes of clarity, as exclusive and exhaustive, i.e. as *contradictory* concepts. In other words 'secular' means 'having to do with this world' in a *non*-religious sense. But to make this exclusive and exhaustive logical distinction between contradictories does not in the least imply that *people* can always be labelled under one heading or the other. No doubt some people can be so labelled and some people so label themselves. There are those who call themselves scientific humanists—or sometimes just humanists. And there are unnumbered religious (e.g. Christian) people who call themselves humanist—though with some such added adjective as 'Christian humanist' or 'true humanist' (Maritain). But more often the position is not so clear cut. The same person may hold inconsistent views, or may tend sometimes to one side and sometimes to the other, or may be genuinely uncertain or agnostic, or simply vague.

Nevertheless, used with due caution, the logical distinction is important, as are its implications for education. Both views insist on the importance of human beings. But for secular humanism, personality is the highest form of being that we know. There is no supreme mind, no supreme being, no creator of nature and man, no God. Man is the measure of all things, and man's life has been evolved over an immense period of time by entirely natural causes. We are told that in time human life will disappear from the face of the universe and be as nothing. The days of man's life are as grass: the wind passes over it and it is gone. These are the psalmist's words, but for the secular humanist they have a finality for the human race which the psalmist did not intend.

For the Christian humanists the transitory life of man has an eternal setting. God created nature, and created man in his own image; man did not merely evolve (though he has evolved) but was made by God for his own purposes which were revealed to be that he should love God wholly and his neighbour as himself. Christian humanism shares with secular humanism the care for human persons, and the sense of human importance. But for the Christian humanist these things turn on man's dependence upon God.

What are some of the logical implications for education, of these contrasted views?

Moral education will (logically) be looked at differently from the two standpoints. *Some* secular humanists (and some only) hold that the final source of moral authority resides in society (so that moral education is education for conformity to society's moral authority). This would, of course, be contradicted by Christian humanists, who believe in the final moral authority of God, not man. Other secular humanists (whom I judge to be more enlightened), *together with* some Christian humanists, hold that moral obligations—to truth, fidelity, compassion, etc.—possess moral authority in their own right, and that this moral authority is recognized as autonomous alike by the secular and religious conscience. But the Christian sees this in a background of belief in a good God of love. Everyone (religious or not) is under categorical moral obligation to treat human beings—in various ways—as persons. But for the Christian this is set in a perspective of divine love, which does not exist for the secularist. So the Christian is conscientiously bound *in this sense* to interpret moral education religiously, whilst the secularist is equally bound not to. Further, for the Christian there exist additional moral obligations, to religious humility, worship, prayer. . . . These are not recognized by the secular humanist.

Human nature is weak, wayward and lazy, and moral education is concerned to fortify the irresolute will [1] against temptation. Here the secular humanist emphasis will be upon self-reliance. Human beings must, in the last resort, rely on themselves—since there is no Being outside themselves upon which they can rely. They must be taught this. The Christian humanist educator, on the other hand, believes in the cultivation of a sense of dependence on God. While the secular humanist asserts himself and pits himself against his own wayward impulses, the Christian humanist believes that moral power comes from God, that prayer is the central activity of moral and religious life and that if the sinner submits and surrenders himself, he will receive the power to do and be what he otherwise cannot of his own accord attain to. It is not suggested that the Christian humanist disparages the strengthening of the will by effort; it is rather that he affirms that it cannot be adequately strengthened if the effort is not also infused by divine grace. Or, in a way, the hardest effort of will is to submit the will to God: but in this very submission divine power is received and the will is strengthened. 'When I am weak, then am I strong.' But to be 'weak' in *this* sense is hard. The secular humanist quite honestly holds that these beliefs are delusions (or illusions) and even, sometimes, that they are degrading. It follows that each side will be bound, when the occasion arises in moral teaching, to be influenced by its own underlying beliefs.

One might expect subtle differences of influence in the attitude to *nature*. The religious teacher who believes that God created nature, and is in some way manifested in and through natural events, physical and biological, must approach these things in a rather different way from the teacher who, when he is being logically consistent, is bound to say that nature is strictly speaking

---

[1] The term 'will' is philosophically out of favour. I am here, as often elsewhere, using popular language.

meaningless (as opposed to the religious affirmation of Divine 'meaning'). For the religious person, the word 'reverence' has quite a specific reference; it is related in the first instance to God. If the secular humanist teacher uses such a word at all, he must be reierring to a sense of 'wonder', admiration, sometimes awe, which qualitatively cannot be exactly the *same* as that of the religious teacher. And these words, expressing attitudes, must have a subtly different influence upon his pupils. The person in whom religion is deeply infused is essentially a 'worshipping' person; some of this is on occasion bound to be caught by those whom he teaches. In a similar way the secular humanist's characteristic attitudes (however described) to life and nature are caught. The teacher's attitudes, whatever they are, are important, and it is well to be aware that beliefs make a difference.

This kind of thing could be worked out further; but enough has been said. It need only be added here that the effect of religious beliefs will of course vary with the particular form of religion. Within the Christian orbit, the fundamentalist will insist on going to Scripture for his *ipsissima verba*. The Roman Catholic will take certain fundamental instructions claimed to come from Scripture on the authority of the Church. The Protestant Liberal will insist that it is the spirit of religion which is shown in the Bible, and that the interpretation must be left to individual judgment and conscience. On the secular humanist side, again, some will stress more the warmth of the humanities and the importance of imaginative activity, others will stress the importance of being rational in everything.

(*iii*) *Non-religious metaphysical beliefs.* The metaphysical beliefs mentioned so far have been those in which the question of religion is involved. But there are many forms of metaphysics in which religion is not involved, at least directly. There has been much metaphysical discussion, for example, about the nature of causation—whether there is a 'real' objective power 'causing things to happen', or whether the idea of cause is only, as David Hume taught, a 'lively expectation in the mind', induced by habit which is formed from the continual experience of uniform succession. This kind of question is not of any obvious educational importance—though it is always dangerous in speaking of philosophy to deny the possible relevance of anything. But there are other metaphysical questions which are very much bound up with assumptions behind what we do in education.

One's attitude to children as *persons* is bound up with assumptions which we make about the human person. In psychological studies, so influential upon educationists, we usually take up an 'objective' attitude to personality, by which I mean that we study human beings as objects with a history. We are bound to take into account, in addition to 'innate' capacities, the historical family, social and other environmental conditions which have influenced this or that person, and have, so far, helped to 'make' him what he is. We are bound to treat this or that child as a 'going' concern, and it is naturally part of our task as teachers to help children to 'go' farther, and to go in the direction which we believe to be right. An extreme form of this belief is the 'behaviourist' assumption that education is entirely 'conditioning.'[1]

But far short of 'behaviourism', we are bound to recognize important elements of determination, of cause and effect, in education. This presupposition, legitimate up to a certain point, can, however, be very dangerous if it discounts in its practice the possibility, the important possibility, of *freedom*. The consideration of freedom presents a different picture. The person has a history, true. The present has been shaped by the past, and the future will be shaped by what happens now. But an idea of 'shaping' and 'moulding' in education, which assumes that the living child is simply an object to be moulded and shaped according to our or society's desires, is an idea which leaves out what *may* be the most important fact about a human person. Is there not, it may be asked, another aspect of every personality which is in some sense independent of its history, which can in some measure at least stand off from its own states, its own history, judge it, criticize it, choose, and, perhaps, move off in a *new* direction?[2] We as teachers can, no doubt, do much to help children to learn in the ways we want. But, says the critic, is

---

[1] Reflection on this is not always carried to the point of asking *why* the teacher wants to condition as he does. If *all* human action can be conditioned, so can the desires and actions of the teacher himself. Is the teacher's 'conditioning' of children in certain directions itself simply determined by the teacher's own conditioning? Is this a satisfactory 'reduction' of his 'aims' of education? Is it not a reduction to absurdity? Should not the teacher think again about the limits of 'conditioning'? See *below*, Chapter VIII.

[2] This is discussed in Chapter VIII below, pp. 115 sq.

there not always something which the child as a person has to do for himself, to choose freely to do? Furthermore, does not the treatment of children as 'objects' to be moulded set up great barriers between us and them? It can well be contended that to *meet* a person, a child or any other, is to experience an encounter between person and person, which is quite different from looking at or manipulating an 'object'. One may come to *know* another person in this way as in no other. The full appreciation of this kind of knowing of a person is of the greatest importance both for the 'metaphysical' understanding of personality, and for the practical success of teaching. When we say that a teacher ought to *know* his children as persons, or that 'good personal relations' matter more than anything else, we certainly do not merely mean that the teacher must be a good objective psychologist of personality (though that is important), but also that he must treat them, and meet them, as free persons in their own right.[1] This is an important 'metaphysical' assumption about personality which, at some stage of a teacher's career, needs to be looked into carefully.

Our metaphysical assumptions (of one sort or another) will affect many practical things we do in education. To take one example only, *punishment*. If we punish, *why* do we? On a purely determinist or 'conditioning' view, we ought to punish only in order to alter, by conditioning, a child's behaviour in the *future*. To punish him for what he *has* done would be irrational and could only be a kind of revenge. The poor child was conditioned to do what he did. On the other hand, if one thinks of a child as having some measure of freedom to choose to do or not to do, we can consistently regard him as responsible for what he did. Here, *if* punishment is ever justifiable, it is justifiable for quite a different reason, that he responsibly did wrong. (For further discussion, see p. 141 sq. below.)

Another example of metaphysical assumptions which affect the practice of education is the assumption about *body and mind*. We normally treat these, and with much justification, as two different sorts of things. The light-hearted 'Mens sana in corpore sano' is what philosophers would call a 'dualistic' assumption. In practice we talk about educating *both* mind and body; the two tasks are allocated to different teachers, and we have been

[1] See below, pp. 134-5.

used to saying that there ought to be a proper 'balance' between these two branches of education (a metaphor). And so on.

This is again a mixture of metaphysical assumptions and practical policy. The metaphysical problem is complex and difficult; it can be confidently said that at present we hardly know how to ask the right questions. But there are some signs, both in educational practice and in philosophical thinking, of an attempted movement towards a more organic view of the relationship of body and mind. The philosopher may talk of the person as an 'embodied organism', or an 'embodied self' or 'embodied person', and some educational practitioners are acting as though they believed in something of the same kind. The patent differences between the 'bodily' and the 'mental' are not denied, but it is sought to insist that the person is a single indivisible unity.

This hypothesis (if that is not too grand a name for a very vague supposition) bears some interesting deductive and practical fruits. Doctors, clinical psychologists, educationists, are tending to conceive of 'health' as neither a purely physical nor a purely mental conception, but as a fusion of both. In pathology the term 'psycho-somatic' medicine may conceal more than it reveals, but it is at least an index of direction. In education two examples occur to one's mind. One is the 'art of movement', initiated by the late Rudolph Laban (and now carried on by Lisa Uhlmann): the other is the broader field of æsthetic education.

A spectator of Miss Uhlmann's pupils at work can feel strongly convinced of the inseparability of feeling, desire, striving, and bodily posture, attitude, stretching, reaching, moving to fill three-dimensional space. The observer seems to *perceive* before his eyes the dynamics of spirit.

The thoughtful teacher of the arts, too, ought to ponder seriously upon this 'organic' view of the relation of body and mind. He should consider how far what he is doing involves the recognition that the life of sense—the perception of colour, sound, rhythm, dramatic action—is charged with spiritual significance. What of drama? It does not seem to be simply ideas *or* human-beings-moving-upon-a-stage, but embodied spirit acting. The idea seems to come to life in its incarnation. Those who are experienced in an art like pottery speak of the profound symbolic significance of handling and shaping the clay which has come out of the earth. The proponents of art education contend that art can employ and develop the whole person as no other single activity quite can. The metaphysical *theory* of the unity of mind and body is certainly hard to formulate; but the facts are impressive, and should certainly open the teacher's mind to the possibility of a new conception of the unified person which could transform much of education.

(*iv*) *Beliefs about knowing:* (a) *Subject knowledge.* I have, so far, referred to three of the four headings mentioned on page 19. The fourth sort of assumptions which can have important relations to education are assumptions about knowing and knowledge.

Theory of knowledge may seem, of all subjects, to be the most remote from education. A moment's reflection shows that it is not so. One of the important functions of education is the acquisition of knowledge; this knowledge covers a number of fields such as science and mathematics, history, geography, literature and other arts, languages, and so on. They are very different. It is surely important to understand the nature of these different studies if one is to teach them. Behind this, there is the more general question of the nature of knowledge itself. I shall say something briefly about these two topics in turn.

First, the various 'subjects' themselves are taught in schools and universities. Yet it is exceptional to find university graduates who are expert in science or mathematics or history who have any philosophical understanding of the nature of the knowledge of their own subject. The graduate teacher in science will sometimes talk of 'proof' to his children where there is no proof. Professional historians are notoriously bored when philosophical questions of the nature of history are raised. There are distinguished literary critics as well as critics of the other arts who have never attempted to think systematically about some of the quite elementary questions of æsthetics. This indifference prevails among many university teachers in the different fields. But if one is going to teach these subjects, particularly to children, how in the world can one do it well if one does not try to examine what one is doing and why one does it?

Mathematics is commonly supposed to be a subject which some people by nature can 'do', and other people can't. There must be something in natural ability, no doubt; but one is repeatedly told by teachers of mathematics who have given attention to the philosophy of their subject that this view is greatly exaggerated, that it depends upon how mathematics is taught, and that it is so often taught badly because it is thought of simply as the learning of rules or tricks for the manipulation of symbols in order to get answers. There is little understanding even among graduates of the 'why' of the rules, we are told. Again, it will make a difference to the teaching of mathematics how far one thinks empirical procedures relevant to it or to the teaching of it. Finally, there must be understanding of the processes of abstraction, of the nature of the abstract ideas and forms of mathematics, and generally of the function of symbols. These questions do not belong to pure philosophy: of course they require competent mathematical understanding, as well as psychological knowledge. But they are partly philosophical in character.

The same applies to the teaching of *science*. Many children are given the impression that you must begin science by learning, in textbooks, definitions which are in fact the result of the highest abstractions of the most advanced thinking. Or, at the opposite end, they are led by their teachers' procedure to think that science is a carrying on of certain manipulations under instruction, in order to get a foreknown result. Much so-called 'experimental' work seems to children pointless, because it is not *experiment* or *discovery* at all: they are not themselves finding out anything, but obediently conforming. Moreover, they quickly notice that even when their seniors and betters carry out in demonstration these so-called 'experiments', 'results' which are *supposed* to appear very often do nothing of the kind, and are cooked or passed over hurriedly by some sleight-of-hand or depreciatory joke. They quickly learn to cook their own experiments or to draw not what they see, but what the book or the blackboard shows. This is a vast pity, for these little apparent 'failures' can be growing-points for interesting, living science—even simple philosophy of science. The sense of reality is missed: pseudo-attitudes are bred. And, as I have said, how often does one hear teachers introducing a 'therefore' or 'this proves' where there is no such inference?

Further, beyond the shortcomings in understanding of this or that science, there is the whole question of the fundamentally abstract and self-limiting character of science. Many people realize nowadays, with one part of their minds, that science employs highly developed techniques for answering certain defined and limited questions, and not others. But the enormous success of science and of its technological applications often leads, and has led historically, to an irrational generalization that science—which is for ever advancing—can in principle advance till it compasses all knowledge. The mature and experienced scientist himself seldom makes any such claim, and a mature philosophy of knowledge is bound to raise serious—I believe fatal—objections to this claim. But the science teacher is often sadly uneducated in critical understanding of science as one kind of knowledge, and even despises this kind of critical thought. For philosophy of science is not science: and if science is the universal 'cat's whiskers', why bother? If this is his attitude, is it much wonder that his pupils sometimes turn out culturally half-baked, even in scientific understanding?

History again: Is it what exactly *did* happen? or a *record* of what happened? or an *interpretation* through a record of what happened? Does it take in material events, or only human affairs? And if it is an interpretation, say, of human behaviour in the past, how far does it require psychology? How far are we allowed to select, and how far is our selection determined by our own bias? Again, how far is history justified as a study for its own sake? Is it only important in so far as it is, directly or indirectly, 'teaching lessons' or helping action now—as Dewey seems to suggest? Should it be a part of 'social studies'? Again, how far is history a 'science' or an 'art'? How far is all history 'contemporary history'? Is there 'objective history'? . . . On the way in which one thinks about and answers these questions will turn the emphasis and direction of one's teaching.

When we look at education in *literature* and the other *arts*, we find a medley of often vague, confused and contradictory assumptions. The arts are to be taught for moral or religious uplift, or because they sharpen the senses, or because they develop the life of feeling, or because they educate the imagination. Practical art is often encouraged because it is an outlet for 'self-expression' or 'expression of the emotions'. Is this the important thing about art? Is it just a kind of safe release for emotions which would otherwise run riot? How far should it be encouraged because it is useful to the teacher with psychological tastes as showing the children's real natures, their fantasy life, and so on? Or if children paint, do we judge it as good or bad by realism, or by sophisticated æsthetic standards, or, at the other extreme, do we say that no standard must be applied at all, and that everything which is spontaneous is wonderful? Is it right, or wrong, to apply artistic criteria to what should be primarily educational? This is a conglomeration of some among a much larger possible number of questions. The questions are on one side practical questions: What should I, as a teacher of the arts, do? What should I allow? What should I encourage? But they are, also (once again) questions whose answer will in the end be determined by our presupposition about education and about what the arts are, and what they do for and to human beings.

Finally, a word about *languages*. Behind the teaching of languages there are many fundamental questions to be asked about the nature of language, of symbol, of meaning. If (for example) language is, as Wittgenstein says, a part of our biological living, one would expect the teaching of language to assume a very different form from that which emphasizes the learning and application of grammatical rules.

(b) *General Theory of Knowledge.* These are all questions about the particular 'subjects' of knowledge and skill. But there are more general questions about the nature of knowledge itself, assumptions which greatly affect the thought and practice of education. If knowing is identified with activity, as it is by the pragmatists (or 'instrumentalists', or 'operationalists'), a central stress of education will be naturally laid upon 'activity methods' (in the widest sense). Experiment, discovery, problem-solving, will be knowledge in action. The possession of a body of *established* knowledge will be at a discount. So will the existence of *passive* elements [1] in our knowledge be doubted. The contemplative and meditative sides of education, quiet un-active enjoyment, may tend to be regarded as a waste of time, as 'doing nothing'. If children are not doing something they are idling. There is another interpretation of knowledge which is very different.

This is loosely connected with the distinction which Bertrand Russell made long ago between 'knowledge by acquaintance' and 'knowledge by description' (though I shall not use it here in his exact sense). Many teachers are converted to the importance of children's direct acquaintance in experience with that which

[1] See below, pp. 177-8

they are studying. They have projects, make local surveys, see and handle—in short, have knowledge by acquaintance with what they are learning. This is very essential indeed. On the other hand, the world was not born yesterday; even in making direct explorations of this kind children are bound to draw enormously on the store of knowledge that there is. This store is embodied in knowledge 'by description', which must constitute a large part of our knowledge. There is no opposition or contradiction between the two kinds; knowledge by description need not consist of 'inert' ideas. There is an important sense in which *all* knowledge really assimilated must be assimilated through active 'acquaintance'.

There are subtler and more technical traditional oppositions in philosophical theory of knowledge—such as the controversy between 'realism' and 'idealism' and compromises between them. Different metaphysical assumptions on these matters do make differences to the thought and practice of education, and differences which are in some ways comparable with those just mentioned. If one is a radical 'realist', one will believe that there is a world with a structure *there* to be known, and that knowledge consists in some sort of mental representation of this. Learning will be a kind of conforming of oneself to what is. If, on the other hand, one is an 'idealist' of the type of the late F. H. Bradley, emphasis will be laid upon the constructive activity of the mind out of what is given in immediate experience or feeling. This may seem technical and remote, and the educational implications of these views (which have many and subtle variations) cannot be worked out here. But they do, I think, suggest different trends, realism perhaps standing on the side of traditional formal education, 'idealism' allowing for greater freedom in imaginative insight.[1]

Behind all this there is a basic question. How widely do we want to extend the conception of 'knowledge'? A very common assumption (an unexamined one) about knowledge is that it consists only of what can be expressed in *statements*—of common sense, science, history, etc. This view would certainly put a premium upon written examinations, which can test what people have to *say* about things. Yet, without denying at all the absolutely crucial importance of symbolic statement of different kinds for

[1] These trends are examined in the *Fifty-fourth American Yearbook of Education*, 1955, (*op. cit.* p. xiii *above*.)

the growth and development of human understanding, one can also say that knowledge, although partly expressed in statements, never *consists* of the statements. It is what is *possessed* by the living mind of the person who makes the statements; and the knowledge possessed by the living mind is always much more than can be contained in any number of statements. The knowledge, for example, of the scientist or historian, is not identical with the sum of the things he says or can say, but is a synthesis made by him which enables him to see new questions in a scientist's or historian's way. If this is true it applies all along the line, and the recognition of it can affect the aims of education and our idea of the limitation of examinations. To recognize the development of personal growth and understanding through statement-making does not imply that understanding can always be adequately assessed in terms of statements. Sometimes the ferment which stirs a new 'untidy' life in a pupil's mind is much more valuable than the assimilation and tidy reproduction of statements given to him. It is doubtful whether by present standards we do justice to this. The concepts of 'knowledge' and 'knowing' need attention.

Further, if it is true that intellectual knowledge (expressed in statements) is the possession of the living mind, it is worth considering whether there is not a much wider range of knowing, of the mind's possessions, not expressed in 'statements' in the ordinary sense at all.[1] There is, for example, the insight which one may come to possess through the making or reading of a poem, the making or appreciating of music or drama or the plastic arts. This possessed knowledge is for the most part not expressible in statements at all. Or again, we may speak, with existentialists, of the 'knowledge' which comes through personal participation and decisions, the 'knowledge' which one person has of another, the 'knowledge' of good and evil, the 'knowledge' of God. There is a tendency among scientists and philosophers—and educationists influenced by them—to 'corner' the word 'knowledge' and to exploit it for important but limited ends. The ordinary uses of the word are much more liberal. Reflection upon the more liberal uses may liberalize the concept of the increase of 'knowledge' which we seek when we educate.

[1] On this, see my *Ways of Knowledge and Experience* (Allen & Unwin, 1961).

3. The Philosopher and the Teacher of Philosophy: Commitment

I said earlier (p. 18) that there are two distinct but related questions—what the *philosopher* of education, as such, ought to aim at doing, and what the *teacher* of students of philosophy of education ought to be doing. In this chapter, so far, I have indicated, through many examples, some of the basic questions for the philosopher of education which arise out of the thought and practice of education, and have suggested that reflection about assumptions can clarify and illuminate, and that practical education can be influenced for the better. The two functions distinguished above have thus been mixed together—the function of pure thinking, and the function of teaching students to reflect in order that they may become better practical educators.

Questions of principle arise there. Is it not the philosopher's function to *think*, to follow the wind of the argument whither it blows, without concern about practical results? Is not the 'philosopher of education', therefore, being false to philosophy if he lets practical interests enter and perhaps direct his thought? Secondly, are we not assuming too much when we say that thought is likely to *improve* practice? Once one starts philosophy one can be led anywhere, perhaps even to the point of scepticism about the value of education itself. And do not different philosophers, equally competent, arrive at different, often contradictory conclusions? If so, is not our last condition worse than our first?

Let us consider the philosopher of education as such, and then as teacher of students. The first, central and final loyalty of the philosopher (of education or anything else) is to the best philosophical thinking he can achieve, come what may. But there is no incompatibility between this and the fact that his concern is with education, a very practical affair. Reflection about education need not be biased (or 'false to philosophy') because of the practical concern about education any more than cancer research is biased because the cure of cancer is of great practical import—though there are temptations. The objection cited in the earlier part of the last paragraph begs its own question by assuming that the phrase 'practical interests . . . direct his thought' is interpreted in the pejorative sense of 'biasing'. But to affirm that an interest (say in education) 'directs' my thoughts, can quite naturally mean that the problems of education, practical and theoretical, occupy my attention, or, if you like, that my thoughts are 'directed' *upon* education. And the philosopher of education must believe that if ever his philosophical thinking can help to better education, it must be as good thinking of its kind as he can make it.

If he is a writer, he can perhaps leave it at that. If, however, he is also a teacher of students, it will be, at times, his duty to do more. Sometimes he will exhort, even 'preach'. He is certainly encouraging his students to think philosophically for themselves, but he is also aiming to help them to be *better* teachers and educationists. He is trying to encourage them to look sympathetically in certain directions in the hope that they may find—freely and for themselves—a better mode of teaching and education than they would otherwise have done. In all this he aims to touch not only their intellects but their feelings and wills also. This aim is no part of the work of the pure philosopher as such, but it *is* part of the work of the teacher of philosophy of education. Education, the practical enterprise, involves holding beliefs and values, beliefs that what one is doing is *worth* doing; it involves *commitment*. The uncommitted teacher has no business to be a teacher. Any teacher who is worth his salt has a *concern* for his job; he cares about it. This is equally true of the philosophical teacher of teachers. He has a concern for education and for education of teachers, and he implements this concern by conveying to them the educational values in which he believes after long reflection. He does not impose them. He is as fair-minded as he can be in presenting different points of view about which he wants his students to think honestly for themselves. But he does not pretend to an indifferent neutrality. From time to time he expresses his own genuine beliefs and hopes to influence his students, not to believe them uncritically on authority, but to *consider* them both sympathetically and critically. At times he has a duty to inspire them if he can.

It is at this point that caustic remarks about 'preaching', 'edification', 'uplift', 'high-sounding platitudes' are heard. 'What has philosophy to do with this propaganda stuff?'

I think that it ought to be said that the objections are made rhetorically rather than rationally. No doubt all these words can be used as boos of abuse, and no doubt lecturers and writers on education at times deserve abuse. But most of these words are of a coinage which was once genuine, though it is now debased. If 'edification' or 'preaching' means 'talking down to', or the evocation of cheap emotion by shallow appeal (a kind of trick of conditioning) then of course nobody wants it. But *on occasion* to proclaim (=preach) reflective convictions about fundamental educational values, and to present them for the reflective consideration of others, is part of the duty of the teacher of philosophy of education.

The other questions remain. Granted that a teacher of philosophy of education has an obligation occasionally to preach or proclaim what he believes—as well as to encourage persistent questioning—it is just possible that he may become a sceptic about the value of education, and proclaim this; or he may proclaim 'pernicious' views. And it is possible, too, that the contradictions between philosophers may shake the belief that is essential for a committed teacher. We have been assuming that reflection upon the assumptions of education will affect practice in the sense of *improving* it. What if considered reflection leads a teacher of teachers to proclaim a view which is nihilist or solidly against the stream of what we assume to be 'enlightened' opinion about education? If anyone then says, 'He must not be allowed to', what becomes of the freedom to think, write and speak which is the *sine qua non* of philosophy and democracy alike?

It is very unlikely that anyone will be led by reflection on education to a nihilist view that *all* education is useless, a waste of time, and that it should not be carried on. If there ever were such a case, it would seem clear that although the nihilist may say and write what he thinks, he should not be employed in a Department of Education or in a Training College, for these exist to promote the study and furtherance of the very thing which he thinks worthless.

This is an extreme hypothetical case, but useful in showing that there is *some* legitimate limit to the freedom of an academic teacher at least in a professional course. What are we to say of more likely cases, of those who proclaim views which are against the body of educational opinion? A person might think (I have known such a person) that there was a lot to be said for Nazi education, and for its adaptation here. He might be anti-democratic, or anti-humanist, or he might hold (again an actual case) that children and teachers are natural enemies, and that the classroom should be organized as a natural field of battle. It is not impossible to put up some sort of case for each of these views, and they might be quite sincerely held.

However much one disagrees, it cannot be denied that anyone who holds opinions like these must, in a democratic society, be free to think and to state them. But it is possible to say that if he holds *some* extreme views, he should not be appointed as a teacher of teachers, and (though this is much more difficult) that if he holds such an appointment, he should resign from it.

The exact and precise point at which resignation should be demanded is impossible to define out of context. Academic freedom is a precious principle. There is, within academic precincts in Great Britain, a great deal of latitude, without strictures on what may after all be a passing phase. It is easier to consider the conditions of academic appointment.

If a committee is considering a candidate for, say, a lectureship in philosophy of education, it will certainly and rightly be concerned with the candidate's general opinions about, and his attitudes to, education, as well as with his intellectual prowess. For the lecturer will be appointed not simply as an academic scholar, but as a teacher in a department or college for professional education. The department has a commitment to and a responsibility for the promotion of good educational *practice* as well as educational *thought*, and it is in duty bound to make its appointments in the light of its commitment. The candidate's beliefs about education, therefore, must be, very broadly, in line with that of the responsible institution, which is working within a climate of educational public opinion. This is, in fact, the way in which such committees do work. There is no reason to question their ethics.

The 'beliefs test' (for it is that) will be, if the committee is wisely competent, a very broad one. The committee *will* expect signs of acceptance of the generally accepted ideals of the common educational enterprise; but within that, it will recognize the importance of freedom for vigorous, independent and it may be unorthodox thought. In this country there is an immense regard for almost unlimited academic freedom. Even if an appointed teacher of students comes to hold what the bulk of his colleagues think to be pernicious views, the principle of freedom will restrain them from intolerant action; and it will be thought that, on the whole, extreme or unpalatable views provide, in an atmosphere of freedom, their own healthy reactions.

This last remark applies equally to the fear (see p. 36 above) that contradictions between philosophers may unsettle beliefs which are necessary for the committed teacher. Certainly they may, for a time. This is one of the risks of thinking at all. But the faith in freedom to think carries along with it the faith that within the necessary broad commitment of education, the uninhibited pursuit of truth will in its own good time lead to deeper insight into truth about education, and therefore to better practice. The faith is that truth and goodness in the field of educational values support each other in the long run.

I conclude, then, that though the teacher of philosophy of education works within a broad commitment to education, his freedom as a philosopher to think is completely untrammelled. Within the commitment, so is his freedom to say what he himself thinks—subject of course to the usual stipulations about being fair in his presentation. If, in an extreme and unlikely case, he ceases to accept the general commitment to education, he should resign, for he has no business to be compounding with what he disbelieves in. But if, still within it, he develops views which are sharply opposed to the prevailing trend of opinion, he should be permitted the utmost latitude to develop these views. The limit of this 'permission' is just short of infinity.

CHAPTER III

Values in Life and Education

1. PLAN

So far I have been saying that the practice and thought of
education is affected by assumptions of many kinds, that teachers
ought (at times) to think as philosophically as they can about
these assumptions and their implications, and that practice is
illuminated by thinking. 'Assumptions' have been illustrated,
but none of them have so far been examined in much detail.
We must now go farther and look more closely at a selected few
of them.

Assumptions about 'values' are, of all assumptions, the most
obviously important for education. What we think 'good' and
'bad', right' and 'wrong', 'important' and 'unimportant', will all
the time be guiding us (often unconsciously) in our educational
practice. These assumptions affect not only the direction of the
moral guidance we give, but the direction and emphasis of the
curriculum, the colour of our attitudes (so important in their
influence) from day to day, even from hour to hour. Educationally and philosophically, therefore, it is right to give consideration
of values first place. I shall do this in two main stages. The
first (in this chapter) will investigate the uses of the term 'value',
the meaning of 'value', 'values' of different kinds, and the comparison between different kinds of value. The second (in Chapter
IV) will ask whether, how far and in what ways we can give
rational *justification* for judgments of value. If, for instance, I
believe that the arts have an important part in education (that
they are in some sense 'good'), and you believe that they are
pleasant but unnecessary frills (that other things are in comparison
more 'important)—is this just a matter of feeling and temperament? Perhaps we can't finally settle our differences but can we,
if we choose, discuss *rationally*, and progress towards the *truth* of the
matter? *Is* there a truth about judgments of value?

2. MEANINGS OF 'VALUE'

Our main concern here is with the values of education. But education is a part of life, and clearly our questions about values in education are inseparable from larger questions of values in life; life values are embodied in educational practice. That is why I have called this chapter 'Values in Life and Education'. The more particular educational questions must be discussed in the context of the more general ones.

There is an enormous literature on 'values' and 'valuation'. I shall not draw upon it here, but merely indicate at the outset the sort of way in which the word is going to be used. Many of my statements are controversial and could be disputed.

'Value' is a word applied in use to an actual or possible complex factual state of affairs, to which we attach the adjective 'valuable'. For example: 'The interchange of views today was valuable (had value).' 'It would indeed be good (valuable) if war could be abolished.' 'To treat children as persons is surely right (morally 'valuable').' In all these cases the actual or possible matter of fact or state of affairs is distinguishable from the adjective 'valuable'. In ordinary usage, however, we mix them up. We talk of 'values' as meaning *things* or *states of affairs* which are thought valuable. 'Success, power, money, these are his values.' This may be called the substantival, as opposed to the adjectival, or sometimes adverbial, use.

The normal use of 'valuable' is positive rather than negative. In other words, 'valuable' means 'good' or 'right' rather than 'evil', 'bad', 'wrong'. But the word *can* be used to cover these as well, by employing the concept of *negative* value: though philosophers sometimes use the ugly word 'disvalue' instead. I shall here use 'value' mainly in a positive sense, of states of affairs thought to be 'good'. (The question whether they 'really' are good or not is the second question to be discussed later). Further, when we say that an actual or possible state of affairs is valuable or good, we also imply that it is a state of affairs which—in *one* of several senses of the word—ought to be supported or promoted.[1]

Another common distinction is between 'values'—valuable states of affairs—which are simply *means* to other values (e.g. going to the dentist), and values which seem to be good in themselves (e.g. happiness or virtue)—though sometimes a valuable state of affairs may be both. Health is both valuable as a condition of being able to do other valuable things, and in itself. This is the distinction between 'instrumental' and 'intrinsic' values.

It is an ordinary and legitimate distinction. But it can be dangerous in practice if we divide too sharply in fact what is only distinguishable in idea. In education, for example, it is often useful to make the distinction between means and ends. For example, it is a desired and valued 'end' that children should learn to read, and by reading become more educated; and it is perfectly legitimate to attend to the question of the best *methods* (or means) to this end. Much research in psychology has been devoted to it. On the other hand, although the distinction is valid it is dangerous to isolate ends from means in education, since the educative end we seek is not simply something in the future to be attained by doing something now which is a means to it, but in a sense is operative all the time, and operative through the continuing relationship of teacher and children. If that is not a good relationship, application of scientifically devised methods (or means) will not work. Dr W. D. Wall, in a paper on teaching methods,[1] speaking about psychological investigations into learning and teaching methods, points out that 'attempts to apply their findings to the real situations of the class-room, draw attention to their incompleteness. The learning-teaching situation is a highly complex one in which pupil to pupil and teacher to pupil relationships play a large, probably even dominant part'. And he goes on: 'Children certainly do progress more rapidly and effectively with some methods than with others; certainly the stimulus of a change of method acts at least as a temporary spur; but by far the most important factor in bringing about progress in those things which are measurable is the teacher himself. It seems in fact almost true to say that while a good teacher and a good method will produce the best results, a good teacher with a poor or indifferent method will do almost as well, and good method alone does not compensate for an indifferent teacher.'

The observations I have made so far on the uses and distinctions of 'value' are commonplace and perhaps familiar. Let us now look at the different kinds of value and their relationships.

[1] *Studies in Education*, University of London Institute of Education, pp. 157–158 (Evans Brothers, London, 1955).

3. Three Ways of Comparing Values

The word 'value', substantively employed, may mean, in the broadest sense, *any* object or state of affairs which satisfies desire, which gives pleasure or satisfaction of any kind. This is a purely matter-of-fact, descriptive sense of 'value'; we may call it for convenience 'fact-value'. In this use there is no distinction between 'lower' or 'higher', 'bad' or 'good'. If food, or drink—or poetry—give me pleasure and satisfaction, then they are (in this sense) as a matter of fact 'valuable'. Or if I enjoy injuring some-one, that is as much a 'value' to me at that moment as would be on another occasion the satisfaction of doing someone a good turn. The same applies to values which in another context we should call perversions, the satisfaction of unnatural desires, e.g., homosexual or incestuous desires, or the satisfaction of drugs to a drug addict. The examples make it clear that here the use is not normative; no moral 'ought' is implied.

Accepting that there is 'value' in this purely factual sense, it is clear that we may begin at once to compare, and sometimes to contrast, different values with one another. I want to dis-tinguish three main ways in which values may be compared and contrasted.

(*i*) We may compare values in a morally normative way in which things morally *good* are opposed to things which are morally *bad*: positive, opposed to negative. In this sense human kindness is opposed to cruelty, the conservation of one's health is good whilst drug-addiction is bad. Generosity, the pursuit of truth and beauty, are judged good, or better, whilst their oppo-sites—greed, error or lies, ugliness—are regarded as bad, or worse. Generally speaking, we believe that we *ought* to cultivate one set of values, and *ought* to avoid the others.

(*ii*) We can, however, compare pairs of values in which they are not opposed as good *versus* bad, but (in some sense), as '*higher*' or '*lower*'. It is said, for example, by the Catholic neo-Thomists, that values of the 'spirit' are 'higher' than those of the intellect, and those of the intellect 'higher' than those of the body. We may think this is vague, or arbitrary, but we shall probably agree that the values of cultivating the arts—music, literature and so on—are 'higher' than the values of passive amusement, and the satisfactions of science and philosophy 'higher' than the satisfactions of eating and drinking, playing games, pugilism. And most of us, again, would think the value of responsibility to be 'higher' than the value of purely external obedience to authority. I shall say later that, generally speaking, the 'higher' values are deeper, more far-reaching, stretching human capacity, making for personal growth. But in the meantime let us note the distinction. Let us be quite clear, too, that the contrasts are not the same as the contrasts between 'good' and 'bad'. If the arts, science, philosophy, responsibility . . . are 'higher' in one's scale than eating and drinking, amusement, playing games . . . that is not at all to say that the items in the second list are in any way 'bad'. The distinction between 'higher' and 'lower' is a *general* one, and gives no particular rules for conduct.

(*iii*) In the third place we may compare values with one another without judging that some are either better or worse, *or* higher or lower than others. Different values may claim our attention on different occasions, and the fulfilment of them on some occasions may be required if human life is to be lived fully. We are comparing values which are simply different, broadly speaking 'on a par'. Thus the values of possessing and exercising skills may be put side by side with the value of health, and there need be no opposition between them. On the other hand, values which are on a par may *seem* to be opposed in the sense that they are values of, in some ways, opposite kinds of activity. Thus the educational value of absorbing a tradition of culture is in a sense opposed to the value of criticizing it. Likewise the values of order and its conservance can be contrasted with the values of initiative and adventure. The analytic intellect can be contrasted with the roving imagination. The value of truth-seeking can be contrasted with the value of enjoying and making of works of art. The value of personal development may be contrasted with the values of the social virtues. In this we should probably all agree, in theory at any rate.

4. Moral Values: 'Full Satisfaction': 'Ought to be': Commitment

Let us now return to the first basis of comparison—the morally normative comparison, in which the 'good' or 'better' is opposed to the 'bad' or 'worse', in which 'ought' is opposed to 'ought not'. Are there *grounds* on which we make such judgments, and if so, what can they be?

We began by saying that in the widest sense values (fact-values) are objects of satisfaction, or, alternatively, the satisfactions or the pleasures we get when desires are fulfilled by an object. Since this applies to all values, 'bad' as well as 'good', desire-satisfaction as such cannot be the criterion of difference between morally good and bad. If 'bad' values are wanted or desired, we add at once, 'Yes, but they *ought not* to be wanted', or perhaps, 'though they are desired, yet they are *"undesirable"* '. Contrariwise, if morally good values are wanted, we say that it is *desirable* that they should be wanted, or that they *ought* to be wanted. On what grounds do we say this?

Desire-satisfaction as such cannot in itself be the ground of a judgment of moral desirability; it is too wide, applying to all satisfactions; there are desire-satisfactions which are not moral. But it is possible to look, not at single desire-satisfactions (such as the satisfactions of food or a drug), but at human satisfaction as a whole, to take a long-term view of human satisfaction. We can look for some balanced pattern of existence in which human beings would live, personally and interpersonally, in a full and rich way, in what might be called a 'truly human' way. (This is doubtless only an ideal, but something of it can at least be imagined, if we extend in thought the best we know.) We should be thinking, of course, not only of our own personal experience and that of our friends but also of what Aristotle called 'the wisdom of the ages'. The idea of the supremely desirable good might be said to be equivalent to the most complete fulfilment of abundant and growing inter-personal human life. And this might be taken as a sort of criterion of more particular moral values. Thus the keeping of a promise or an act of kindness might be judged as right or good in as far as it is conductive to, or is an integral part of, this pattern of personal living, a pattern which is judged after long human experience to satisfy most fully.

This looks all right. Greed, cruelty, oppression, it seems, do not in the longest run satisfy, socially or individually. Generosity, kindness, mercy, do. And if we look at the great moral figures of history, we might say that they were deeply satisfied people (which is not contradicted by the fact that they may have suffered greatly and in some cases were martyred), and that the kind of satisfaction they enjoyed is just what we mean by morally good satisfaction. It is the kind of satisfaction which, morally, *ought* to be. Reference to the many great ones of history supports our own subjective, tentative, feeble adventures in moral good.

But if we take this line we must not suppose that this reference to deeply satisfied good people of the past and present is based on anything like an empirical scientific investigation, impersonally discovering that the most humanly satisfying life is the life of the morally good. It would not be possible to find out, in a purely impersonal scientific inquiry, what the facts are, what *is* the 'most truly humanly satisfying' life, since there is no impersonal scientific means of measuring what must be a personal judgment. If one is already committed to the values of love, justice, integrity, etc., and then proceeds to inquire into the views of the 'wise men', one may indeed judge that those who have most practised these virtues are the most 'truly happy'. It may be so: that investigations like these—into the lives of good men, saints, etc.—do reinforce a personal belief that the 'truly good' is the most 'satisfying' on the longest view. But it is a reinforcement, from *within*, of a belief already tentatively held. It gives greater objectivity to one's judgments, greater support for personal belief, but not wholly impersonal truth. If the investigation of the 'truly satisfying' were of an impersonal scientific sociological kind, we should have to record equally all opinions—of Don Juans, Borgias, dictators; of ordinary men—as well as 'wise ones'. The reports might give us a total summary of contradictory opinions, and we should learn nothing about moral good.

We can only find out about that if we address carefully formulated questions in respect of the only people who would understand them. Only if we come to the consultation of the store of moral wisdom with some idea already of where we expect to find that wisdom, and what we expect to find in it, shall we be convinced that the sort of human life which we believe *ought* to be is indeed the most deeply satisfying life. The wide consultation does indeed release from subjectivity, and confirm belief through wider and worthy support; but it does not *prove*.

In fact, the very word 'prove' suggests establishing an invariable connexion between two things which are separate from and outside one another—the 'truly good' (in the realm of value) and 'the most humanly satisfying' (in the realm of natural, psychological fact). But if we do believe that there is an invariable connexion between 'truly good' and what is most deeply satisfying to human beings, it is because they are seen to be two faces of one thing, a pattern and quality of total human living. The account of human satisfaction and fulfilment is just the account of the *content* of 'good'. The developed description of a pattern of personal and interpersonal fulfilment makes concrete what we *mean* by the truly human good. We are not saying that the fulfilment of some hypothetically neutral, naturalistic pattern of satisfactions is the criterion of the truly human good. This would be a fiction, for human satisfaction is already within the context of moral good. We are, as human beings, inescapably within the context of good from start to finish. The 'justification' of judgments of good is a rational survey, from inside this context, of long-term moral viability.

It should be added here that this account of the search for a wider ground of human good is not meant to indicate that the search can be completed. It never could be completed, because the content of moral obligation is not comprehended and finalized in the past, but is in detail constantly changing as the world of things and knowledge and people (individuals and societies) change. The *particular* content of ideas of what it is good to do and seek must change along with other change—with change in social structure, the position of women, the emancipation of formerly backward races, new understanding of human potentialities, scientific and technological advance. To take only one or two obvious examples; the satisfaction and ethics of marriage must be altered by better understanding of persons and personal relations, or of the techniques of family planning. The ethics of participation in war is radically altered if war means total self-destruction. New moral dangers, satisfactions, obligations arise out of the developments of mass media. . . . The content of human satisfaction and moral wisdom alike have to grow continually, to keep pace with continually new challenges. The sifting of the genuine from the spurious goes on endlessly.

The judgment that a pattern of human living is *good* is a judgment that it *ought* to be. This judgment immediately implies that there is a moral obligation to try to promote it. Further, this recognition that what ought to be implies *an* obligation to try to promote it, is in some measure a recognition that *I* have at least a potential obligation to do something about it. There are, of course, many degrees of difference between the rather general recognition that 'ought to be' implies moral obligation and commitment, and my own sense of immediate and urgent obligation and commitment. Whilst recognizing that a certain state of affairs ought to be, I myself *do* little or nothing about it, either because of my human negligence or because it is beyond my immediate power. (It might for example belong to past history.)

Finally, the recognition of 'ought to be' and 'ought to do', though rational, is not *proved*. The penny drops. It is not proved, for the sense of obligation and commitment (in any degree) is the taking up of a disposition or attitude to *action*. This is the kind of thing which is *done*, and which is not susceptible of proof, as a statement may be. On the other hand, what can be rationally considered (though never strictly proved) is *what*, out of various alternatives, ought most truly to be. And here the consideration of different value-beliefs, beliefs about the satisfying life, may be very relevant.

5. PRELIMINARY SURVEY OF DIFFERENT VALUES

Consider now some of the things which we in the contemporary world think valuable in life and education. They can make a motley list. Some of the values are more immediate ones, relative to immediate individual and social needs. Others are less immediate and more general. Some of them are moral, some of them are religious, some claim partial or occasional allegiance, one or two may claim absolute allegiance, some are both means and ends, a few claim to be ends only. They can, however, purely for convenience, be classified under three or perhaps four main headings: (*i*) values which are *agreed* by civilized people as being basic to individual and social living: (*ii*) values which are *broadly agreed upon by responsible educationists in Western Democracy*: (*iii*) values which are held to be importantly valuable by *some* schools or leaders of thought but not by others, values which are more under dispute. They might be disputed (*inter alia*) for two reasons: (a) because one party holds the other's values to be projections of personal or group 'temperament' (e.g., the arguments between those who like 'tough', and those who like 'sensitive' values) or (b) because one party asserts, and the other denies, the 'absoluteness' of certain values.

(i) Under the first heading come the basic skills—e.g., reading, writing, simple mathematics, speech skills, etc. These are agreed to be necessary, for obvious social reasons. But although they clearly have utilitarian value they are not, of course, merely utilitarian in a local sense. Language, communication, the use of symbols—these are fundamental to all characteristically human living; one would not be properly human without them, and without them it would be impossible to progress to further knowledge. In this class, too, we must place the values of vocational preparation, interpreted in a very wide sense. Every young person ought to receive an education which has some sensible relation to the life and work of his own society, and to the place he is likely to take in it; this does not mean that he should necessarily learn book-keeping or the use of engineering tools at school. Another indisputable value is health, and all that is required for good health. Health is desirable in itself, and is a condition of attaining many other desirable things.

(ii) Then there are the values which are broadly agreed upon by responsible educationists in Western Democracy. Most of us believe that the acquisition of knowledge by our pupils is one obvious good; we believe also that it should be received critically and intelligently and should not be learnt parrot wise. We believe again that one of the indisputable aims of education is to pass on a tradition and a culture—social, moral, intellectual, aesthetic, religious. . . . In democracy we subscribe too to the importance of individual personality. Persons are to be treated as persons, not as mere means or instruments; to treat persons *as* persons is sometimes put as a central condition of all good education. Again, we all believe that good moral character is important, and that there should be a sense of responsibility. Finally, in our speeches and writings and lectures we all praise 'freedom' and 'maturity' though it is not always clear what we mean by those important but elusive ideas.

(iii) We now come to those values which are espoused strongly by some parties or individuals, but which are disputed by others. I suggested that this might be (a) because they may seem to be projections of personal or group 'temperament'.

Professor P. H. Phenix in his book *Philosophy of Education* [1] gives an interesting and rather unusual list of aims of education, some of which would seem to come under this heading. The relevant ones are: *Order, Intensity, Security, Variety, Activity, Peace, Power.* To this list one might add *Adventure*, and the 'tough' or the 'sensitive' virtues. Some people have a temperamental love of *Order*, both individual and social; so have some societies (e.g., the Germans?). This is something associated in the individual with the need for security, much felt by some temperaments and less by others. (Clearly 'temperament' is being used loosely: an individual's desire for order and security may be derived from his personal history rather than from any native endowment. And it is highly inaccurate to speak of the 'temperament' of a society: we include here what is sometimes called 'climate of opinion'). On the other hand, order and security may seem dull excellences; some prefer intensity and vividness of experience, fullness of life rather than safety and order. Again, we can contrast the love of variety, of *adventure*, or of the 'tough', active and enterprising patterns of living, with the 'values' of peace, quietness and confidence, serenity . . . sensitiveness . . . love. . . . Some people would put these latter high in a list of aims of education; to others they seem soft and sentimental. The belief in at least some of these values may indeed be based on a great deal more than 'temperament'; but it seems clear enough that temperament can have a good deal to do with it. Obviously temperament has a great deal to do with love of *power*.

There are other value-beliefs which are not so obviously connected with 'temperament' and which yet do seem to be influenced by it. One example is the emphasis in education upon *intellectual* development and in particular the value of intellectual clarity, as distinct from concern with *feelings* and the *imagination*. Every sophisticated educationist will of course say that it is important to educate feeling and imagination as well as intellect, or intellect as well as feeling and imagination. But one can often sense in a school the temperamental emphasis on the one side or the other. The same is true of the claim for education in greater *depth* of awareness, and for education in greater self-knowledge. The advocate of these may protest against the shallowness of personal impact in much learning. He is suspect

[1] Henry Holt & Co., New York, 1958.

by the extroverted teacher. ' Let us be up and doing, let us face the world', they say, 'this digging down inwards is unhealthy stuff.'

Then, finally, there are those values (b) which are disputable because some claim, and others deny, their *absoluteness*. The two important examples are the moral categorical imperative, and the absolute imperatives of religion: 'Be ye holy as I am holy, saith the Lord.' Some moralists, as we have said (above p. 24) have believed that moral imperatives are socially derived and relative to social needs and demands, or to some desideratum such as the general happiness. Others have held the moral imperatives to be underivative, final. Patterns of moral education will vary according to the two views. Likewise, as we have already indicated, belief or disbelief in final religious authority will greatly influence the shape of education.

6. THE JUSTIFICATION OF JUDGMENTS OF VALUE: PRELIMINARY.

These, then, are some of the many value-beliefs involved in education. The question (already referred to above, p. 41) now arises how we *justify* judgments of value, how we reason and argue about them, how they can be defended in case of attack. Disputes do not, obviously, arise over the first set mentioned; we are agreed about the need for the basic skills, etc. Again, within democracy there are many things which we are agreed about among ourselves—though the values of democracy cannot simply be taken for granted; human rights are apt to slip or to be stolen away unless there is constant vigilance, and some of the things we in Great Britain take for granted are far from being possessed or understood in many other parts of the world. Even we ourselves, in taking them for granted, may understand them and the reasons why they are precious much less than we think. This is true too of the so-called 'temperamental' values; but 'heat' here may be in inverse proportion to 'light': because we feel so strongly, we dislike the exposure of cherished beliefs to cold sceptical reason. On the other hand, the disputes between protagonists for 'temperamental' values (say between security and adventure, or sensitiveness and toughness, or contemplation and activity, or 'artistic' and 'intellectual') are not usually of an 'either-or' sort. The conflict is not between good and bad, right and wrong, or between 'higher' and 'lower' values, but between values which are very much 'on a par'. We can usually agree to differ about our varying personal emphases, and conclude, with fair comfort, that we need *all* these values in a rounded education at different times and places and in the right proportions: 'it takes all sorts to make a world'. It is otherwise if it is claimed that the beliefs call forth *absolute* loyalty, if the values are held to be *ultimate*. Indeed it seems good sense to say that if a belief is truly ultimate, there can be no compromise.[1]

This may be quite true. But the ultimate is not to be found on every—or perhaps any—blackberry bush; it requires searching out and much reflection. What we are immediately faced with is a multiplicity of values making various claims upon us. Every day and hour (in education and other modes of living) we have to make choices, to decide between this and that alternative. On what principles, when there is a conflict, do we decide? Can we converse about values in a rational way, arriving at a deeper and more 'objective' understanding of them, getting nearer to a common 'truth' about them, and so beyond our mere private feelings and opinions? Can any single dominating key idea be found under which more particular choices can be ordered? Is there a hierarchy of values, ruled by some supreme ordering principle? In education in particular, is any single dominating principle discoverable to justify our educational actions as appropriate and right?

[1] But we should here distinguish between a *practical* attitude of loyalty and 'no compromise', and the *theoretical* consideration of what we should be loyal to. This latter is in principle open to further reflection. See below, p. 59.

CHAPTER IV

The Justification of Judgments of Value

I. PLAN

The questions roughly put at the end of the last chapter can be restated under several headings. First, there is a question which underlies the others; it concerns the rational basis of any discussion of values. It is: 'Can we hope to attain to any degree of objective truth in judgments and decisions concerning values? Or are "values" so inescapably subjective that we can never get further than talking about our feelings (or something of that sort)?' This question must be looked at before we can deal with the others.

The other questions are connected aspects of one larger one, which is, 'How, when we have to choose between alternatives, do we arrive at more nearly "objective" decisions supposing, for the time being at least, that we can do so?' The first aspect of this is that of the general order or *hierarchy* of values, which includes the question of whether there is some dominating or key principle which enables us to place the values in some order or orders. This is a *general* question, and will be discussed in this chapter. The other (which will be discussed in Chapter V) is a *particular* question: 'How do we ("reasonably") decide what we ought to do in such and such particular circumstances *here and now*?' And how do we *do* it? How, for example, do we decide whether this boy, with his natural gifts, personal character, social background . . . should be punished or let off, encouraged to specialize in history or science, stay at home or go abroad next summer? Clearly decision here requires full knowledge of the circumstances, as well as some general principles of value (perhaps guided by some 'key' idea). The particular decision, that is to say, is made on the basis of a more general system of belief.

54

But this is not quite all: it is rather an intellectual way of putting it. We do not only *decide* to do something; we *do* it. And there is always more in doing than in thinking about doing. All these questions must be considered in turn.

2. RECENT SUBJECTIVIST VIEWS CRITICIZED

Is it possible to work towards an *objective* apprehension of values? Is there a *truth* about values which our judgments are endeavouring to express?

Traditional philosophy has given varying answers to this. In recent times the 'objective' view has, for various reasons, come under criticism. (It is impossible to expound and criticize these in detail in a chapter of this kind. The following pages give a bare indication of some of them.)[1]

The attack on the objectivity of ethical knowledge arose out of logical positivism and was popularized in the first edition of Ayer's book, *Language, Truth and Logic*. The reader will remember that significant statements were there classified under two headings, analytic or tautological statements, and empirical statements such as 'the book is red', or empirical statements of science. The validity of the former is dependent upon definition: the latter are verifiable in sense-experience. But ethical statements fall into neither class; they are neither analytic nor empirical. 'Stealing is wrong' *seems* to be saying something; it is not analytic or self-evident; it looks as though it had the same logical form as 'the book is red'. But the statement is unverifiable in sense-experience, by making some observation. Therefore it is in the defined sense 'meaningless' or 'nonsense'. The account of statements like 'stealing is wrong' was as follows: 'If I say to someone, "You acted wrongly in stealing that money", I am not stating anything more than if I had simply said, "You stole that money " In adding that this action is wrong I am not making any further statement about it. I am simply evincing my moral disapproval of it. It is as if I said, "You stole that money" in a peculiar tone of horror. . . .'[2] In other words, an ethical judgment is a statement of fact plus a certain kind of emotion.

[1] The reader is referred to S. E. Toulmin, *The Place of Reason in Ethics* (Cambridge, 1953), and A. C. Ewing, *Second Thoughts on Moral Philosophy* (Routledge, 1959). [2] *Language, Truth and Logic, op. cit.*, p. 158.

This view was seen at once to be obviously unsatisfactory, if only for the reason that although, when we make ethical statements, there may be no doubt about the facts (e.g. that X stole), we yet argue about morals. And since the facts are not in question we must be arguing about our own emotions. But as we never, when we are in our right minds, argue with one another merely about our private emotions, the theory must be wrong. If I am horrified and you are indifferent or pleased, these are just facts—there is no contradiction involved. What we dispute about is not our emotions, but whether the admitted act (say of stealing) was right or wrong. This takes us back to the common-sense view. But the 'emotive' view was not abandoned but developed in rather a different way by C. L. Stevenson in his book *Ethics and Language*.[1] Stevenson attempted to transcend the extreme subjectivism of the first view and to give some more rational account of it. He distinguished between ethical disagreements and disagreements about facts. Apparent ethical disagreements may include disagreements about facts: (we might, for example, think an act wrong if we did not fully understand the circumstances). But ethical discussions really concern favourable or unfavourable attitudes, attitudes of approval or disapproval. Ethical statements are 'emotive', in that they have a meaning which is commendatory, or imperative, in that they are used 'more for encouraging altering or re-directing peoples' aims and conduct than for simply describing them'. For these reasons, ethical statements cannot claim to be true or false. They do not on this view affirm that anything is the case. There can thus be no genuine reasoning about moral judgments. What appear on the face of it to be reasonings and arguments are not really attempts to show that an ethical statement is true, but are devices for altering emotional attitudes, either in oneself or in others. Various writers emphasize different aspects and use different key-words to indicate subjective states. Sometimes (as has been said) the emphasis is upon feelings and emotions, sometimes on desires or wishes. Here it is 'attitudes', there it is 'decisions', or 'imperatives', or 'prescriptions'. . . .

The fundamental trouble about all this is the same as before, namely, that the characteristically ethical has slipped through the meshes. If we disagree with another person on some ethical

[1] Yale, 1945 (repr. 1953).

question, surely we do not *merely* want to *persuade* the other person to agree with us, unless indeed he is 'persuaded' by the ethical validity of the statement to accept it for himself. Otherwise persuasion is a mere propagandist trick. Certainly we may in ethical argument want to 'persuade' in one sense, but only because we claim our belief as valid and desire the other person to see that it is. Again, if there is, as certainly there is, an imperative element in some ethical statements, the use of a sheer imperative, as such, is not ethical. Ethics legitimately raises the question of reasons why, sheer imperatives do not.[1] It is the same in the other cases. Ethical statements do not simply express or persuade to 'attitudes'; they do not simply 'decide' or 'request' or 'commend'. Some or all of these may be present, but unless the ethical notion of 'right' or 'good' or 'ought' is—explicitly or surreptitiously—introduced, none of these words accounts for ethical discourse at all. It is wholly unsatisfactory to speak of 'ethical' approval or disapproval without recognizing that there must be something irreducibly ethical in the actions or characters of which we approve or disapprove, without assuming that there is some ethical truth about which we dispute. An ethical truth is admittedly not like a truth about ordinary matter of fact. 'Valid' may be a better word than 'true'. But without *some* sort of assumption of 'ethical truth' and 'ethical fact' the most ordinary discourse about morals is impossible.

Nevertheless, although these views are utterly inadequate to account for the ethical judgments which ordinary robust commonsense must acknowledge and which we make every day, the various forms of subjectivism have made it clearer than before how closely ethical judgments—which when too simply regarded look like plain statements of ordinary fact—are related to feelings, approvals, recommendations, persuasions, commands . . . and, as I said earlier, to sense of obligation and commitment.

3. 'OUGHT TO BE', 'INVOLVEMENT' AND OBJECTIVITY

I pointed out (pp. 48–9 above) that whilst there is an ultimate and irreducible moral recognition of the 'ought to be', this recognition is not of something from which we can be detached in the same way as we can be detached from ordinary matter

[1] S. E. Toulmin, *The Place of Reason in Ethics*, p. 52.

of fact. The very recognition of 'ought' contains some degree of recognition of *obligation* to try to promote what ought to be. This recognition of obligation does not, we said, necessarily imply that we immediately proceed to do something about it in a practical way, that we commit ourselves to immediate action. We may do so; but we may not, for many reasons, some of them good, some not so good. But one must insist that there is a recognition of obligation bound up with the recognition of 'ought', a challenge to action which is, in some measure or degree, *personal*. Recognition of 'ought' involves, whenever it is genuine, some kind of moral tension in those who apprehend it.

To say this is to say that the recognition is not just an intellectual one; it requires feeling and conation. We do not merely coldly 'recognize' that such and such (say, honest truth-seeking, or compassion) 'ought to be'. It is doubtful whether moral recognition which is not, *at some stage*, integral with feeling and with potential or actual resolve, is even possible. (In the extreme case of the psychopath, the lack of power to feel seems to constitute part of the inability to recognize the difference between right and wrong.) In the very recognition of 'ought to be' there is, then, personal involvement, the consummation of which is a firm commitment of belief, and resolve to action. Recognition of 'ought' thus instantly brings into being a *bias*.

It is not the bias of an unexamined prejudice; it arises from free open assent. This is very important. If the bias were mere prejudice, or if our recognition of ought were simply something conditioned in us by our environment and upbringing, we should be caught up in a hopeless mesh of determinism. Education in any sense of a reasonable purposive enterprise would be an illusion. We should go on being driven in directions beyond our control, and our 'drivers' would be driven by *their* drivers—and so on.

But if the moral bias is the bias of a free assent, an open-eyed recognition of 'ought to be', with its sense of obligation and potential commitment, the question still remains—'How rational can the bias be made?' If we start with moral bias, can we progress from a more subjective to a more objective apprehension of *what* ought to be? I may have a narrow and parochial conception of what ought to be. Can I broaden and criticize and check and improve my moral understanding? I believe (as I have already suggested) that the answer is clearly 'yes', and that this is what we in education and life are constantly trying to do.

But if we take this line, we should be quite clear about two things. The first has already been stated generally; it is that our progress towards a more 'objective' view is a progress from within an already tentatively accepted *personal* point of view.[1] If I slowly reconstruct my conception of what ought to be and attain a more objective understanding than I did, it is still an 'objective' construction which *I* make. It is a sincere attempt to get beyond my own private limitations in one way; but it is still *I*, thinking more objectively. I started within a commitment with a provisional content; my conception of it has now (let us suppose) become more illuminated through communication with other people's points of view. But it has not therefore become a wholly *impersonal* thing. I was committed at the start, and I am now re-committed, only on a securer and more rational basis because I have opened my mind to opinion and wisdom larger than my own. This is in essence one of the cardinal aims in the education of any teacher (or any human being).

In the second place, it is the *substance* or *content* of my conception of what ought to be (affecting later what I *do* in particular circumstances) which is changed for the better, and not the recognition of 'ought' itself with its sense of obligation, etc. Recognition of 'ought' and of obligation is itself simple, irreducible, ultimate, and, in so far as it can be abstracted from its content, unchanging. It can be stronger or weaker, but it either exists, or it does not exist, in me. I may, for example, change my views about warfare, or sex behaviour, or voluntary euthanasia, or about how I should treat a particular person. But if I am conscientious, and have a serious sense of 'ought' and moral obligation, the recognition of 'ought' is still the same in its serious character throughout, even although I have changed my mind about *what* ought to be, or *what* ought to be done.

4. PROBLEM OF THE 'HIERARCHY' OF VALUES

With these preliminary questions out of the way, let us now consider some of substance or content, of competing claims

---

[1] I assume of course that the person grows up in society.

between different values in life and education, asking whether they can be put in any order or hierarchy, and whether there is any key principle which can give overruling guidance in moral and educational judgments and decisions.

Returning to the distinction (above, pp. 44–5) between 'higher' and 'lower' values, it can surely be said that there is no doubt that many of the judgments of 'higher' or 'lower' which we make have a considerable degree of objective truth. The values of the spirit and intellect, generally speaking,[1] are 'higher' than mere bodily values; the pursuit of the arts, literature, science, philosophy, are 'higher' than the pursuit of amusement, games, eating and drinking; responsibility coupled with freedom is 'higher' than mere obedience to imposed authority. And within this or that range of values, we can admire, and with good reason, the higher developments of any one of them. Long human experience has shown us the difference between 'high' and 'low' intellectual values, between the eminent and the commonplace. We can, by some measure of participation, extended by imagination, enter into the intellectual magnificence of the great thinkers, philosophers, theologians, scientists. We can admire the superiority of the comprehensiveness and depth and illumination of their minds. Once again, we can say with virtual certainty that the intellectual excellence of Plato, St Thomas Aquinas, Kepler, Newton, Kant, Huxley, Einstein . . . is 'greater', 'higher', 'better' than that of a child, or of you and me. The same kind of thing can be said of the imaginative superiority of the great artists, Sophocles, Shakespeare, Milton, Goethe . . . Leonardo, Rembrandt, Cézanne. If we as educationists set a high store on the cultivation of intellectual and imaginative excellence, we are acting upon ground which is as secure and 'objective' as anything could be.

Then there are the peculiarly personal and interpersonal values—love, integrity, responsibility, freedom, and a good many more—to which I shall return. Within our commitment, we can confirm their supremacy by consultation with many worthy witnesses.

Maritain sums it up as follows, from his own Catholic commitment.

---

[1] Judgments of 'higher' or 'lower' do not give rules for *particular* actions. See above, p. 45, and below, pp. 72 sq.

There is no unity or integration without a stable hierarchy of values. Now in the true hierarchy of values, according to Thomist philosophy, knowledge and love of what is above time are superior to, and embrace and quicken, knowledge and love of what is within time. Charity, which loves God and embraces all men in this very love, is the supreme virtue. In the intellectual realm, wisdom, which knows things eternal and creates·order and unity in the mind, is superior to science or to knowledge through particular causes; and the speculative intellect, which knows for the sake of knowing, comes before the practical intellect, which knows for the sake of action. In such a hierarchy of values, what is infravalent is not sacrificed to, but kept alive by, what is supravalent, because everything is appendent to faith in truth. Aristotle was right in sensing that contemplation is in itself better than action and more fitted to what is the most spiritual in man, but Aristotelian contemplation was purely intellectual and theoretical, while Christian contemplation, being rooted in love, superabounds in action.[1]

This account would certainly in some parts be questioned by those who approach from other points of view. But enough has been said to indicate that differences arise within a framework of *reasonable* discussion.

5. KEY IDEAS: SOCIAL COHESION: PERSONALITY

If, then, there is sense in the distinction between 'higher' and 'lower' values, if there is some order or hierarchy, the question arises whether there is any supreme principle or conception in relation to which the values can be ordered. If one says that, generally speaking, the values of spirit and intellect are 'higher' than those of the body, or than mere amusement, it cannot be simply that one likes some of them more than others. One may, but even that depends upon the time and occasion, and one's general presupposition. The order which we give to the values must depend, it would seem, upon commitment to some dominating belief. Maritain's dominating belief is in a religious meta-. physic as expounded by Thomism. It postulates time and eternity, the love of God and the love of man, and the Aristotelian distinction between the speculative and the practical intellect, all comprised within a Christian framework. The values fall into

---

[1] *Thomist Views on Education.* The fifty-fourth Year-book of the National Society for the Study of Education, *op. cit.*, p. 54.

their places within that scheme. If one rejects that scheme one
may opt for another.

An alternative dominating belief, for example, may be belief
in the importance of the survival of a society, or in its harmony
or cohesion. This is what Dr Toulmin argues for in his book
The Place of Reason in Ethics. His ideal is 'social cohesion'. All
responsible ethical judgment sets store upon such common
virtues as truth-telling, honesty about property, keeping promises,
justice, and so on. And if one asks, Why should these virtues be
cultivated? or, What is their authority? the answer will commonly
be in terms of social welfare, cohesion, convenience, happiness,
harmony. If we break promises or are unjust . . . 'Society' can't
carry on. The common virtues keep the wheels oiled; when they
are neglected the social machinery breaks down. Dr Toulmin
writes: 'The function of ethics is to reconcile the independent
aims and will of a community of people. . . . All the principles,
which together make up a moral code, can be related to some
institution within the society, the code as a whole to the complete
social organization.' [1] The very idea of community, he argues,
is the idea of a group of individuals who habitually avoid types
of behaviour liable to inconvenience others. 'The concept of
"duty", in short, is inextricable from the "mechanics" of social
life, and from the practices adopted by different communities in
order to make living together in proximity tolerable, or even
possible . . . And we can fairly characterize ethics as a part of
the process whereby the desires and actions of the members of a
community are harmonized.' [2]

This is perfectly sound as far as it goes. Social cohesion does
represent a regulative idea. But it does not go the whole way.
There is a wide range of values operative in private *personal* life,
or in small inter-personal groups—between friends, in families,
between teacher and children . . . which 'social cohesion' and its
common virtues do not finally explain at all. It can be retorted
that 'society' is made up of persons, and that the common virtues
making for social cohesion are virtues required and exercised by
persons. Nevertheless one can find quite different *reasons* for
observing the common social virtues if one looks at them from
the angle of private personal relationships rather than from that
of social mechanics. If I as your friend break my promise to

[1] *The Place of Reason in Ethics,* p. 170.   [2] *Op. cit.,* p. 136.

you, or am unjust, untruthful, or dishonest, this is 'wrong', not simply because such acts erode 'social cohesion', but (more importantly) because they erode something much less abstract, formal and general, much warmer and more intimate, namely, my personal relationship with you. So that without in any way denying the need for more impersonal moral principles, without denying 'social' justification, there is another line of explanation.

The personal principle seems to be, morally speaking, of a more fundamental order than 'social cohesion'; the latter providing only what Kant would have called a 'hypothetical' imperative.[1] It is only a reasonable expediency. '*If* you want society to run smoothly, observe the virtues.' (Moreover, cohesion and 'smooth running' may not always be good.) It can be claimed, on the other hand, that imperatives arising from the nature and needs and rights of persons are much nearer to unconditional or 'categorical' imperatives. In spite of the fact that so much (too much) writing upon ethics is almost exclusively in terms of social cohesion, there is also a widespread recognition that some duties are not simply relative to this or that society's need for cohesion, but as *human* duties, transcend it.[2] The protests, for example, against colour-discrimination in different parts of the world come from a conviction that there are human rights and duties which are above and beyond this or that society or political loyalty.

6. AN IDEAL OF PERSONAL LIVING AS A KEY

Persons is certainly a keyword in education and life. But we have to be on guard in talking about this subject. 'Respect for persons and personality' is a truth, but it is also a cliché. 'Persons' can mean nearly anything and almost nothing—centres of wisdom, imagination, heroism, love: witches' cauldrons from which come forth every evil thing, cruelty, persecution, envy, greed, orgies of perversity and wickedness. Religiously speaking, the person is often conceived as an empty vessel waiting to be filled with God's grace or the Devil's evil. When we think of

[1] See *Fundamental Principles of the Metaphysics of Ethics*, Immanuel Kant Abbott's translation, p. 35 and *passim* (Longmans, 1911).
[2] Or as near to it as we ever get.

young children, or of our good kind friends, or of saints, we say, perhaps, 'What a piece of work is man!' But it is also 'persons' who demand and lap up the horrors of the cheap press, and 'persons' who supply the demand for sensation by intruding upon private love and private sorrow. It is 'persons' who jostle and push, drive maliciously, shoot policemen in the stomach, 'cosh' old women. . . . 'Persons' means all men, the outstandingly good, the abysmally evil, the ordinary motley-coloured people like ourselves. Man is made, we are told in Holy Writ, 'in the image of God'. In the same Writ the prophet declaims, 'The heart is deceitful above all things and desperately wicked'.

So, if 'person' is to be used as a key idea in the understanding of the order of human values, we have to ask carefully, 'How?' In what way?

The broad answer is, I think, that it is not so much 'personality' or 'persons' as an abstract idea which is a key to the understanding of the order of values, as a very concrete idea, developed out of long experience, of what human growth and development at its best should be. Or, to put it another way, it is not just the *fact* of 'personality' which is important (and it is important) as the *values* which the expanding growth of personality can make real. It is through an idea, or an ideal, of what personality can be, and *ought to be*, that we can judge the relative value and importance of the various values that have been mentioned. Indeed, although we are bound often to speak of 'the values' as though they were self-subsistent entities, they are in fact abstractions from human enterprise. The 'values' of justice, truth, charity, and the rest, have no meaning except in so far as they are realized in the life of persons: and what we have to see is how they contribute, in different ways, to that life at its best.

Of course the *fact* of personality, with its freedom and all that this entails, is of utmost importance.[1] It is the fact of human beings, with all their potentialities of thinking, feeling, loving, hating . . . of freely choosing . . . which is the condition of all the values, and disvalues, that there are (at any rate within the human sphere). But, as we have said, the 'human being' can become almost anything; and it is a particular ideal conception of human nature and its development in certain direc-

---

[1] See below, Chapters VII and VIII.

tions, which alone can give an evaluative 'key' to the various claims of the values.

In this context we can see why, speaking generally, we, with our own ideals of human personal living, rate some values 'good' or 'bad', 'higher' or 'lower', and why we may even rate some as absolute. Cruelty, drug-addiction, greed, lying, injustice, are destructive of the expanding and growing life of persons and the relations between persons: love, generosity, truth, justice . . . make for fuller human life. Freedom and responsibility (in the measure and degree in which they are possible) are the conditions of every kind of human growth, and their final denial a final wrong against man anywhere. If we rate the values of the intellect and imagination and character as 'higher' than those of mere pleasure, amusement, eating and drinking, it is because through the former, human understanding, experience, and action have been extended in range, depth and quality. Through them has developed, largely, through the ages, the richness of 'the piece of work' that man is. The 'lower' [1] pleasures certainly have their place, but a life devoted chiefly to them would be less than personal.

7. 'PERSONALISM'—AND THE IMPERSONAL

The considerable study of the person and of personal relation-ships in recent times has brought out the complexity and subtlety of personal life and personal relationships, and has shown how personal development is very largely *inter*-personal development. The philosophy of 'Personalism', better known in France and Germany and Switzerland, but developed in Great Britain in an original way by John MacMurray [2] and others, is worth the attention of teachers. Martin Buber, though difficult, has been fairly widely read. Gabriel Marcel has become recently better known in England through his Gifford Lectures.[3] Emmanuel

---

[1] Not the evil ones. See pp. 44–5 above.

[2] Professor MacMurray's Gifford Lectures, 'The Form of the Personal', are his most recent and mature work. They are published in two volumes (Faber, London, 1957). Volume I, *The Self as Agent*. Volume II, *Persons in Relation*.

[3] Gabriel Marcel's Gifford Lectures were published under the title *The Mystery of Being* (Harvill Press, 1951).

Mounier [1] deserves to be known. Some of these writers look in a fresh way at the ordinary virtues from the standpoint of 'personal' living. They also examine minutely the nature of personality and the personal, and they greatly illuminate what can only be called the finely spun ethics of intimacy. They show new and often profound insights into the conditions of human freedom and growth and into virtues and disciplines not to be found in the ordinary lists of such things. We are made aware of how the 'fundamental nature of the person is not originality nor self-knowledge nor individual affirmation . . . but in communication'. We are told to learn consciously to accept the difficult fact of the *obstacle* of other people. 'Love . . . is a mutual disease, and inferno.' 'The world of others is no garden of delight: it is a perpetual provocation to self-diminishment or aggrandisement.' (For Sartre, it is plain Hell. 'Hell is other people.') In self-defence against it, some 'narrow all their social contacts'. Others make themselves into objects, or, alternatively, restrict their circle to people who will consent to act as their own mirror. But a person can only grow by making himself, as Marcel says, 'available' to other people. The first condition of the person's true existence is his 'decentralization'. 'The person only exists thus towards others, it only knows itself in knowing others, only finds itself in being known by them. . . . It is in material nature . . . that we find mutual limitation and exclusion because a space cannot contain two things at once. But the person, by the movement which is its being, *ex-poses* itself. . . .' [2] 'The economic of personality is an economic of donation, not of compensation nor of calculation. Generosity dissolves the opacity and annuls the solitude of the subject, even when it calls forth no response: but its impact upon the serried ranks of opposing instincts, interest and reasonings can be truly irresistible. It disarms refusal by offering to another what is of eminent value in his own estimation, at the very moment when he might expect to be over-ridden as an obstacle, and he is himself caught in its contagion: hence the great liberating value of forgiveness, and of confidence.' [3]

[1] Readers are referred to Mounier's *Personalism*, trans. P. Mairet (Routledge, 1952), and to a truncated edition of his *The Character of Man*, trans. Cynthia Rowland (Rockliff, London, 1956).

[2] *Personalism*, p. 20.   [3] *Op. cit.*, p. 22.

The categorical importance of treating persons as persons and not things is stressed. 'Whenever I treat another person as though he were not present, or as a repository of information for my use, an instrument at my disposal; or when I set him down in a list without right of appeal—in such a case I am behaving towards him as though he were an object, which means in effect, despairing of him. But if I treat him as a subject, as a presence—which is to recognize that I am unable to define or classify him, that he is inexhaustible, filled with hopes upon which alone he can act—that is to give him credit. To despair of anyone is to make him desperate: whereas the credit that generosity extends regenerates his own confidence.' [1]

Mounier's teaching is that the way of growth is a direction outward toward the world and other persons. It is important that in asserting the relationship with persons we should not forget that there is also the *world*. There is much that is *im*personal in our universe, and there is some danger in being one-sided in the emphasis on persons and personal relations. Even within the human sphere there are, as we have seen, some relatively impersonal social and political values. The teacher (or examiner) has his duty to academic standards. Law, justice, clear-headed administrative action, are examples of proper loyalty to somewhat impersonal good. Then there are important interests in logical and mathematical structures, there is the world of natural science—physics, astronomy, geology, biology. . . . And there is the world of the arts. Martin Buber has a good deal to say about the 'dialogue' with nature—although it might be argued that he covertly personalizes nature.[2] If it is true that we find ourselves in losing ourselves, the study and contemplation of the vast mysterious and largely impersonal universe is an example of it. In concern for the impersonal, man has increased his spiritual stature not only intellectually but imaginatively, æsthetically and sometimes religiously. (Though here again he may believe himself to be confronted ultimately with the not-less-than-personal.[3]) In the range of the 'higher' values, there are contained many which feed total personal growth through encounter with the impersonal. Human good is personal, but much more.

[1] *Op. cit.*, p. 23.
[2] See below, pp. 178–81
[3] See below, pp. 179–82

8. MORAL UNIVERSALITY: TWO EXAMPLES OF 'JUSTIFICATION' ARGUMENTS

It is, then, in the context of human growth and development, and the expansion—in every kind of way—of personal and inter-personal life, that the general 'ordering' of the values is determined. This is the *reasonable* working out within our own 'commitment'. Being formulated inescapably within a commitment and within a culture, it is touched, as always, with human fallibility. The breadth and depth of the concrete idea of 'the supreme good for man' is so immense that no human person and no society can rightly claim that it has been adequately comprehended even as an ideal. Human reason, illuminating the insights of experience, has to do the best it can under its own limitations, which are in part cultural. A Chinese or Indian sage may view very differently the importance of the individual personality and the obligation to respect it, *vis à vis* the claims of the family. His system of values has a different focus and a different perspective. Yet for reason, local culture cannot be the last word. Reason seeks universals, common human elements beneath and beyond cultures, though seen through them and necessarily manifested in them. Reason, exercised from within a cultural setting of experience which in a sense limits it, is, *qua* reason, struggling after objectivity, in this case the truth about the good of man as man. Our own struggles after objectivity, in the pages which precede this, point in the direction of a good for man which is focused upon and realized in personal and inter-personal life. If this is in fact our orientation, then, practically speaking, it implies an unconditional or categorical imperative to pursue it in all ways open to us.

The way in which the attempt to justify value-judgments reasonably may be carried out can be further illustrated by two examples, the first a negative one.

Let us take (i) the claims of power, domination, self-assertion. The exercise of power is not in itself good or evil. Domination is on some occasions required; so is self-assertion. But when any or all of these are loved and sought for their own sakes, or when they become dominating motives, supreme ideals, everything humanly good goes wrong. Throughout history men have acted under these 'ideals'. They have been pushful, ruthless, cruel, often with great success and effect. The strong have exulted in their power and have given thanks to their own particular god for the glory of it. Nazism is only one recent example. But a claim to the supreme good is a universal human claim. The good must be for the good of human beings as such, and not only for *some* human beings. The ideal of power and domination *therefore* cannot be the supreme human good, since power and domination are morally legitimate only in some circumstances for some people, and not for all. If it is claimed absolutely it becomes tyranny at the expense of others. Intrinsically, as a universal ideal it is self-contradictory, since all cannot dominate. Further, the exercise of power and domination for its own sake is humanly destructive. Human nature in the grip of it does not grow and mature but shrinks and perishes in regressive infantilism. The pathological vanity and progressive isolation of tyrants is well known.

The power ideal, again, destroys the very possibility of truth. One might imagine, for example, that one could *argue* with the Nazi, and that he could argue back. But if argument means reasonable discourse, he could do nothing of the kind. The Nazi could not argue; he could only shout or beat up. To argue in any real sense means that you assume that there is an objective truth which can be discovered—at least to some degree—by argument or discussion. This implies a certain openness of mind and a certain humility. But if you once have forsaken truth for power propaganda, there is no more argument, but only force, and it may be in the end, war. Certainly Nazi propaganda pretended to argue, pretended to say what was true and to claim truth. In order to be effective it had to start upon the basis of the human value of truth if it was even to appear to convince those who were not yet wholly indoctrinated. But of course even this trick of pretending to speak and to care for truth is soon seen through. So we had a system which was not really a system of ideas claiming truth at all, but an anti-human organization for power setting out to persuade by tricks of rhetoric, backed up by the machine gun and the concentration camp.

(ii) As we said before, arguments and convictions about values are not simply a matter of 'seeing' or of abstract intellectual conviction. Some recognition of obligation, some feeling, some conation are involved. In order to illustrate this I shall take another example nearer home of a difference of opinion where two disputants are, broadly speaking, on the same (humanistic) side, and yet hold rather importantly different opinions about education. One is more 'old-fashioned'. He believes that what he calls the efficient teaching of academic subjects in a set curriculum is the chief aim of school education. He believes in the discipline of obedience, as in the discipline of 'subjects', stresses class teaching, hasn't much use for the arts, regarding them as expensive luxuries, is suspicious of too much freedom. His values are 'stern' or 'tough'. The other is suspicious of 'subjects' and of what is often called 'discipline'. He believes in as much freedom to explore and solve problems as possible, in a flexible curriculum, in the growth of personality through experiment and social living, in art and 'creative' activities. It is a familiar, if commonplace, contrast. If the two are discussing the character of a school known to them both, it will be less of a discussion than a succession of statements and counter-statements on every point.

Is this the last word? Must it be simply left at that? Is argument thus bound up with differing value-judgments therefore so subjective, so closed to the further opening up of truth? I do not think so. It is certainly true that the beliefs on each side are not readily changed by purely intellectual or dialectical disputation. Two opponents of the kind mentioned do not convince each other, or not very much, by argument. One says of the other, 'Oh, he will never change his mind'. This may be true. But if so, why? It will not necessarily be from lack of logical acumen. It may be from a defect of will and character and voluntary choice, an unwillingness to be open to new experience, a complacency and lack of humility which closes the way to possible growth and change of opinion. In such a dispute about 'toughness' and 'freedom' the truth is no doubt complex, combining or transforming the truths over-stated on one side or the other. But to see the opposing truth requires virtues of character, *and* education of feeling, as well as clearness of intellect. The defender of freedom may very well be blind to the important convenience (at any rate at later stages of school) of defining 'subject' areas, because he is emotionally biased towards the less 'tidy', less decisive approach of 'activity' methods. Again, he may not, in his own personal experience, have discovered the emancipation of a mental discipline, where one has to go on doing for a period what one heartily dislikes and protests against. Or he may not have honestly faced the fact that there is on occasion an excellence in sheer obedience to a properly constituted and respected authority. In order to change his mind he has to be prepared experimentally to enlarge his experience, either actually or in imagination. This is difficult. It demands character and deliberate choice. On the other hand, the 'tough-minded merchant' tends to lack imagination, to be insensitive, to be complacent. He may seem sometimes to be almost invincibly ignorant because he wills to be ignorant. He likewise will not change his mind without a change of heart. And he will not allow his heart to explore. Perhaps he is secretly afraid. All this is not just his unlucky fate. He too can choose to be more open if he wills to. Certainly he is self-debarred from a better insight into the truth if he is not ready (as the rich man in the Gospel was not) to sell all his goods (e.g. his complacency) and give to the poor, in order to enter into the kingdom of educational truth. How can any teacher *know* how important it is for a child to develop faith in himself by having his own bungling discoveries accepted and appreciated, if the teacher has never sympathetically entered into the life of this child, and will not deign to do so? Or how can he evaluate the effects of music, poetry, flowers in a room, if he is not only blind and deaf, but proud of it? If he is an authoritarian with an air, what does he know of the sensitive tender values of a child's experiment and initiative?

I have been saying, then, that although judgments of value in education and life are not impersonal to the same degree as the statements of science, because in order to be aware of them we have to be 'involved', yet it is possible to develop a much greater understanding and objectivity about values, about what we are involved in. This progress towards greater objectivity is one which entails the use of reasoning of different kinds (and is in this sense 'rational', though always short of 'proof'). But it also requires a revision of our commitments and involvements themselves; this requires qualities of feeling, will, character, as well as of intellect. Whether or not it is true of all thinking, it is certainly true that in this kind of thinking humility, which is a basic attitude of will, is required. If a theologian were speaking, he might say that *some* error at any rate is due to 'sin'.

CHAPTER V

The Nature of Right Decisions

1. General Principles and Particular Occasions

If we look in one direction our judgment of the order of values, and our particular decisions, depend (according to the view expressed here) upon a *general* belief in the supreme importance of persons and personal life and development. If we look in another direction our judgments and decisions depend upon our knowledge and understanding of *particular* circumstances. The case of the Nazi is an illustration of the first kind. But if I advocate Course A for this child and you advocate Course B, we may both be in fundamental agreement about values, but our knowledge and judgment of the material facts may be different and so we decide differently. I may be mistaken because you know more about the child's background, make-up, emotional qualities, intellectual capabilities. Or if I disagree with you about 'streaming', or the proper age for transfer from primary to secondary school, it may be because I have more or less information about the facts, the effects, than you have. Differences of sheer experience and knowledge of fact may be the sources of differences of decision which look like, but are not, differences between judgments of value.

It is clear, therefore, that however necessary it is to have general beliefs about the order of values, and about human needs and rights, these give us no sufficient directions about what we ought to do on particular occasions. An exception may seem to be a rule that we ought to cultivate the good or better values in contradistinction to the worse ones. But this rule is so general that it is not itself enough to give sufficient guidance in particular decisions; it might be called a principle of all morality rather than a rule; there is always an element of individuality in particular situations of choice which demands attention on its own behalf, and which is not covered by any rules.[1]

The need for very particular consideration is seen clearly when we consider how the belief that this value is 'higher' than that is to be 'applied' to individual cases, or even whether it is accurate to use the word 'apply' at all. One may ask whether a very *general* belief can be 'applied' to a particular situation, if only for the reason that one is general and the other particular, and that the general is always too general to fit the particular. 'Poetry,' you tell me, 'is "higher" than beer and skittles.' I reply testily, 'But not *now!*' Indeed it can seriously be argued that any attempt to apply rigidly the hierarchy of 'higher' and 'lower' to particular questions of action, would lead not only to ridiculous priggishness but even to moral mistakes, and would in fact amount to a kind of irresponsibility to the duty of living in the best way in our actual world as it is. I would go further and say that any attempt to turn into rules of thumb the most important beliefs about values, leads to absurdity and complete chaos—and in effect to great *im*morality.[2] For instance, the principles of mercy, justice, duty to oneself and duty to others, care for human life—are all of them important moral values which claim allegiance. But they cannot possibly be turned into rules about what I ought to do here or now. For in a particular situation their claims may be sharply opposed. Sometimes if one is merciful, one cannot be strictly just, and *vice versa*; or it may (most would judge) on some occasions be morally justifiable to tell a lie in order to save another's life; on another occasion it might be wrong to save one's own life if one could only purchase life by uttering a lie which would be a lie in the soul. Or on one occasion it may be right to put one's parents' happiness before one's own claims to personal development. On another, it may be right to do the opposite.

Again, although there are 'higher' and 'lower' values, the 'higher' are not *against* the 'lower'—as the *bad* are against the *good*.[3] And they are not exclusive of one another. If I enjoy my food and drink I am not betraying my love of good poetry or my belief that I ought to have good will towards all men. It is, surely, rather that the 'lower' values take their proportional

[1] See below, pp. 79 sq.   [2] This is developed further below, pp. 83 sq.
[3] See above, pp. 44–5.

place in a pattern of living in which the 'higher' values give the general direction of emphasis. All have their proper place in the proportions of the good life, the 'higher', though not excluding the 'lower', being in general control. And if this is so, then it is not just *permissible* to enjoy the 'lower' in their time and place, but positively *right*. Not only are the 'higher' in a sense dependent on the 'lower' (one has to eat in order to pursue philosophy), but at times it is right to go all out for relaxation, enjoyment, and sometimes, extravagance.

The same kind of thing is true of what we called the values 'on a par'—security, adventure; energetic activity, peace. . . .[1] They are not opposed to each other except in idea, and we can say (as we did) that all are good in their place, time and proportion; the proportion being that of an ordered pattern of life with certain predominating keys. In their place and time we need both order and adventure, both intelligence and imagination, both absorption of the tradition and criticism of it. It is the particular place and time and occasion which have to be appreciated responsibly. To these particular times and occasions we come with our sense of values in their proportion: responsible deciding is the coming-together of these two things.

2. CONFLICTS AND PERSONAL DECISIONS

'To these particular times and occasions *we* come . . .' The form of this is important. It is we who come to the occasion and make the decisions. This is a personal judgment and there is no adequate analogy to describe it. The particular decision is not to be described simply as a conclusion of a practical syllogism, nor as a particular instance of a generalization. In stating it one sometimes uses language like that. But it is really too logical a way of expressing it: moral responsibility cannot be reduced to a piece of logical thinking. Although there are plenty of ordinary moral rules which are quite useful and which absolve us from the necessity of having to make frequent agonizing decisions, yet personal deciding is a thing which has to be done not seldom. It is a process which, involving the personality, takes in feeling as well as thinking. We have seen that values have to be known through involvement. If respect for persons,

[1] See above, p. 45.

justice, truthfulness, intellectual integrity . . . are to be expressed
and made real within the pattern of actual moral living, these
values require not only intellectual understanding and assent.
They need to be *believed* in. We have to feel them, and the pull
or demand of their obligatoriness must create a kind of tension,
a conative disposition in us which, when assimilated, becomes
part of our make-up. The man who really believes in the obligatoriness of justice and truth does not say to himself as a disembodied logician might: 'I ought to pursue justice and truth;
here is an instance in which the rule ought to be applied, therefore I must act in this way.' Or at least if a man ever did say
such a thing to himself, as he conceivably might, he would not
be making a genuine moral decision if there were not a great
deal more to it than that. Deciding is not just inferring. It is
rather that a moral person, apprehending, feeling the goodness,
'oughtness' and obligatoriness of justice or truth, comes to this or
that particular situation with already formed sentiments, disposi-
tional tensions in him; then, in these circumstances, he does the
just or the truthful thing.

But this is a simplified case. If there is a situation in which
justice is called for and I, because of my formed sentiment for
justice, do the just thing (possibly in spite of the fact that I may
be for some reason tempted to be unjust), that is perfectly straightforward. But there often arise moral perplexities, in which we,
in all conscientiousness, are in conflict, and do not certainly
know what to do. I have (let us suppose) built up within me
a sentiment for truth on the one hand and mercy or compassion
on the other. But perhaps I cannot act both mercifully and
justly. I have to make painful decisions. Or I hate violence
and have a strong sentiment of respect for human life and
welfare; but I have to decide whether or not to take part in
the violence of war for what I genuinely believe to be a good
cause.

Many conscientious people in Germany before the last war
were faced with a real dilemma. Should they go on pretending
to be loyal to Hitler whilst at the same time doing all they could
to use their influence against him without declaring it openly?
Or should they make the use of their influence impossible by
declaring themselves openly, and being at once arrested? In less
agonizing situations, the ordinary teacher in the classroom is

every day confronted with the need for quick decisions. He
believes in avoiding punishment as far as possible and in encouragement rather than reprimand. But ought he here to
punish or reprimand in the long-term interests of the pupil, or
perhaps for the sake of example to others?

3. MORAL SUFFERING AND DECISION

In situations like this, which could be multiplied indefinitely,
there is bound to be a kind of suffering and tension because of
real conflicts or because the ideal course of action which we
should like to put into operation is not practicable in the circumstances. (This is a particularly common experience of idealistic
young people.) So much moral choice is not the clear decision
between clear 'right' and 'wrong', but between one good and
another, or between two evils, between the lesser and greater
of two evils, or between what is ideally desirable and what is
actually possible in the world as it is. There are no exact rules
for guidance. We have to come to the particular situations with
our responsible tensions within us; and we must suffer the
inevitable consequences of this.

It is important to be clear about the nature of the suffering
even if only for the reason that the suffering of conscientious
conflict is sometimes confusedly interpreted as a kind of failing,
even as immorality. We have to distinguish in a clear way
between the kind of suffering we ought to experience if we know-
ingly choose *wrong* rather than right, and the kind of suffering
inevitably involved when we do what we conscientiously feel to
be right, and have to do it, perhaps, with a heavy heart. Men
have participated in war in this way—or have refused to participate in it. Teachers have in this way punished, or refused to
punish—in either case being aware of and accepting the pain
involved. It may lead to wrong or shallow decisions being made
if we confuse *this* kind of suffering with the pain of wrong-doing;
or think that it *is* the pain of wrong-doing. Most people (not
everybody) would agree that there are very occasionally morally
'justifiable' deceptions. If deception of another person is carried
out, this *ought* to involve moral pain. But this *moral* pain (of
justifiable deception) is not to be confused with the pain of
wrong-doing. It is very easy to be so confused, and it is some-

times because of this confusion that people act rigidly and un-imaginatively (and perhaps in effect immorally), refusing to utter a deception because it is morally painful to do so, and thinking mistakenly that this refusal is therefore right. An opposite example of the same thing is the confusion between what one ought to do and that which is the painful thing to do. A man or a woman may, for example, forgo marriage for the sake of a parent, wrongly thinking that the *difficult* course, something that makes one suffer, must be the *right* one.

In general I have been saying that there are no exact rules for particular situations of conduct, and that it is a mistake to try to turn general principles of value into exact rules of conduct. They can, of course, be counted as very general maxims which are useful. But it is the *person* who comes to this or that situation, the person self-shaped and moulded by his considered beliefs about values. The teacher in particular should ponder his values, especially asking himself about his key-ideas. He must feel these values as well as conceive them; he must experience in his own being the moral tension of their obligatoriness, assimilating them so that they become part of himself. He must possess them and (always under his final control and judgment) they must possess him. This is well put by Jeremiah, speaking religiously, of the 'New Covenant' of God with his people. 'I will put my Law in their inward parts, and will write it in their hearts.' [1] But 'the Law' is, according to the views expressed here, not a rule or a set of rules, but—to adapt the text—the very pattern or form of the 'inward parts', written upon the 'heart'. It is the formed and shaped person who comes to the individual situation of ordinary life or classroom, intelligently aware of its demands and limitations, and who chooses and decides here and now. Sometimes in the decision he has to accept an inevitable and moral pain.

4. 'RIGHT' AND 'GOOD'. UTILITARIANISM, AND THE TRANSCENDENCE OF MEANS AND ENDS

The conditions of decision need, in conclusion, to be stated a little more precisely—but necessarily in a summary way. The general questions of values which we have been discussing may be called questions about *Good*. The question of what one

[1] Jeremiah xxxi. v. 33.

ought to do in particular circumstances is the question of *Right*. We speak of benevolence, justice, honesty . . . as being good. We speak of a person as good: 'he is a good man'. We speak more naturally of doing right, of choosing the right course of action, of (e.g.) its having been right to tell the whole truth on that occasion. These are legitimate and useful distinctions; but clearly there is a close relation between 'right' and 'good'. There are a number of traditional views on the nature of right, only one of which need be mentioned here. It is the 'teleological' view, sometimes called utilitarianism.

The teleological or utilitarian view gives a very clear answer about the principles of decision when one is faced with a conflict of duties. It says we must look to the probable *consequences* of our actions. The best-known form of utilitarianism is the hedonistic form: in any conflict, that action is most right which tends to produce the greatest amount of happiness (in some forms of it one's own happiness, more usually 'the greatest happiness of the greatest number').[1] Generalizing, we may say that, for the utilitarian, *good* is the primary notion, and *right* actions are those which produce most good. And this is no doubt a great help when we are faced by a conflict and have any time to think about it. (Even if we have not time, assimilated experience of the past gives useful guidance.) We do in fact in our ordinary everyday life very frequently consider just this question: 'If I do this, what will be its effects on myself and other people? Will it be for the best, or for the most good, if I do X rather than Y?'

The distinction between good ends and the means to those ends is certainly a valid one within certain limits. On the other hand, it is not adequate to think of right acts merely as means to some end outside them. If (for example) we give money away, we certainly ought to be reasonably sure that it will be used for a good purpose. But the probability of its achieving a good purpose would not be an adequate measure of the 'morality' of the act. One might, for example, give money away in order to see one's name in a subscription list, or if it were a very large gift, in hope of a title. Every ordinary person would surely agree that the motive makes a difference,[2] and that it is not merely results or probable results that count morally. Or if a teacher has to use punishment it will not be a sufficient moral justification to say that

[1] See J. S. Mill, *Utilitarianism*.   [2] See below, pp. 82–3.

it will act as a deterrent; [1] the teacher's action is also an expression of his attitudes and beliefs: I have argued that this is of major importance. Again there are many difficulties, into which I will not enter here, about the 'end justifying the means'. It is a mistake if ends and means are conceived as too external to one another. Even if the end is good the means may be bad, and if they are they may corrupt the end.

In other words, the aim, the probable consequences of the action, the action itself, the way in which it is done, the mood and motive of the person acting—all these are together parts of a single phenomenon. We have to consider moral action as something which is motivated in a certain way and directed and intended in a certain way.[2] In moral action there is a mutually interpenetrating influence of end upon means and means upon end. And every action is action in a larger context of the pattern of human living. To violate a promise or to act unjustly does not mean simply that a *prima facie* moral rule has been broken, or simply that bad consequences will follow. Such wrongdoing, we have already suggested, undermines the 'health' of the person, and personal and social relations, which require integrity, fidelity, justice and a great deal more.

How positively are we to conceive of right and its relation to good?

5. DEFINITION OF 'RIGHT': ÆSTHETIC ANALOGY

I shall define the Right [3] briefly as the character of an action which is 'the best possible in these particular circumstances which could be done'. 'Best' is the superlative of good: 'best' means 'most good'. The Right (to repeat) is the character of the action which is the best possible in these particular circumstances. In this definition there is meant to be a strong stress on the two parts, and a dominating stress on 'best'. There is, on the one hand, the stress on the particular circumstances. The moral agent must be aware of the actual situation and must use his practical judgment

[1] The point is arguable. See my *Creative Morality*, pp. 58 *seq.*, 71 *seq.* (Allen & Unwin, 1937).

[2] Here see my *Creative Morality*, *passim*. Esp. Chapters III to VI.

[3] This passage is a selection from a fuller treatment in my *Ways of Knowledge and Experience*, pp. 212–222 (Allen & Unwin 1961).

about what needs to be done here and now. There is no escape
from this responsibility. It is true that approximately similar
circumstances often recur, and that one can in many cases apply
well established rules without much or any reflection. I made a
promise yesterday to go and see a certain person today. Of course
I shall do it, unless there appears some fresh circumstance which
may make me morally reconsider my decision. But this proviso
in itself indicates that the circumstances challenge some amount
of reflection or judgment, even if it is only the judgment that
there is no reason to depart from the original moral rule. What
is important—if I may labour the point—is that we should
realize that no rules or general principles ever finally absolve
us from the serious moral responsibility of attending to particular
circumstances.

On the other hand, there is the stress on the *best*, or the 'most
good' in the circumstances. If there is a serious moral responsibility to attend to the particular circumstances, and very often to
make a considered judgment about what to do, there is, if possible,
an even more serious responsibility to do what is judged *best*
in those circumstances. To be guided by immediacy only, or
by what seems obvious or easy or pleasant or convenient, would
be expediency. But the doctrine suggested here is not that of
expediency but of *moral* fitness. The Right is the *very* best that
can be attained or realized in *those* circumstances. There is, in
other words, a tension between right and good. The very best
in the circumstances is not of course the whole ideal of man's
good (that goes without saying). And it is not even that expression of it which might be possible in other, perhaps more favourable circumstances. The right is what, with all its limitations, is
possible here and now, which is *not* the ideally good: but, unfortunately, quite frequently the least among evils. The 'pull'
of the obligation to be fully aware of the circumstances, means
that to do right is to be realistic, to be moral in a real world
and not an ideal one. On the other hand the 'pull' of the ideally
good emancipates rightness from expediency. Attention to the
circumstances is not the only duty; the circumstances have to
be as far as possible morally infused by the agent's deep care for
good. This is, of course, in a sense a doctrine of 'compromise'.
But a word should not bemuse us; it is utter confusion to be
misled by the popular emotional aura of 'compromise' in which

it means expediency, and to suppose that it must be immoral. (If it were, most elections of candidates to posts would be immoral.) It is immoral to compromise if this means that you forget altogether about good and pay attention only to what is convenient and expedient. But it is equally immoral—or immoral in a different way—*not* to compromise if this means that you are not ready to face the necessity of acting realistically, that you prefer either to keep your ideals in heavenly cold storage waiting for ideal circumstances which never arise, or that you are ready, in supposed loyalty to your ideals, to act in some way which will not be for the best possible good *in those circumstances*. Right action is realism transmuted and illuminated by living care for the good.

The Right is the character of action which is the best possible which could be done in the particular circumstances. The circumstances of the moment merge into both past and future. The challenge of the immediate situation arises in part from circumstances in the past; and we have to take into consideration the effects in future of what we do. Keeping this in mind, let me turn to an analogy for illumination on the nature of right and its relation to good.

The analogy is that of the relation of a part of a work of art to the whole work. We may say of a work as a whole that it is *good*. Of a part of it—such as a pattern of brush strokes within a picture, or a passage in a piece of music or a poem, we may say, 'this is "just *right*" ' or æsthetically fit. The rightness of the part lies in its æsthetic relation to the whole. It is so related that (speaking rather ideally) the whole is æsthetically 'implied' in the part and the part finds the completion of its meaning in the whole. The complete æsthetic value or æsthetic goodness can only be apprehended in the whole work.

The rightness of the brush stroke arises from its relatedness. That in itself is a purely abstract and formal statement. In æsthetic experience, however, the relatedness is enjoyed in the actual experience of parts in relation to the whole. So likewise, formally stated, the rightness of a right act arises through its relation to a larger situation in an indefinitely stretching context of life. But rightness as experienced does not of course consist in making such an abstract statement or thinking of an abstract formal relationship. I said that it is *we* who come to decision.

Rightness as experienced is *felt* [1] as part of a larger good (as the brush-strokes are felt to be 'right' in the experience of the whole 'good' work.) For example, supposing that in some situation it is right to lend a helping hand to a child who is in trouble, the rightness of the action, formally speaking, is its fitness to meet the situation in the best way. But to a man infused with humane ideals, the helping act is a natural and spontaneous expression of his humanity. Its rightness as experienced is just a part of the meaning of a much wider good, focused at this point; and something of that good is infused into the right act.

I stress the distinction between the purely formal and abstract approach to right, and the realization of right in moral experience, because one of the perennial curses of thought is the making separate of what is only distinguishable. The philosopher must distinguish between right and good; having done so he finds it all too easy, and convenient, to deal with each in isolation and to forget their unity in experience. Having set up artificial isolates he then constructs an equally artificial statement of their relationship. Right, for instance, being separated from good, is not-good. Sir David Ross once wrote: 'If we contemplate a right act alone, it is seen to have no intrinsic *value*.' [2] The teleologist makes a similar mistake in making right a mere instrument to good. If it were, the right as such would possess no goodness. All this is utterly foreign to moral experience in which good and right, though distinct, belong together. The view I am suggesting is one which, whilst distinguishing right from good, makes good *ingredient* in right and right ingredient in good. The good of the picture or the poem is realized partially and at a point in this or that passage; so the goodness of a general ideal pattern of human living is partially realized at this or that point of right action.

This is an analogy of the moral with the æsthetic—and it must not, of course, be pushed too far. The moral and the æsthetic are not the same. The perception of rightness in a quasi-æsthetic act of moral apprehension is not as simple as the

---

[1] If one says 'felt', the feeling must be taken as the mode in which, at this moment, the assimilated effects of the previous experience, and rational thinking are operating. 'Feeling' is not to be taken as divorced from the whole personal context.

[2] W. D. Ross, *The Right and the Good*, p. 132 (Oxford, 1930).

immediate perception of a brush-stroke as 'right' within a picture before the eyes. The edges of the situation of 'right' are not sharp, and the moral good stretches outwards as the framed æsthetic 'good' does not. In moral situations we may have to take into account the more remote past and more remote future. Again, though the categories of means and ends are morally speaking inadequate, they cannot be excluded: and there are many actions in which it may be more true to say that we have to calculate or weigh up the possible effects, than that we judge æsthetically (or quasi-æsthetically) that this is the 'right' thing to do.

I have said that the right is the very best that could be done in the circumstances. But one may not know what is the best in the circumstances, and even if one does, one may not, at this moment, have the power to do it. Some moral decisions are terribly difficult to make, and even in the more straightforward cases one may not have the moral strength to do what one ought to do in the *way* one ought to do it. Ideally, perhaps, I ought not only to treat my neighbour justly (which is within my power) but to love him as myself. But at this present moment, the moment of action, I certainly do not love him, and I know that if I pretend to do so, I *am* pretending. But if I do not know X, or cannot now perform it in the spirit which I know is morally demanded of me, it is irrational to say that I ought now to do X, or that it is my duty to do so. All that can be fairly be said is that I should act according to my best lights and powers now, aware that they are fallible and feeble, and that I have a basic underlying moral obligation to improve my lights and powers with all that in me lies. My immediate duty is to do the very best I know and can, and my *general* duty is to make every effort to increase my insight and to educate my motives. This is what a moral person must say to himself. (A religious person would have a good deal more to say.)

6. THE IMPORTANCE AND DANGERS OF 'RULES'

There is an essential element of relativity in the account of rightness which has been given. And so there should be. No one knows better than the teacher how the circumstances of the classroom from day to day are scarcely ever exactly the same.

Yet though I have said that there are no unexceptionable rules of rightness giving directions to particular actions, rules do play a very important part in moral life; and in educational practice one ought to look at their functions and limitations.

There are plenty of moral rules which are obligatory in many circumstances. Approximately the same circumstances often recur, or at any rate recur in such a way as makes no relevant moral difference. Roughly speaking, what is right today will be right tomorrow. It is safe enough to follow rules, though there may be circumstances—not so very exceptional—in which there is a conflict between rules. Broadly speaking, moral rules ought to be respected and obeyed unless there is some *moral* reason (repeat *moral*) to the contrary. There are a number of reasons why rules ought to be respected. They are general expressions of frequently recurring obligations. They embody collective moral wisdom which rightly has prestige and authority. The individual's experience is limited, and the collective reservoir is useful. Further, the rules have importance for many people who have not much capacity to think things out for themselves. And of course there is not always the time to think. Again it is said (as we have seen) that obedience to certain rules makes for social cohesion. The rule is a safeguard against individual impulse.

On this last point, we have seen that the social cohesion criterion, though important, is not ultimate. It may be *sometimes right* to act in such a way as to endanger social cohesion. In this case, therefore, there is an element of moral danger in paying too strict attention to the social rule. There is nothing intrinsically moral in the opinion of society—which may sometimes become ruthless and overbearing. Even if it is not, there is always the danger that the individual's obedience may be a morally ineffective conformity because it is motivated not by responsible choice, but by a sense of conventionality or even fear. Obedience to socially approved rules can thus keep people in a state of moral immaturity. Worse than this, insistence on obedience to the ordinary social rules about truth, justice, honesty, chastity, etc., may produce over-simplification and complacency; and this may lead to the neglect of the less obvious rules and even to complete neglect of the individuality of moral situations. If society insists too much upon its rules it may prevent maturity, foster shallow acquiescence and leave undeveloped a sense of moral responsibility. It may even induce shams. The individual, acting under fear of social disapproval, may produce the *appearance* of socially approved conduct, whilst going his own way as far as he can in private.

But we ought to distinguish between this insistence by *society* upon conformity to rule, and the private, *personal*, responsible decision to conform to rules for the sake of the common good. One reason for rules, I hinted, is that they protect the weaker brethren who are not highly capable of judging responsibly for themselves, and who need to be 'kept on the rails' by rules. If an authoritarian *society* insists for this reason upon strict universal obedience to rules, it can, as I have suggested, be dangerous. But an *individual* may judge responsibly on some occasion that it is right to obey a common rule for the sake of his weaker brother when, if it were not for this, he might act differently. This is quite different from simply living by rule; it is a responsible individual decision.

It is often assumed, without sufficient reflection, that an account of morality which insists that there are some particular rules of right which *never* ought to be broken, is a more respectable, reputable and 'moral' sort of theory, than an account which accepts them as *prima facie*, which emphasizes the relativity of right, and which seems liable to the charge of being a mere 'expediency-morality'. But we have already seen that for many reasons strict insistence on rules leads to a complete *impasse*. If, for example, the duty to truth conflicts with the duty to protect life, one *cannot* obey both. They cannot possibly each, or both, be absolute. It is not morally superior to say that one should live according to absolute moral rules: it is to demand the impossible. One could only succeed in feeling morally superior as an absolutist by being quite blind to the fact that in obeying one 'absolute' rule one may in fact be ignoring another, refusing to face real circumstances. Strict 'working to rule' is, in fact, immoral counsel.

On the other hand, although there are no particular rules which are unexceptionable, it is perhaps as well to close on a positive note by reminding ourselves of the binding *general* rules of duty—to act up to one's light and powers, seeking to know the good as well as one can and to make it real in the right, to pay conscientious attention to the rules, and to do whatever duty is appropriate to the circumstances.

CHAPTER VI

The Idea of 'Application' of Theory to Practice

1. PRELIMINARY: OPINIONS ABOUT 'APPLICATION'

Classroom situations are infinitely individual. A prepared lesson, a prevailing purpose, becomes, in the hands of a good teacher, transformed into an individual pattern of conduct like the play of an artist's brush. A teacher, for example, who has to teach English composition, may find a class not necessarily ill-disposed, but bored with what seems meaningless. One of my colleagues tells the story of one such bored class which became suddenly interested in the fact that their young teacher was going on to teach African children. They questioned him about it, and thought it would be a good idea to find out about life in an African school. They then decided to reverse this order of procedure, and to write a journal (they called it their 'Memoirs') telling the children in the African school about their own life. The scene was instantly transformed, and can be imagined. The best boy was elected by the others (with unerring perspicacity) as editor; each boy had an appropriate job to do. The children became meticulous and self-critical about style, spelling, punctuation. The teacher was now besieged by eager pupils wanting to be taught. This is only one instance which could be paralleled by a thousand others.

There are two ways of looking at this transformation. It can be thought of as the teacher's skill or 'art' of turning to good use what is to hand, a skill which is discovered by 'intuition'. Or one can take what might seem rather a pedantic line, and call it an 'application of theory to practice'. In a sense, it *is* clearly this. The young teacher in question had learnt during his professional year that to engage and develop interests already there is a sound general principle. That is 'theory', in that it is an idea, and in this way it is obvious that the 'theory' was here being 'applied', being 'put into practice'. Yet this description is much too crude. No inference from the theory of the development of interest, however precisely formulated, would in itself by 'deduction' tell a teacher exactly how to handle a complex individual situation. The *individual* situation is not just a *particular instance* which the theory can prescribe for without falling short in some way. The theory is general and constant and the individual situation contains imponderables and variables (to use rather too-mathematical language). In education these are of the most crucial importance. I am not suggesting that there is not an important sense in which, say, carefully formulated psychological theory, based on research, can be 'applied' to teaching situations: there certainly is. I am only suggesting that whilst there is a factor of 'application', there is much more.

If this is true of the application of scientific (or near-scientific) theories, it is even more true of philosophical ones. These are so general, and the individual situations are so individual and so remote from what seem (to some) to be 'vague generalizations', that hard-headed people calling themselves 'practical', pooh-pooh such theory, regarding it all as practically irrelevant. Some years ago *The Times Educational Supplement* wrote: 'It is humbug to pretend that a person cannot teach perfectly well who is not simultaneously wrestling with the great perennial issues.' Ignoring the point that 'simultaneous' is a misleading rhetorical word here, the sentence pinpoints a frequent contemporary attack on the relevance of philosophy of education to practice. Since these attacks are not merely of academic interest, but have in my opinion a corrupting practical influence upon many who are too ready to be led by irresponsible catch phrases, it is extremely important to see how, if at all, general ideas of education can be applied, or can become relevant to classroom situations. We have, I believe, to work from the idea of 'applying' *theories and concepts*, as such, to practice, towards the idea (already developed in a general way) of a *person, charged with ideas*, deciding and acting in an enlightened way in the individual situation.

2. 'Theories.' The Application of Scientific Theory—from Engineering to Educational Psychology

'Theory' is a blanket term and there are theories at very different levels. In education there are 'theories' which are mere rules of thumb derived from practical experience. They are the 'hints and tips', of various grades. 'Write clearly on the blackboard', 'Speak so that you can be heard by everyone', 'Remember the back of the class', 'Keep them active', 'Don't (or do) "put on an act" ', 'Keep your temper', 'Be firm', etc. etc. This is, strictly, 'theory', since all these are ideas; but they are very *thin* and snippety, and for the most part are claimed to be merely horse-sense. There is no important problem of 'application' here. Then there are more complex and developed practical empirical generalizations, sometimes carefully made—for example about ways of teaching reading effectively, stages of development, etc. (We shall refer to the 'applicability' of these below.) At a much higher scientific level there are the very general theories of science (e.g., of gravitation, light, electro-magnetism, etc.), or the particular concepts, say, of the chemical structure of this or that substance. If we talk of the 'application' of these theories and concepts within pure science, we shall probably be thinking only of particular examples of them or their incidence.

Our interest here is not in pure science, but in the possibility and meaning of the 'application' of science and philosophy to practice. In order to understand this better, I shall take a number of graded instances, a sort of scale of examples of 'applying' theory to practice. I shall try to show that at one end of the scale the concept of application of theory is fairly simple, because application is little more than deduction from theory. At the other end of the scale such a complete transformation of theory is taking place through its assimilation in the person, that 'application' tells us hardly anything and becomes the wrong word.

The scale of examples starts from application of theory to practice in engineering, and considers (very briefly) in turn application of theory to practice in clinical medicine, clinical psychology and psychiatry, educational psychology, and finally educational philosophy. I shall try to show, as we go along this scale, that with increasing complexity and with the multiplication of individual and personal imponderables, the idea of 'application' becomes less and less appropriate.

In *engineering* there is the application of scientific theories (e.g. statics, dynamics, metallurgy) to, say, the building of bridges or aeroplanes. Here, the forces involved, the stresses and strains, the properties of metals to be used, can be scientifically worked out in advance by the usual hypothetical-deductive-experimental ways. The idea of application is relatively simple. The engineer designs girders (say) in an appropriate material, and with a structure which takes account of calculated strains, allowing for a margin of safety. He knows fairly precisely what he is doing; the laws which he assumes are taken as constant, the materials fairly constant. This metal, this girder . . . this bridge . . . is nearly (not quite) [1] an *instance* (or complex of instances) of a theoretic concept.

In *clinical medicine* the doctor is, like the engineer, not a pure scientist but an applied one. But his patient (or, more accurately, this patient's disease) is much farther from being a logical instance of a general idea than even this piece of steel is a perfect instance of its general type. The doctor 'practises' with patients. Patients are individual people, organisms and more, which are not nearly so constant as metals. The scientific theories, or the empirical generalizations which he judges to be relevant to this or that case, have to be applied tentatively. They have to be tried out, and they do not always work. The patient is an individual; responses vary, case histories are needed. To know what 'theory' is relevant enters into diagnosis and treatment, but all this is very much of an art—incidentally largely learnt in the first instance by working together with a master rather than by book instruction. If (e.g.) an antibiotic (a product of scientific research) has to be applied, its effectiveness is chancy: it has to be tried cautiously—much more cautiously than, say, a rust-proofing treatment applied to a metal. The good doctor has to know his patient in a different way from that in which an engineer knows his metals. The patient is (at least) a varying responsive organism.

In *clinical psychology* and *psychiatry* this is more so still. There is a great deal of general theoretical knowledge in the background—of general psychological principles, of psychopathology, of personal 'types', of motivation, conscious and unconscious, of

---

[1] The girder is not quite an instance—as nearly as a ball rolling down an inclined plane is an instance of a certain kind of motion. In pure science the instance is an abstracted particular which by definition is related to the general concept. But the engineer is not a pure scientist and has a practical interest not so much in abstracted particulars as things for *use*, with their potentially dangerous variations.

the extraordinarily tangled intimacy of mind and body, of types of mental aberration (neurotic, psychotic, depressive, schizophrenic . . .). But any wise experienced clinician knows that, although all this information is necessary, it is most dangerous to regard a patient simply as an instance of a 'type' or to pigeon-hole individuals too confidently. 'Type' is a useful abstraction; but there are no human individuals who are simply types. The generalizations, *when assimilated into the mind of the psychologist*, are useful, but only as illuminating a person who is always an individual with an individual history, needing at best, personal attention. 'Application' becomes here a subtle and complex idea.

The idea can be taken still further. Anyone who has read *Mr Lyward's Answer*,[1] or knows the person whom that book is about, will understand that there are occasions when a clinician's understanding may be limited by the formality of his relation to the patient. In Lyward's institution the 'doctor' (and that is not the right word[2]) *lives* with the people whom he helps to become adjusted to ordinary living. Though in control as Head of his 'school', Lyward maintains close relations with the maladjusted or disordered young people whom he is helping. Those who have read Michael Burn's book, or who have visited Mr Lyward's school, come to realize that it is in part through this personal—sometimes very 'costing'—self-giving that the successful 'application' of wide and deep psychological knowledge is achieved. This has important relevance to the good teacher, whose experience must sometimes be costing too.

Let us turn now to the 'application' of *scientific psychology* to *education and teaching*. Everyone knows that child psychology, developmental psychology, studies of learning, of temperament, of personal and social relations, of methods of teaching, as well as psychoanalytic studies, have been of enormous service to education. There is a real sense in which scientific (or near-scientific) knowledge can be and is in some sense 'applied' to education. It is also obvious that the understanding of physics or chemistry and the understanding of children are not of the same kind, and that the application of scientific theories to things is not the same as application to persons. Children are not 'instances', or things, or objects, or even patients: and the teacher

---

[1] Michael Burn (Hamish Hamilton, 1956).
[2] Nor are 'teacher' or 'psychotherapist' adequate.

is not a scientist or an engineer or a doctor. Applying psychological theory to teaching and education is not at all like applying scientific theory to building a bridge or an aeroplane. It is not so much the 'application' of science to a particular instance as the *use* of science by a teacher who has assimilated it, in helping him to come to terms with his practical problems. The teacher, like the doctor or the clinical psychologist, must have so absorbed what he knows that he comes to particular teaching situations with his possessed knowledge, sees them in a more illuminated and understanding way, and so acts differently from what he would have done otherwise, using his judgment like the artist.

There is even more in it than this. He is not just a personal artist in dealing with the human situations in which children are involved. The artist is, after all, dealing with *material*, and children are not material. Material has its own obstinate nature, as the artist well knows, but material does not answer back in quite the same way that human beings answer back. Material does not challenge oneself as artist in the *same* way as a person challenges oneself. In his encounter with children, the teacher's own personal life is inevitably involved, and this involvement can be deeply disturbing. In coping with this disturbance the teacher has to come to terms with himself. Part of this coming to terms is, as the psychoanalytic educationists keep reminding us, a coming to terms with the child in himself. So now the idea of 'application' becomes very remote and crude.[1] It is in encounter with other human beings that much education takes place.

All this is true, but much more so and in a more complicated way, of the 'application' of philosophy. In order to treat this properly we must notice something which has so far been assumed but must now be made explicit.

3. Values Implied in Applying Theory to Practice

Whenever there is, anywhere, application of theory to practice, a judgment of *value* is implied. In all the cases mentioned

[1] To reduce the idea of strict 'application' to absurdity, imagine an electronic brain 'fed' with a compendium of theories translated as rules such as might be 'fed' into teachers in training. Would the electronic brain be an 'efficient' teacher? Perhaps the fact that electronic brains cannot be strictly said to suffer may be one little thing to offset their present tendency to get swelled heads!

it is so obvious and so uncontroversial that it is not usually noticed, or it is unnecessary to affirm it. We assume, for example, that it is good to cure people bodily and mentally: health is 'good'. Of course we want to cure; so we do it. Again, we want in education to teach better, to help children. Therefore we set about applying psychology.

These values of application are assumed. Nevertheless, when the application is to *human* welfare (medicine, psychiatry, education), it is easy to fall into compartmental thinking, to forget the human personal needs of the patients, or children, to think of the application of formulæ, to forget that the first aim or value is to help them as human beings. It does not matter in an engineer, but it does matter in a doctor or a teacher, if he gets too much into routine habits, or becomes a hack, because that tends to make him a bit inhuman in doing his job. Many doctors still take the Hippocratic Oath (a magnificent code of ethics), but it is all too easy to become a little callous in routine dealings with patients as cases—or so one hears doctors say. Again, new treatments have to be tried out, certainly, and I as a patient may consent to be a 'guinea-pig'. But the doctor has to be on his guard against 'guinea-pig attitudes' on his own part. (Hospitals and medical teachers vary in their emphasis here.) The psychiatrist *can* be very hard-boiled; the educational psychologist *can* seem scarcely human.

4. The 'Application' of Philosophy to Education: Personal Involvement

What now of the values of the philosopher and of the application of philosophy of education to educational practice? I want to suggest that if philosophical thinking is to go any distance in transforming educational practice for the better, it must be hard and thorough thinking, and that both on its intellectual and practical sides it must be the activity of a *person*.

In this context it is really the last emphasis which is the key to everything. Of course one wants thorough philosophical thinking—thinking ideas through, in and out, up and down—as thorough as one can make it. That seems obvious enough. The distinguished names in philosophy at least think thoroughly, though they may do much more. But thinking as the activity of a person? Is this another truism or a rather fishy idea? Philosophers themselves vary, as I suggested in Chapter I, in the account they give of thinking, some regarding it almost as if it were a pure disembodied act of the intellect, others conceiving of thinking as a distinguishable act, but an act of the whole person, himself inevitably involved in those things in which human beings are involved—freedom, values, etc. In emphasizing here that philosophy is a particularly far-reaching kind of thinking, and that it is a function of a person, I am urging that this is the kind of thinking which alone is likely to make much difference to the practice of education.

I referred earlier to the critical tone of some philosophers in writing about philosophy as a possible help to human beings in practical situations. 'It is not the business of philosophy to give moral guidance; philosophy belongs not to the sphere of moral faith, but of the intellect.'

I need not repeat myself, or enlarge on this unduly. There is an important truth behind this attitude. Philosophy *is* of the intellect; it *is* thinking, not in itself moralizing, sermonizing, uplifting. . . . And emotion should not muddle thinking. But though philosophy is thinking of a certain kind, and the philosopher as such is a thinking functionary, his thinking (as we said earlier) is that of a man who feels and values and acts and experiences in every kind of way. If the thinking philosopher goes too far in attempting to divide himself, the range of his own thinking suffers. A certain tense form of repression is not unknown among some too exclusively logical philosophers, and shows itself in a 'conversion-symptom' of a sort of monocular mental vision. In sharp opposition to this I want to repeat that philosophical thinking (for example in education) is an activity of the *person*, and that the attitudes and feelings and interests (or the limitation of these) of the person affect intimately not only the way in which he behaves, but the range of illumination of the thought itself.

Thinking, of whatever kind, is not only an activity of the person; but thinking does much to the persons who think. Hard thinking makes them what they otherwise would not be, subtly affecting their action for better or worse. And I suggest that the sincere thinking about education which I have been advocating in this book, ought to do something in itself to educate a person, to make him more reasonable, less blind in thought and action. This is true of any philosophical thinking—about the self, freedom, knowledge. . . . But it is perhaps most importantly true of thinking as clearly as possible about the important *values* in education and life. As I have repeatedly said, one cannot *think* or apprehend the meanings of these ideas without at some stage being *concerned* about them—feeling, being moved, recognizing obligation, becoming committed. This concern of thought and feeling has a carry-over into active life.

But one must not exaggerate this carry-over. It needs to be reinforced. For the teacher, upon whom practical decisions constantly depend, it is not enough to think with as much integrity as he can muster: he has to make a deliberate orientation towards making real his values in practice. This is not in itself philosophy, but it is important.

Compartmental thinking and living, everyone knows, are all too easy. On Sunday I may see clearly and intend sincerely what I ought to do: on Monday the glow has faded into the light of common day. The doctors have their Hippocratic Oath, and they need it. The engineers need none. The committed teacher certainly has his own oaths of commitment, but they are for the most part silent, personal and private.

They must be his own. There are not just simple obvious rules set out in a code for anyone to see, universally accepted and straightforwardly applied. In the first place, values accepted for education have, as we have seen, been so *different* at different times and places, and are so today. (We can recall the differences about 'subjects', freedom and discipline, arts and science, the secular and the religious.) In the second place, the meanings and practical implications of such values as are accepted need— because they are so fundamental and interpenetrating—to be thought out at a deeper level than, say, the more obvious values of 'applying' science to engineering or medicine, or even the values of teaching arithmetic or reading more efficiently—all of which are indisputable. And in the third place, most important of all, the teacher has to think them and dwell in them and make his thoughts and commitments peculiarly his own. The great danger in education is tags and catchwords, what may have been living wisdom reduced to a formula for all to copy (and to fail miserably in copying.) We can think of the magnificent, or subtly fine work done in education by those who have made ideas like 'freedom' or 'activity' really their own—contrasted with the silliness of camp-followers who have never got farther than the emotive catch-phrases. It is quite useless to learn the 'correct' codes—even if they were all agreed upon—to mug up the summary statements. Each person has to sweat them out for himself. They have to be written on his own heart and mind— and he, in this case, has to do much of the writing himself. The teacher's Hippocratic oath is written on the mind and heart and not on a tablet or a piece of paper or parchment.

It is basically, then, through the deliberate time-taking integration of thinking and belief into personal living, that practice, and in particular the practice of education, is changed. We have already seen how the idea of 'application' of scientific principles, quite straightforward in engineering, becomes less and less adequate as the involvement in human affairs grows, and that personal decisions are required. But although this is certainly true of the 'application' of science, the need for *personal* transformation in the 'application' of philosophy to education is more radical still. Patients or children are, we said, far from being mere 'instances' of scientific ideas; yet medicine, psychiatry and educational psychology, in so far as they can be 'scientific', are using for their purposes relatively impersonal, 'publicly' formulated, 'publicly' verified knowledge. *Qua* scientific (and in so far as scientific), the knowledge is accepted by the practitioners on this kind of *authority*, and rightly. But philosophy of education, although it is a rational endeavour, cannot claim, as I have tried at length to show, this kind of scientific verification or authority. The authoritative ideas must be taken seriously, but always they have to be interpreted by the individual thinker, so that in the end not only has the *practice* to be a very personal decision (as it has to be for the good 'scientific' doctor or teacher), but the very ideas, the *theories* which affect the practice, are discovered finally through personal involvement. The person is involved from beginning to end.

We saw at length in the last chapter that principles of value, personally assimilated, cannot be turned into particular rules, and that judgment of the individual situation in all its relativity is demanded in right decision. The main burden of this chapter is simply an application of this to education. The teacher, we have been saying, has to think through (to the utmost of his ability) his principles, particularly his principles of value, and with his feeling and will and imagination as well as his intellect. If he does so, then through time these principles become so assimilated into his personality that all his dispositions are subtly changed, and his outlook illuminated so that he *sees* situations differently, notices new aspects and relations, and (with some reinforcement of deliberately willed effort) acts differently. He does not merely *deduce* what he ought to do now from theoretical concepts—though I am certainly not denying that deduction may have a part in the total process. But mainly, the teacher has through his thinking become more of an educated person; his orientation is changed, and his actions bear the stamp of himself. The teacher, once again, is much more the artist than the applied scientist—both in his 'application' of science and of philosophy. This is not itself 'philosophy', but character, leavened by philosophy, in action.

CHAPTER VII

The 'Personal Self'

1. ASPECTS: PERSON—SELF: THE LOGICAL POSTULATE OF SELF

The development of personal and interpersonal life has been taken as a key-idea of good education. But one needs to clarify as far as possible one's idea of a person and personality. This chapter is an attempt to sketch out one conception of personality; it will be followed by a consideration of responsibility and freedom. This sketch—and the chapters which follow—are merely outlines meant to give material for further thought. I shall make no attempt to summarize, textbook-wise, all the various views which ought to be taken into consideration in any adequate treatment.[1]

First, a matter of terminology. I shall speak of the 'personal self' rather than of 'personality'. This is not merely a verbal preference. The word 'personality' is a name for something which is studied by the empirical psychologists, a name for an 'object' of investigation, an object which has a history and which can be examined—in part at any rate—by scientific methods. From the outset, however, I wish to contend that this necessarily represents only one aspect of the human being, and to affirm that the 'personality' which is the subject matter of empirical psychology cannot be thought at all without presupposing something else—which may be called the 'self'. Therefore, in order to avoid begging any questions it is safer to begin by speaking, not of 'personality' or of 'the self', but in a portmanteau way of the 'personal self'.

Three aspects of the 'personal self' may be distinguished. Two of them can be studied objectively by science, by human

---

[1] See C. A. Campbell, *Selfhood and Godhood* (philosophical) (Allen & Unwin, 1957); G. W. Allport, *Personality* (Constable, 1938); Gardner Murphy, *Personality* (both psychological) (Harper, N.Y., 1947).

biology and psychology. The third is of a different kind and is known in a different way; it is, in fact (as I have already hinted), presupposed by the first two.

There are, in the first place, innate or inherited individual characteristics, such as intelligence, physique, temperament (importantly connected with physique). These innate or inherited characteristics have to be accepted as given; their recognition is important in education, since they set some limits to education and may set acute problems. The limitations set by intelligence are familiar; so are those of temperament.

Secondly, there are the many acquired characteristics built up in the course of an individual lifetime. Examples are, acquired competence in history, art, human relations, skills, attitudes, character. Smith has learnt patience. Jones has become an intolerant person. Robinson is now a good artist. What is commonly called the 'education of personality' would generally be taken to be the development, through time, of characteristics thought desirable (by whoever sets the standards) built up on the basis of native intelligence and temperamental make-up.

These innate and acquired characteristics, we said, can be described and studied scientifically. Empirical psychology can give a fair account of the structure and development of personality in a particular person's history.

But there is another aspect (the third mentioned) of the personal self which does not belong to its objective history, or at least to its history in the *same* sense, and which is not in the same way accessible to objective scientific study as is the structure of character or the causal sequence of personal experiences. This other aspect is in fact the presupposition of there being a structure and a history of personality at all, even of there being anything properly called experience or knowledge. Knowledge, experience, and their development have a temporal or 'process' aspect; but the process aspect presupposes an activity of something which is not itself activity and which may be called the *self*. There must be a self which is distinguishable from its passing states and which can possess, own, apprehend, know these states, both as passing and in relationship.

For example, I got up this morning, drove to work, read my correspondence, and am now writing this sentence. At the moment I am aware of what I am thinking about and at the same time aware of my room with its furniture and pictures: I am subconsciously aware of organic, tactile and other sensations. In order that I should be able to write these sentences as a true account of recent experience, there must be one 'I' who possesses or owns these experiences, who apprehends them as different, as successive, and as related. *Logically*, there must be such a single 'I' or 'self', since without it there could be nothing called experience or a sequence of experiences, no knowledge, no personal history. Philosophers and psychologists do often speak of mental states, or of the 'stream of consciousness', as though these data were somehow apprehended as existing by themselves. Thus Hume spoke of the mind as 'Nothing but a bundle or collection of different perceptions, which succeed each other with an inconceivable rapidity, and are in a perpetual flux and movement.' [1] But this analysis leaves something essential out, something which must be postulated logically, and which can also, I believe, in *some* sense be immediately apprehended by us. This latter contention is more controversial; let us look at the logical point first.

It is an extremely familiar one in the literature of the subject; the examples are well known. One of them is the striking of the clock. If the clock strikes three, it is impossible even to recognize the second and third strokes *as* the second and third, unless there is a self, the *same* self, distinguished from the temporal experience of the sounds, to apprehend all three as a sequence. If there were simply discrete 'experiences' of the sounds, each would be extinguished instantly it occurred and there would be no three-in-sequence. It can be said that all this (more clearly shown when the clock strikes twelve, not three) is a function of memory, which is quite true: nevertheless, memory in its turn logically implies a self distinct from its memory contents. Rather desperate attempts have been made by some contemporary philosophers to reduce the subjective awareness of sequence to objective terms, i.e. to a relationship between the sequent terms, to reduce the self's awareness of sequence of experiences to a relationship in time of the experiences to one another. But this begs the question. The relationship of myself, who possesses these experiences, to these experiences, is a unique relationship (first made clear by Kant) which cannot possibly be reduced to

[1] *A Treatise of Human Nature*, Part 4, Section 6.

the relationship in time of the experiences to one another. It has to be repeated that the relationship in time cannot be conceived at all unless we presuppose the self in unique relationship to its states. The idea of the self, that is, is the logical prerequisite of temporal experience.

2. Awareness of Self-activity: 'Enjoyment' and 'Contemplation'

This, if we like, is a metaphysical postulate, logically required. But it can also be argued that we discover the self in action in actual experience, though this is difficult to express without falling into the error of supposing that the self is part of the object of experience, whereas in fact it is always the subject, and never the object. William James said somewhere that when he tried to discover himself he could only discover his eyes converging before him, frowning. Much earlier, Hume had said, 'For my part . . . I can never catch *myself* at any time without a perception.' [1] To this, the witty and I think penetrating reply has been made, 'But can he not catch himself *with* a perception?'

I think he, and we, can. I believe we can be said to be aware, not indeed of any 'transcendental ego', which is a logical postulate, but of the identity of ourselves in experiencing: throughout a sequence of experiences one can be aware of the singleness and sameness of oneself as possessing experiences. One may be aware also in experience of the operation of what has already been logically described, namely, the holding together as one a succession of experiences. If I count five, I can be aware, not only of the sequent beats or only of the synthesis of them as five: I can in some way be aware of my own act of synthesis and of myself as the same throughout the sequence. I do not know *what* I am, but I can immediately experience *that* I am, that I am active, that I synthesize, etc.

An opponent may say, 'Yes, but you are doing the very thing that you have said we ought not to do, namely, making the self an object of awareness of the self, making the subject an object.' This objection is difficult to meet satisfactorily. But two things can be said in reply. The first is that awareness of

[1] *Op. cit.*

synthesizing, activity, self-identity, is not awareness of temporal sequence. *If* 'the self 'is 'being made an object' that is to say, it is not an 'object' of the *same* order as the 'objects' which are the temporarily sequent contents of consciousness. In the second place, the immediate awareness of self-activity, synthesis, identity is *not*, we said, awareness of the self in the sense of a 'transcendental ego'. It is not being claimed that we can be aware of *that* as an object of experience. That is a metaphysical postulate made necessary, it may be, by logic. What we do know in experience is the existence of the same continuing self which is experienced as possessing its experiences, as holding them together and synthesizing them. To say this is not at all the same as to talk about the sequent contents of experience at one end, or the transcendental ego at the other.

It is true that the self's activity and identity are being claimed as experienced, which seems to contradict the earlier veto. But the earlier veto was of making the self an object of experience in exactly the same sense as one speaks of the story of the day's experiences or of the striking of the clock as objects of experience. It can be claimed that there is in fact a difference between the way in which we apprehend the sequence of experiences and the way in which we apprehend ourselves as single, enduring and active. The difference was long ago given a name by Samuel Alexander,[1] in his distinction between 'enjoyment' and 'contemplation'. 'Enjoyment' does not mean *pleasurable* enjoyment (though it could be pleasurable). The meaning corresponds more to the German word *Erlebnis*. We may 'live through' or 'enjoy' the possessingness, the identity, the synthesizing activity of the self, be aware of it in that way. This is distinguished from the 'contemplation' of the related succession of experiences which the single actively synthesizing self possesses. The words 'enjoyment' and 'contemplation' are only words, but they conveniently pin-point this distinction.

3. PARADOXES: THE MYSTERY OF SELF

Certain observations must be made at this point—though they are observations which will raise more questions than they answer. (*i*) There seems to be a contradiction. We have said

[1] *Space, Time and Deity* (Macmillan, 1920).

that, in order to account for the experience (e.g.) of sequence, of history, there must, logically, be a self which is distinct from the process and which apprehends it as a whole. And we have said that although there is no direct awareness of a self, as it were, out of time ('transcendent' or 'transcendental', to use the jargon) we nevertheless 'enjoy' the singleness and the activity involved in apprehending the states which we possess. The contradiction seems to be that we are saying both that there must be a self which is at least in some sense distinct from time (in order that time sequence should be apprehended) and are also saying that we are aware of identity, ownership of our states and activity, which being part of our experience occur in time. They are not in time in the same way that successive states are; yet they cannot, even as 'enjoyed', be said to be *out* of time. This is paralleled by the common yet apparently paradoxical statement, that whilst the self of a minute, a year, thirty years ago . . . is the *same* self, yet this 'same' self has *also* changed, even in modes of activity, its approach to thinking, synthesizing. . . . In one way, I am the same self as I was when I was eight years old (and have a single history of experience which I can call 'my' experience). In another sense, my self—in respect of my outlook, my 'attack' on things—seems to have changed a great deal. It is perhaps better to call this a paradox than a contradiction, because both the statements appear to be indubitably true. I must, logically, be the same, as a condition of there being personal history. And yet, though there is one 'I' throughout life, there is another sense in which the 'I', in so far as I can 'enjoy' it in a sideways fashion, is affected both by the succession of what it contemplates and by the succession of what it enjoys. Though both sets of statements seem to be true as far as they go, they are, however, inadequate and frustrating because we can understand so little of this mystery of the self. It appears that we must simply accept them in their imperfection without understanding *how* they can be true or not. It *is* mysterious, and the intellectual statements have, it seems, to be left side by side as a puzzling paradox. I am—I must be—the *same* at the beginning and end of the symphony, or at the beginning and end of a course of education, and yet I know that I am *different*.

The paradox may look less like a contradiction if we remember that the temporal and changing aspects, and the extra-temporal and unchanging aspects, are to be thought of as *aspects* of what was originally called the 'personal' self. The term 'personal' represents the emphasis on the changing aspect, and the term 'self' the emphasis on the unchanging aspect—though as far as the activity of the self can be experienced it must be experienced in time. If we obstinately refuse to transform the necessary distinction into a separation, the paradox, though still made in a background of mystery, seems less contradictory. We may say that the 'personal self' is the same *qua* its aspect of self but different *qua* personal. This admittedly sounds a little near to word-juggling: it can only be accepted in so far as it clarifies, and discarded as it obscures. As before, the inadequacy of the words is simply symbolic of the incompleteness of the understanding. Professor C. A. Campbell, for example, writes: [1] 'The self may function when the person does not [perhaps, e.g., in insanity?]. But the person cannot function when the self does not. The person *is* the self, *qua* functioning in terms of definitive and normal character. Indeed the person, so far from being an entity, different from the self, may be said to be a something which the self gradually tends to become.' I certainly do not think it is easy to understand this language either. But Campbell is trying, as I am,[2] to draw a distinction which is necessary in order to get nearer to understanding of the personal self, but which must not be made into a separation.

4. THE PERSONAL SELF AND FREEDOM

(*ii*) The second observation to be made on this view of the self is that it leaves open, and does not bar, the way to the acceptance of personal freedom. The empirical psychology of personality, studying structure and history, is necessarily deterministic in its methodological assumptions. As with the study of other natural events, what happens now must be accounted for in terms of causes in the past and conditions which already exist. Explanations of behaviour, psycho-analytic accounts of motivation, etc., are deterministic in the sense that causal explanations are naturally and necessarily looked for. Empirical scientific psychology must be like this. On the other hand, the assertion

[1] *Selfhood and Godhood*, p. 88.
[2] And I have learned much from his thought.

of the *self* aspect of the personal self is an assertion of an element
in the personal self which is not identical with the time sequence,
but is detached from it. The logically necessary 'self' must be
conceived as in a formal sense *free* from past personal history,
standing off from it. If this is so, it may well be that self, in
addition to being able to apprehend sequences already before
the mind, may be able to alter the sequence of future experiences
and actions through its power of detached activity. The self,
by reason of its power of synthesizing, of thinking together (and
extensions of this), may be able to modify future action in a way
which is quite different from the determination of future events
by past natural events in time. Suppose we think of an action
where moral responsibility is involved. On the one hand, I may
let the natural inertia of my moving personal history take its
course: or I may reflect, after which its course is altered. I may
be naturally lazy or selfish and go on acting in a lazy or selfish
way. On the other hand, if I stop to reflect, if I employ my
power of surveying my ideas, not only of my own selfish pre-
ferences, but of other people's claims and needs, my resulting
action may be quite different from what would have happened
had I not reflected. In other words, the necessary detachment
of the self can be a detachment of wide-ranging thought in the
course of which new ideas, fresh alternatives, other points of
view are disclosed. The self as detached is 'free' from the sequence
of events and its condition. Thinking is free, or it would not be
thinking, and the effects of free thinking may be seen in decisions
and choices which can fairly be said to be 'conditioned' by this
free thinking. As conditioned, they will be in a sense 'caused'
by it, but if caused, caused by the intervention of the self which
is the thinker, and not one among other events. Much of our
conduct goes on of its own inertia; but some of it may be 'caused'
by a 'cause' which is, in an important sense, free from determination by the self's past history. It might be called a 'free cause'. I
shall return to this question of freedom quite soon.[1] The point for
the moment is that the view of the personal self sketched here does
open out the way to an acceptance of a measure of personal
freedom of choice.

Without developing this further now, let us note some of
the immediate educational implications of our thoughts about

[1] See below, pp. 111 sq.

the personal self, and of an assumption (at present provisional) of personal freedom.

5. EDUCATIONAL IMPLICATIONS *i*. RESPONSIBILITY, *ii*. 'EFFORT IN LEARNING', *iii*. FAITH IN A PERSON, *iv*. THE TEACHER'S HUMBLE RÔLE

The assumption of the pupil's freedom is educationally of the first importance. (i) It is necessary if one is to insist coherently on moral responsibility. Teachers can never wholly determine the growth of their pupils, who (I am here assuming) in part make their characters by freely choosing, and it is good for young people to realize this—perhaps through the influence of their teachers. It is a good corrective to the tendency of some adolescents to wallow in self-pity, blaming everyone but themselves. I am not, of course, suggesting that young people are not importantly conditioned by their circumstances, and everything reasonable ought to be done to improve conditions of living. But it is easy to overstress conditioning, and so to undermine the sense of responsibility.

(ii) The assumption of freedom is important if we are to find a proper place for *effort* in new, perhaps difficult, perhaps irksome learning. 'Activists' are perfectly right in stressing the importance of interest in learning, but they have sometimes blurred the distinction (made a long time ago by Ribot) between 'spontaneous' and 'voluntary' attention. Spontaneous interest and attention automatically involve the already-mentioned activity of the self which is the *sine qua non* of any learning or experience at all. This, because spontaneous, requires no deliberate effort of choice. But we all know that all the time, and particularly with new and unfamiliar work, voluntary effort of attention is necessary. No education which underplays the responsibility of conscious voluntary effort is being realistic.

There are some more general implications for education of our general view of the personal self. (iii) The clear recognition of the *self* aspect of the total person, as distinct from the *personality* aspect—in the sense in which that means built-up personal characteristics—makes it possible for us as parents or teachers to have faith in the continued existence of the same self, when the 'personality' seems altered or in abeyance. Surprise, sometimes shock, when someone we know seems to be acting in a strange or unexpected way, leads us to say, 'He doesn't seem to be the same person'. If it were simply true that he is not the same person, then, of course, we should cease to hold the same kind of regard for the person whom we knew formerly, for the simple reason that he is supposed no longer to exist. On the other hand, if we believe in the self-same (though in a sense changing) self, we can still maintain our regard and perhaps affection for one who seems to have suffered a personal aberration. We may say, 'That was not the real person', and continue to believe in him, and believe that what has happened is some—perhaps temporary —deviation of personal character. This has distinct educational importance; the continuing self makes a claim on us: it calls for the categorical obligations to respect and *caritas*. Faith in a substantial human being, despite personal changes which we may not understand, must greatly affect the way in which we treat people under our charge.

This faith and obligation has wider educational and therapeutic implications. Where the disturbance of personality is severe, as in temporary insanity, the person is subject to delusions, hallucinations, is apparently confined in a psychotic cell which seems completely to separate him from his former self, from the world and from us. Yet in those circumstances one may still have the strongest conviction that in spite of all, the real 'self' is still there, behind and beyond the phenomena. (This, of course, might be an illusory feeling, and in itself it proves nothing of the existence of a continuing self; but given the firm hypothesis, it is a supporting experience.) The conviction is sometimes confirmed from the other side. A mentally deranged patient may *seem* to be entirely inaccessible to communication from friends or doctors: yet afterwards on recovery it has been found that things said— for example, encouragement and sympathy given—have registered and made an impression. To act (at least in recoverable cases) upon the faith and conviction that *he*, though deranged, is still 'there', and to address him still as the same self, may not only be a kind of due, but may help in healing. There are, of course, extreme cases, for example, of people in advanced senility, living an almost vegetable existence, where it is difficult to sustain this faith.

(iv) Another educational implication of the insistence upon

the self with its free synthesizing activity is that it checks the teacher's over-confidence that he can *direct* other people's experience and knowledge. The whole of the process of being educated depends upon the free independent initiative of the self's synthesizing activity. If one is a teacher and forgets this, thinking exclusively of the kind of order one's pupils' minds ought to have, then order may never even exist in their minds because *they* have not been able, or have not themselves chosen, to order their minds' contents. We easily make the mistake of thinking that we can do other people's 'integrating' for them. But the only place where integration can take place is in the individual living mind vivified by self-activity. As St Thomas Aquinas has it, the 'efficient' cause of learning is not (as one might expect) the teacher, but the 'active intelligence' of the learner. The teacher is the 'external proximate cause'.[1]

We have been saying that the assumption that the personal self is independent, free and responsible has important consequences for education. So far, this is only an assumption. The question remains, Does freedom exist? And what is the relation of freedom to responsibility? Let us now look at the word 'freedom', at its meanings, and at its bearings upon education.

[1] Though there is much more to it than that. See below, pp. 149 sq.

CHAPTER VIII

The Freedoms

1. Freedom—Questions of Fact and Value: Three Senses of Freedom: (A) Freedom from Restraint

No word is more frequently or loosely used than the word 'freedom'. We talk, for example, of 'education *for* freedom' and 'education *through* freedom'. We speak of 'free activity'. We speak of freedom as a *condition* of human living and freedom as something to be *won*. Every lecturer on education declaims, 'Freedom is not licence!', and every student in his examination repeats the stirring call. In what follows I distinguish three main senses of freedom: at the outset I shall be contradicting the last of these clichés, and saying that licence is exactly what freedom is.

Freedom, primitively speaking, means licence. This may sound shocking but it is plainly true. The prime, natural, unforced meaning of freedom is essentially negative. Freedom in the first and the basic sense means freedom *from*—from restrictions and limitations, external or internal, from bodily constraint, from regulations and laws, from conventions, from other people's influence, or freedom from internal restraints, fears, wants, impulses, complexes, habits, even conscience. Freedom in the primary sense is freedom from any kind of constraint.

This is of course only an idea and never exists in fact. If we happen to be free from this, we are limited by that. The prisoner freed from his shackles is limited by his inhibitions. If we are free from regulations we may be burdened by responsibilities. If we are under strict regulations we are in that respect free from responsibility. If we are free from impulse we are limited by conscience, and *vice versa*.

In discussing freedom we have to distinguish two kinds of questions, questions of fact and questions of value. The latter are educationally more interesting, but as we shall see, they lead us away from the idea of freedom to other matters.

The comparatively uninteresting questions of *fact* are two: What are we free from? and, What are we limited by? I'm-portant, and more interesting, questions of *value* are: What do we *want* to be free from . . . limited by, and why? Again, What ought we to be free from . . . limited by? What is the *best* freedom, and the best limitation?

That the more generally interesting question is the question of value, not fact, is obvious from ordinary conversations. Free-dom in ordinary conversation is a cheer-word. 'He has been freed from prison'. . . 'He is free from all engagements . . . Hurrah!' 'His mind has been freed through education . . . Fine!' It is not mainly the *fact* of being free from X or Y, but what we are able to *do* through this freedom, which makes it seem important. And what we do through freedom is not a part of the idea of freedom, but something else.

This is ordinarily called 'freedom-for'. Freedom-for stands in a confused way for something important. But it is confused. 'Freedom for' is a compound idea made up of freedom *from* this or that limitation, *plus* using this condition of freedom from, for some purpose thought good. The using of freedom for a purpose *is* not itself freedom, but something else, of which 'free-dom from' is the purely matter-of-fact condition.

This is quite important; it is the commonest assumption that freedom is good in itself. But apart from its potential use for some purpose thought good, 'freedom' in its prime sense is neither good nor bad but a neutral fact. And whether, on this or that occasion, there *ought* to be in existence a certain freedom, depends wholly upon something else, namely what is good or truly desir-able. The presence or absence of fences round electric railways is not good or bad in itself, except in so far as safety is good or bad. School rules, or school freedom, are not in themselves either good or bad, but are only so in so far as they exist for the sake of something else which is not freedom.

The values which are called upon to justify the use of freedom can be many. We can lazily want to be free from obligations and ties in order to live in a lotus-land where we may live on impulse. Or one may want to be free from one's repressions in order to be happier and able to have healthy interests. Or one may wish to be free from too much ordering about in order to be responsible and live the the good life according to our own reasonable ideas. It is clear that the assessment of these values is often ethical. But, once again, this basic freedom in itself is neither good nor bad, but factual.

If, then, the significance of freedom lies in the use that is made of it, the question becomes: What are the most important ethical and human justifications of freedom?

Taking it that the primary notion of freedom is as we have described it, (i) a freedom from restraint, external or internal (attainable only in limited degrees), there are, I think, two intimately connected but distinguishable ethical purposes which justify a reasonable measure of freedom from restraint. Very confusingly, both these purposes can be labelled 'freedom'. But obviously if they are so labelled, the meaning of 'freedom' must in each case be different from the meaning we have so far given to the term. The two new meanings of 'freedom' are (ii) freedom of *choosing*—the traditional 'freedom of the will'. (iii) The third meaning of freedom is harder to indicate in a word or a single phrase. It is perhaps most easily indicated by referring to a religious version of it. This is what St Paul called 'the glorious liberty of the sons of God'. It is a liberty or freedom which (St Paul urges) is attained when a person, using his free will, chooses to accept the 'law of God', and by so doing, becomes 'free' in a new sense. This is religious language. It can be translated into moral terms by saying that a person who *freely chooses* to accept his proper moral obligations, attains or wins *freedom*, in a still further sense.

The relationship between all three senses of 'freedom' which have been mentioned may be illustrated by the following sentence: 'We must leave children a large measure of freedom that they may be free to become (or not to become) free.' This would be clearly nonsense unless the three uses were all different. The first (i) means freedom from external restraint, the second (ii) means freedom of choosing or freedom of the will, and the third (iii) applies to the rather stretched sense of the freedom of which it is said that it can be 'won'. I shall return to the third sense a little later. In the meantime let us consider the question of the freedom of choosing.

2. (B) FREEDOM OF CHOICE: FREEDOM AND DETERMINATION

I have suggested in the last Chapter that the view of the personal self outlined there opens up, or at least does not bar, the way to acceptance of freedom of choice in some sense. One aspect of the personal self transcends the sequence of its states, and in some measure may be thought to be free from their causal determination. These ideas of freedom and causal determination must now be examined. The questions are: Are we free to choose? Are we determined? or, To what extent are we free or determined? [1]

The theory of determinism is usually taken to mean the view that everything a person does is wholly and without remainder caused by what happened in the past, up to the moment of the action. This 'past' includes heredity, environment, the acquired character of the person, his desires, the influences upon him of the circumstances in which he acts, etc., etc. His action is a result (or effect) of all these things taken together. If we think or feel (as we all, including determinists, do) that we are 'free' whilst we are doing what is called 'choosing' or 'deciding', this must somehow be explained—or explained away—wholly in terms of what has happened in the past. In justice to, at any rate, the philosophers who are determinists, it ought to be said that they try to explain, rather than explain away, the undoubted subjective experience of freedom. Freedom, in some sense, to do this or that, or to do or *not* to do, is of great moral importance to all of us. For if we are not free in this way it is difficult to see how we can be called morally responsible.

---

[1] This is an immense subject, and there has been much writing on it in recent years, including defences of determinism. In a short discussion it is impossible to deal systematically with opposing views. I can only hope to open up some questions in a brief advocacy of freedom. But see P. H. Nowell-Smith, *Ethics* (Pelican, 1954), Chapters XIX and XX. This is a defence of determinism. Libertarian views are advocated by C. D. Broad, 'Determinism, Indeterminism and Libertarianism' in his *Ethics and the History of Philosophy* (Routledge, 1952) and by C. A. Campbell, *Selfhood and Godhood* (Allen and Unwin, 1957). The questions are generally examined, at some length, by A. C. Ewing in *Second Thoughts in Moral Philosophy* (Routledge, 1959), Chapter V, and briefly by Mary Warnock in *Ethics Since 1900* (Home University Library, 1960), Chapter VI.

Can this freedom be philosophically maintained? I believe it can—but not along the usual determinist lines.

If freedom of choice is to be argued for here it will not be by a denial of the many important ways in which one's actions are 'determined', but by an assertion that, *along with* much determination, there are some human acts which are properly called free. Again the assertion of freedom of choice need not (indeed must not) imply a denial of causation of choice in *some* sense. However 'free' my choice may be, it is not *un*determined, *un*caused by anything at all that went before. If so, 'freedom' might imply chaos. If it is my choice, at least I choose, and what I do in choosing can be called in *some* sense a cause of the resulting action, though this 'cause' may turn out to be quite unlike causes in other senses—as when an acid 'causes' litmus paper to turn red, or acute hunger 'causes' one to grab food.

We are all certainly very much 'determined' by causes in the past—by heredity, environment (including education), by personal gifts, temperament, by character that has been built up through time. If there is free choice, it is always in a way greatly limited by past and present circumstances. It is obvious that we are not all free to choose to become conductors of an orchestra, or champion runners, or barristers.

But does this mean that our *freedom* is limited? In one sense it does; in another it does not. The field within which we may choose, the area of choice, is certainly limited. But this leaves the question entirely open whether or not we are really free to choose from alternatives *within* that field. I may be free to choose—not anything, but, say, to be a clerk or a worker in a factory, or a doctor or an engineer, or to act selfishly or unselfishly, or to lie in bed or to get up. We all do in fact believe that we are free to choose or not to choose within certain limits. Even if we sometimes complain that choices are too hard for us, that we are 'like that' and 'can't help it' if we aren't as good as we should be, we are not so ready to apply the same argument when we think we have done something bright or praiseworthy or virtuous. We are inconsistent; we blame unkind fate when we do badly, and conveniently forget about fate when we happen to do well.

If freedom is not annulled by limitations of the field or area of choice, neither is it necessarily annulled when—perhaps because of past history—choices are *hard* to make. I may be very sorely tempted to do what I ought not or to leave undone that which I ought to do, and still be entirely free to do the harder thing. Difficulty is not impossibility. There are, certainly, extreme limits where difficulty seems to amount to practical impossibility, though it is not always easy in practice to draw the line. To be tortured, or to be the victim of habit-forming drugs, may seem to make a hard choice impossibly difficult. But even if it is (debatably) held that in such extreme circumstances freedom of choice has disappeared, this does not apply to ordinarily 'hard choices'. If there is freedom at all there is no less freedom even when it is difficult to do.

But is there freedom? If there is, what does it mean to be 'free'?

3. DIFFERENT SENSES OF 'DECISION'

I have spoken of the possibility of 'freedom of choice', or 'freedom to decide'. But 'choice', 'decide' are slippery words; their meanings slide about. A judge in a Court of Arbitration may 'decide' after consideration to make what he thinks is a fair recommendation. This is a fairly intellectual kind of decision, and the carrying out of the decision is left to others. Sometimes, when an ordinary person decides after reflection which of several actions to take, it may again be a fairly detached weighing up of alternatives, done in 'a cool hour'. Where shall I go for my next holiday—France, Italy, Scotland? And if I 'decide for' or 'choose' Scotland, though it is I who will have to carry out the decision, there is no difficulty in so doing. It requires no great powers of 'decision' (in *another* sense) to carry out a pleasant plan which I want to achieve. The action follows easily from the mental decision. In a moral 'decision' (or 'choice') of some difficulty, however, 'decision' acquires new meanings. Though—if I have the time—I may 'sit down in a cool hour' to reflect seriously on which of a number of things I ought to do, I may be (sometimes) in considerable conflict. If I *want* to do this or that which conflicts with what I have a notion I *ought* to do, it will require not only considerable trained powers of reflective detachment to be fair and objective in my 'decision', but 'decision' of a moral kind, to keep my fairness and objectivity of mind up to scratch.

'Decision' here is not only intellectual but also moral decision. Furthermore, even when I have 'decided' (come to recognize), theoretically with the aid of some moral reinforcement ('decision' in a moral sense) that X is the thing I ought to do, there still remains the job of turning myself in the direction of carrying it out. There can be a great difference between recognizing in thought and idea that I ought to do a thing, and resolving ('deciding', 'choosing') to do it. Lastly, there is a difference between 'deciding' to do it, and actually *doing* it.

Though the words 'deciding', 'choosing', can be employed in these various senses, it may avoid some confusion if we use different words to stand for the different aspects of deciding which have been mentioned. The words are, of course, to some extent arbitrary: the justification for their use lies in convenience in making clearer distinctions between ideas.

I shall, therefore, speak of (*i*) the arbitrator's 'decision' as *finding*. (We speak of the 'finding' of a Court.) This use may be extended to the result of any more or less intellectual reflection, particularly where there arises no conflict between idea and action. The arbitrator can leave action to other people. Or if I 'find', after thought, that Scotland is the place I really want to go to most, the action can follow without difficulty.

(*ii*) Where, after some doubt in a moral situation about which course of action ought to be followed, we conclude that X rather than Y or Z is better, we may speak of *recognizing* that there is an obligation to it. We arrive at recognition through an effort partly intellectual ('finding'), partly moral. But recognition, though moral, is still fairly theoretical in stress. We certainly recognize that X ought to be done or generally that we have an obligation to it. But it may stop there.

(*iii*) It is a distinct step further to *resolve* to do X. To make preparations for a hoped-for holiday which I *find* I want needs no great resolve. To do what I *recognize* I ought to may require much *resolve*.

(*iv*) Hell is said to be 'paved with good intentions'—which need not here be distinguished from good resolutions. However this may be, there is a gap between resolving and actually *doing*.[1]

---

[1] The late Professor H. A. Prichard (in *Duty and Ignorance of Fact*, Hertz lecture, Brit. Acad. 1932) made another distinction, between actually doing an action and 'setting oneself' to do the action. Since something uncon-

Today I resolve to write tomorrow an overdue letter. Alas, tomorrow passes, the letter unwritten. To do my duty is not only to find, or recognize, or resolve, but to *do* it.

As these are different facets of human thinking and action, so are there corresponding facets of the freedom and determination issue.

4. Freedom of Choice: Detached Reflection: the Arbitrator

Consider first the human power of reflection and detachment, the power of sitting back from the situation in which we are involved and looking at it all round. No animal, as far as we know, has this power of detached reflection. The animal is moved by impulses and desires (as human beings are, no doubt, for a large part of the time), but the human being can stop acting, can pause, can sit up and look at himself and at the alternatives before him, together with other alternatives not now before him. He can say, 'Here am I, desiring so-and-so, pulled in this direction or that'. He can detach himself to look even at his own bias. It is possible to be something of the spectator of oneself and of the situation before one, and by being a spectator it is possible to see a situation in its proportions, and moreover, to see implications in it which would never appear at all without such reflective thinking. It is, of course, true that this detached contemplation of oneself and of the situation of action is intellectually difficult and comparatively rare. No one who is not highly intelligent and who has not had some practice in it can carry out this process to a high degree of perfection. Nevertheless, it must be firmly maintained that every person of more than sub-normal intelligence is able to think reflectively in some degree—and this may be true even of a proportion of those who are commonly called sub-normal. Anyone within this range, who is not insane or psychopathic or in some other way morally defective, can in some degree become aware (for example) that if he acts selfishly he will be depriving another person or infringing his rights: or he

---

trollable, e.g. an earthquake or sudden paralysis, might arrest an action of mine about to be done, and these are not within my power to control, it is the 'setting oneself' which is morally important. We may accept Prichard's distinction without dwelling on it here.

can be aware, upon a little reflection, that the person who had wheedled money out of him is a rogue who will misuse it, and that this is not 'right'.

Whether a person does or does not in fact reflect will in part of course depend upon his past habits, his education, his general outlook and disposition. The influence of many things in the past is not being denied. Whether and how he reflects will also depend on whether he *resolves* now to be as honest as he can with himself. Reflection—and particularly when our own interests and comfort tempt us to turn a blind eye towards possible duties which might be irksome—is a kind of action which it may require much firm resolution to carry through. I shall return to the question whether this resolve is 'free'. For the moment, the question is whether mental reflection is in any sense 'free', and if so what this means.

Reflection enlarges one's mental perspective beyond the present moment and the present impulse, and so increases the possible range of alternatives of action. I contend that reflection is free, that it would not *be* reflection if it were not free, and that what we think of doing after such reflection is an expression of that free reflection, and in *that* sense the action is free. Reflection (and the action which expresses it) is *sui generis*.

Consider the case of the arbitrator. He listens to all sides, with all the detachment of which he is capable (which we agree depends upon his natural capacities and past training). He then makes up his mind what, in his view, is the fairest 'finding'. If he is doing the job properly, his finding is not predetermined by any personal bias he may have had in one direction or another, but is an act of free, detached, reflective judgment upon the situation as now freshly seen. If we thought that the arbitrator was wholly determined beforehand by his prejudice and bias, he would not be appointed: the whole thing would be a farce. The 'bias' we look for in an arbitrator is a unique kind of bias—the bias for freely 'finding' in the light of truth, fairness, the facts. Unless, before it is finally judged, the issue is *really* open before him, and the arbitrator free to make up his mind on the evidence, arbitration would have no meaning. Every day the scientist is doing the same kind of thing. If there were no really *free* thinking in science, there could be no scientific knowledge at all. The scientist's conclusions could not claim to be knowledge since they would be merely a product of his 'conditioned' bias. The same holds good of the theory of determinism itself which, on that theory, must itself be determined by the make-up of the philosopher who believes it. It cannot consistently claim to be known as 'true'.

5. Is Thinking 'Determined'?

'But,' it may be objected, 'this thinking of the moral person, or the arbitrator or the scientist, is not as "free" as you say. The "finding" of the moral person is, if he is being honest and objective, as near an approximation as he can get to a rational answer to what he ought to do. There is, we may assume for present purposes, some objective moral truth which he is trying to discover. If his search for the truth is a fruitful one it is the truth or very nearly that which "determines" him. Likewise the arbitrator is "determined" in some sense by legal, social, industrial, economic codes, as also by general precedents of fair awards. His finding is not an expression of his, the arbitrator's, freedom of reflection, but of the normative laws of fair dealing in such things. Several really good arbitrators' (it may be said) 'might arrive at approximately similar findings, which shows that it is not their individual freedom which is important, but their being "determined" by what is objectively just and fair. The same kind of thing can be said of scientists, "free" thinking. Their aim is not to express their "freedom" but to submit to (to be "determined by") scientific truth and fact.'

These objections contain a partial truth, and when I come to discuss the third sense of freedom (see p. 110 above) I shall urge that there is a freedom which depends upon the submission to 'order' of certain kinds. But it is a free submission to 'order'. It is certainly not true to say that the 'determination' referred to in the last paragraph is in *any* way like any other sort of determination, comparable to, say, the determination by natural causes, as when a motor car failure is caused by drying up of petrol or disease by a germ, or a sexual act by blind sexual desire. If I conclude after thought that I ought to do X, the conclusion is not adequately explained by saying that there was a sequence of natural events which led up to it. There was of course such a sequence—my sentiments for value, my questions, my logical steps, the mental history of my ruminations, etc. These things happened: but they were the conditions of something of a different order—my reflective judgment of assent. If this is to be called a 'cause' of anything, it is a cause *sui generis*. It might be called a 'free cause' if that is not too confusing. Reflection is upon issues which are genuinely open to the reflecting mind when it begins freely to reflect. The fact that the mind comes to conclusions (right or wrong) after reflection, and that the reasons for (or causes of) these conclusions can be afterwards pointed out, is no denial that they were arrived at by a freely reflecting mind. If they were not they would not be 'conclusions'. The really important thing here is that human persons by voluntary reflection discover for themselves truth, goodness, the 'facts', that their assent is free, not forced or compelled by the inexorable inertia of the events of their personal history.

6. The Freedom of Different Kinds of Decision

This is an appeal to careful examination of the *fact* of free reflection. It says 'look what happens when you reflect', and points out that judgment and assent cannot be reduced to any other kind of 'causation'. The same method must be applied to the different forms of freedom which I called *recognizing* a moral obligation, *resolving* to do it, and actually *doing* it. They can be taken together.

To *recognize* that X is a moral obligation may, as we said, need some *resolve*, since there are many temptations to be dishonest in reflection, to 'find' something which is not the truth when truth becomes uncomfortable, and temptations to avoid recognizing an obligation which requires commitment. And there is needed more than resolve to 'find' honestly and to 'recognize' obligations. This resolve needs to be consummated in the *actions* of honest thinking, recognition of obligation and the carrying of it out.

There is a difference in kind, as we have seen in this and in an earlier chapter,[1] between the sort of deciding involved when we are thinking what we really *want* to do, and deciding that we *ought* to do something. 'Deciding' where to go for a holiday is really discovering, by means of free reflection, something in a sense really there already—namely, what we in fact want most

[1] Above, pp. 46 sq.

(e.g., to go to Scotland). But in deciding that I ought to do a difficult thing X, resolving to do it and doing it, I am not discovering a want already there, but recognizing a new commitment, now, to an imperative which categorically commands me. It is not, 'I really want this and so I shall do it', but , 'This is the moral obligation which commands me; I recognize that I *ought* to do it whether I want to or not: I assent and commit myself to it'. In both cases there is freedom, but the specifically moral freedom shares in the special character of moral obligation, assent, action.

The freshness of moral decisions and actions and their irreducibility to the sum total of past history is most clearly seen in the individuality of particular right decisions, discussed in Chapter V. We compared this to the artist's use of the 'right' brush-stroke in relation to the whole picture. The morally right decision is something which becomes fully born only through action in this individual situation. No given set of rules, no preconditioning, no set of habits already formed are enough. In a real sense, a difficult decisive moral act is a *creative* act, and exhibits its freedom from the chains of the past in its newness and uniqueness. Not every act which is ordinarily called 'moral' is like this. But delicate or difficult personal moral decisions are new unique individual creations, freely created. They are for these reasons free in an additional way in which the other non-moral decisions cited are not.

That they are not just the outcome of character previously built up is reinforced (but not proved) by the fact that a decisive act is sometimes a *surprise* to the person himself or to others. We say, 'Till the event, we shouldn't have thought him *capable* of it'. We may be quite right; he may not have been.

The appeal throughout is to direct experience of the facts of decision, and to the discernment of their difference from all other determined causal sequences. Dr Johnson was right,[1] though he did not say all that there is to be said. We *know* perfectly well that we can choose to make or not make the effort to think straight, to recognize obligation, we *know* that we can resolve or not resolve, do or not do. We *know* freedom in all these senses.

We know that these occasions of freedom can and do occur. It is not, of course, being argued that every human occasion is

[1] 'Sir, the will is free: and there's an end on't.'

an occasion of freedom (for there is much human action which is habitual or otherwise automatic), nor, further, that on all occasions when we think (or say we 'know') we are free we really are so.

7. Introspection: Unconscious and Other Causes

It is necessary to say this, because the sort of introspective evidence I have been appealing to is often discounted as an argument for freedom. One ground for this objection is certainly worth considering briefly. It is that 'unconscious' motivation has been ignored in the sort of account I have given. Depth-psychologists pirated a word of respectable lineage—'rationalization'—and have given it a meaning opposite to its original one. It now means the—often ingenious—invention of 'reasons', which are in fact spurious, for what we do from unconscious motives. I may 'decide' that I ought to make a self-sacrifice for another person. I believe it to be an ethical decision for which I can offer reasons, but really my unconscious motive is to put them in my debt and perhaps acquire power over them. The decision is unconsciously 'determined'. Or in asserting what I genuinely believe to be my moral right I am unconsciously resisting the image of father-domination. The appearance of moral rationality is deceptive. Even more striking is the phenomenon of post-hypnotic suggestion. It is put to me in a state of hypnosis that an hour later in a roomful of people I will open a certain window. An hour elapses; I have an impulse to open the window and do so, saying to myself that it is for the public good. What looks like a decision is the fulfilment of a pre-arranged conditioning.

Certainly these things happen, perhaps more often than we think. In some cases where they do, actions can fairly be said to be predetermined. But (*i*) there is certainly no empirical evidence or self-evident justification for saying that *all* human decisions are irresistibly and totally determined by unconscious motives: that would be an improved dogma. (*ii*) Even if it is conceded that unconscious motives always play a part in conscious decisions, it does not follow that their determination by unconscious motives is an adequate explanation (or explaining away) of choice. Unconscious motives may 'determine' in the sense of limiting or shaping the *field* of choice, or by making some choices *harder*,[1] but these determinations do not annul freedom, as we have seen. There is no reason for denying that freedom of choice may be exercised within limits shaped and constricted by determinations of many kinds. E.g. if I am strongly and irrationally influenced by a father-image or by an unconscious desire for power, no one has grounds for saying that I must forever be a helpless victim of irrationality. Psychoanalysis itself is one affirmation to the contrary. One may come, through analysis or otherwise, to recognize one's own irrationality and by insight and will and choice change oneself and one's mode of living. In the case of hypnotic suggestion there is evidence which justifies saying that if the suggestion is one contrary to the moral standards of the 'patient' it *can* be resisted. Thus, though we may sometimes be subject to illusions about our freedom of choice, the illusions are potentially open to insight and correction.

Introspection, though it does not infallibly guarantee the existence of freedom, is the most important source of evidence for freedom. It is so because reflective thinking and deciding, of which we have immediate inner knowledge, is a crucial differentiating characteristic of man from things or other animals. 'Things,' said Kant, 'work according to laws: rational beings according to the conception of laws.' The hypothesis of inescapable determination is largely derived from the influence of science, from the habit of seeking causal explanations and desiring to find them everywhere if possible. But this is an external, spectator's view, and if it is insisted that this is the only proper way of understanding human motivation, it results in injustice to the peculiarly human phenomenon of conceiving, reflecting and deciding. One could no doubt attempt to prove, for instance, a physiological account of human behaviour. In practice it would be impossible to do it completely, but it is conceivable in theory to describe human behaviour in a systematic statement of brain and other nervous events. But this description, important no doubt to the physiologist, is really irrelevant to the question of freedom, because the techniques of physiology are not competent to deal with it. If one may take an analogy: it is quite possible in physics to calculate and resolve all the forces at work

[1] See pp. 112–13 above.

when a vessel at sea is being steered by a strong hand, against wind and tide. The purpose and intention of the helmsman need not, indeed cannot, enter into the mathematical equations. But from the impeccability of the equations one cannot infer that the helmsman's ideas and voluntary decisions have nothing to do with the direction the vessel takes. This would be silly. Mathematical techniques can deal adequately with their proper subject matter: they cannot comprehend choice. But this certainly does not mean that choice in this illustration has no relevance.

Socrates, in the *Phædo*, shows how philosophically irresponsible was the attempt to explain his presence at his trial in terms of the action of his sinews on his bones, etc., instead of 'the real reasons; which are that since Athens has thought it better to condemn me, therefore I for my part have thought it better to sit here, and more right to stay and submit to whatever penalty she orders'.[1] If I ask you, What made you come to see me today? and you reply in terms of mechanics or biochemistry or physiology, I can tell you not to be so 'clever' and answer my question. If you reply in language of psycho-analytic determinism you may in some instances be near the mark; yet our common recognition of the operation of unconscious motivation is itself the beginning of emancipation from being irresistibly pushed along: we can together proceed from this insight to consider the next step. Insight into oneself is potential power to modify one's behaviour.

8. Determinism, Predictability and Freedom

If determinism were true, human actions should be in theory at least as *predictable* as are other natural events, and with the same degree of certainty. Now since, as we have repeatedly said, there is a large element of determination in human affairs by the past, one can readily agree that it is often possible to predict with reasonable certainty. Men form habits and develop characters of different kinds, and from knowledge of how they *have* behaved we can with some assurance say how they *will* behave. The more stable the character the more likely are we to be right so long as the new circumstances resemble those which have gone before. We could have said with moral cer-

[1] Plato, *Phædo*, 98 C-D. (Socrates is the speaker in the dialogue.)

tainty that during the Second World War Churchill would go on defying Hitler and would not ('could' not) sell his country to the enemy.

Does this predictability mean that the predicted action is not free? It depends on what one means here by 'free'. If the action is done from formed habit or is such an automatic expression of character that no alternative (as in Churchill's case) is seriously considered, then in that respect the action is determined. On the other hand, it is the action of a person who in the past has had (as we have argued) a real say, through making free choices, in the development of his character. In that sense it is expressive of his freedom. Predictability of human action entails causal determination, but not determinism.

To assert that there is much determination by the past (and so predictability) is not, as we have been arguing, to say that every action is completely accounted for in this way, *must* be done, or is predictable. If the 'open' and difficult cases of choice which have been cited are really open and free, then they are not predictable. If I am truly and explicitly choosing or deciding, not only do I not know certainly what I am going to do before I have chosen or decided: no one else *could*. The evidence of 'free choosing' gives the strongest reasons for rejecting universal predictability of human actions. It is not only difficult in practice always to predict: it is impossible theoretically if free choosing has been correctly described. Furthermore, it has to be remembered that universal predictability of human decisions is simply an hypothesis of determinism, which has never in fact been verified by observation. My contention is that this lack of verification is not only due to the practical difficulties of testing it but that the facts of choosing are wholly against the plausibility of the hypothesis.[1]

[1] The attempt sometimes made (by Nowell-Smith and others) to show that 'could have acted otherwise' should be translated into 'would (in fact) have chosen otherwise if (in fact) the conditions had been different', is really an indirect assertion of deterministic predictability. My reply to it here would be (a) a repetition of Mrs. Warnock's objection (*Ethics since 1900*, p. 149): 'It seems to me absolutely self-evident that to say of someone that he was *able* to do something does not say anything at all about what he *would have done* in certain specifiable circumstances.' The two statements do not *mean* the same thing. (b) Furthermore, to affirm that 'could have' is equivalent to 'would have if', as repeating the belief in universal deterministic predictability, is an affirmation merely, and without grounds.

9. CHALLENGE TO DETERMINISM

The challenge, then, is to determinism to explain coherently, without explaining out of existence—that reflection is *not* free, that choosing situations are *not* open but predetermined, that individual moral decision is without remainder explainable in terms of chains of events and conditions before action. The determinist must be asked whether he is not being too exclusively behaviouristic, taking up an external point of view (which must make it appear that the causal chains and the causal nexus are everything). Is he really willing to consider introspection as evidence, to ask himself 'What happens when I appear to be "deciding"?' Does he really think that his own assent to the moral obligations, to which he personally is committed, can be explained *without* assuming some freedom in moral assent or dissent? Can he be consistent? In the complex of the 'personal self' is he not overemphasizing the historical personality at the expense of the self?

Then there is responsibility, and the praise and blame, punishment and reward which we give on the assumption of responsibility. If praise and blame are given, this *seems* [1] to be fair and just only if they are directed towards those elements of decision for which people, as free, are wholly responsible. They cannot fairly apply to circumstances, to heredity and environment, for which the person is not responsible. If we praise or blame a person for his character which has been built up during his past, we are entitled to do this only in so far as he has made his character what it is by free choice in the past. And in all this we assume that now or in the past he *could* (in the ordinary straightforward sense of 'could') have chosen otherwise than he did.

Another related consequence follows. Supposing, for the moment, that radical determinism is 'true', and that radical determinists hold, as they do, that all education, including reward and punishment, is a kind of conditioning,[2] the question arises, 'What *justifies* the conditioning in this direction rather than that?' Educationists, as I have argued, certainly *think* that they can give some reasonable justification for their aims. But on a radical determinist view, since all our opinions and actions are wholly

[1] But on the complex implications of this, see below, pp. 141 sq.
[2] See below, pp. 139–141.

determined by what circumstances, and our own personal past determined by circumstances, have made us—the educational 'ideals' of the determinist are ideals which he is inevitably determined to believe. They are not ideals independently and freely accepted because they seem to be true. There is, therefore, no justification for educating in this direction rather than that. It is only that some people happen to be biased in this direction, and others in that. There is an intolerable contradiction in all this.

The general conclusion, then, is that although there can be no water-tight proof of freedom of choice, the assumption of important elements of freedom accords well with the facts of experience, including moral experience. Radical determinism (equally 'unprovable') appears to represent a limited point of view which just does not fit all the facts of the picture, and can appear to succeed only by explaining them away. And in its most radical form it seems to be self-contradictory.

10. (C) THE THIRD FREEDOM—'GLORIOUS LIBERTY . . .'

So far, we have discussed freedom in two senses—(1) the freedom from external or internal restraint, and (2) the 'freedom of the will'. We come now to the third sense mentioned (p. 110 above).

'Freedom' in this third sense is not simply some measure of freedom from internal or external restraint, nor just the freedom of thinking and choosing and acting. It is a 'freedom' which is attained when, being in some measure released from restraint, and having exercised one's freedom of thinking and choosing, one attains, or 'wins', or 'enters into', a state of 'freedom' which is achieved through voluntary acceptance of some kind of *order* or *law*. This highly abstract statement can at the outset best be understood by referring back again to the language of religion in St Paul—although this 'freedom' is by no means confined to religion. If, it is said, one voluntarily accepts and puts oneself under certain *sorts* of limitations, and *not* others, then by doing so one discovers a new 'freedom'.

As has just been said, a first condition of this third freedom is the exercise of the second freedom, the freedom of choice when in conflict. St Paul describes the conflict clearly in his own language. 'I see another law in my members, warring against the law of my mind, and bringing me into captivity to the law of sin which is in my members.'[1] In our own terms; there is a conflict between the claims of impulses and desires and the duty to choose and accept the law of God. For St Paul the supreme duty is to accept and obey the law of God. In secular language we should probably replace 'law of God' by 'moral law'. But it is the next step which is important for the third freedom. St Paul writes of 'The law of the spirit of life . . . which hath made me free from the law of sin and death', and he goes on to say, speaking of those who accept the 'law of the spirit of life' that 'the creature itself shall be delivered from the bondage of corruption into the glorious liberty of the sons of God'. For the religious person, this third freedom is achieved by the full acceptance of the 'law of life' by whose acceptance alone he can become fully emancipated.

On a Christian interpretation of life, this is *the* answer, and there is no substitute.[2] Nothing but acceptance of the 'law of life' can release a person's full capacity for living. A moral person who, for one reason or another, is unable to adopt this religious language, can still say that the fullest human emancipation can be attained only if a person freely and voluntarily accepts the discipline of the moral 'law of life', of the authority of the good (beautiful, true . . .). To accept and obey love, truth, justice . . . is—it can well be said—both a release from the slavery of impulses and an opening-up of new human possibilities.

The third freedom can be discovered not only in moral living, but through the acceptance of the disciplines of learning, or of craft or art. The thinker or scholar must first freely accept the discipline of thinking or scholarship, the craftsman and the artist their disciplines.

In the earlier stages after acceptance, the 'law'—of God, morality, thought, etc.—may appear to be an extraneous discipline. But as time goes on, through the acceptance of the discipline of 'glorious liberty', new ways of freedom begin to be discovered. The player of a musical instrument, for example, in the early stages finds that his natural impulses and habits are

---

[1] Romans viii. 23, and *passim*.
[2] With some theological reservations, I myself accept this as true.

always getting in the way of the desired skill; he has to submit to some difficult 'rules'. In time his fingers cease to be controlled by impulse and, disciplined by practice in the art, become the means by which new musical meaning can be discovered. The poet learning to write in sonnet-form, moves from the stage of frustration to a new freedom. New worlds open up before him. The master in any art or scholarly discipline, acquires through the voluntary acceptance of the discipline an ability to move about in it, with the acquired 'freedom' of the master.

It may be questioned whether 'freedom' is the right word to use here. Perhaps it is not exactly right; it is, however, sanctioned by use. It is, of course, 'freedom from' the domination of un-ordered impulse as well as a sense of release into new worlds of meaning. As I suggested at the start, 'freedom' is often a cheer-word, and seems so here. 'Glorious freedom' stands for the sense of joy in which order has become assimilated into the person in a way which no longer feels restrictive, but expansive.

To attain a quality of living of this kind is a—perhaps the—supreme end of education and this aim is the justification for insistence on the other freedoms and the other disciplines. We must have freedom (from restraints) to be free (to choose) to be free.

PART TWO

CHAPTER IX

Discipline: Incentives and Sanctions

1. DIFFERENT SENSES OF DISCIPLINE

Our discussion of freedom in its three senses has an important bearing on the idea of 'discipline' and upon the ideas we have of any 'sanctions' or incentives which are thought to be required at certain levels of discipline—those of punishment, reward, competition.

'Discipline' can be looked at in three ways which correspond to the three senses of freedom. We can think of it (1) as the exact opposite of the first freedom—the imposing, by some persons on others, of restraints backed by sanctions of some kind. (2) 'Discipline' may mean the self-discipline which is involved in exercising one's freedom of choice, in which case one must be reasonably free from external restraint. (3) 'Discipline' may mean the discipline which is freely accepted when one decides to put oneself under *order* of some kind—the order of religion, or morality, or of an art or craft, or of the 'discipline' of a subject.

In the widest sense, discipline (in one aspect) may be described as a relationship of submission or obedience to some sort of order, with all the effects of this relationship. This wide sense includes some more limited senses with which discipline may be rather misleadingly identified. There is the literal sense of discipline, being a disciple of a master, in which the disciple accepts, submits, obeys, serves the master, and is ready to endure in his service. Such a use is perfectly ordinary, justified by tradition, and this relationship of disciple to master may enter into many educational situations in different ways. But it would be a mistake to define discipline as this, since discipline has other uses which are wider and which cannot be deduced from the relationship of disciple and master. Rather stretching this meaning of discipline, one may say that a person may become his own master, or that he may be under discipline to himself: the idea of 'self-discipline' seems to imply something of this kind. But it is a stretching; it may sometimes be natural to speak of being 'master of oneself'; but it is unnatural to speak of being a 'disciple' of oneself, except in irony. And the master-disciple idea becomes unworkable when we think or talk about the 'discipline of a subject'. Here one submits to the 'order' of the subject, but this is not a personal relationship of being a 'disciple'.

Another too limiting use of the word is to identify it with coercion and the application of external sanctions. When teachers use the word 'discipline', they often identify it with keeping the upper hand over a class, with reward and punishment in the background. 'Keeping good discipline' often means just this. But we beg the question at once if we identify the idea of what we are going to discuss with one limited form of it. There can be discipline without any external imposition at all and without any external sanction, e.g. the discipline of learning to play Bach.

As I have suggested, there is a relationship between the three ideas of freedom and three ideas of discipline. And an argument parallel to the argument for *justifying* freedom can be applied to discipline. We said (i) that a person must be in some degree free from external restraint that (ii) he may exercise freedom of choice, that (iii) he may choose freely the order which will make him free. So discipline in the sense of external restraint is only justified if, by some means or other, it leads on to the exercise of the 'discipline' of oneself choosing, in this way opening up the way to the third freedom which is a freedom of a chosen discipline. Negatively speaking, externally imposed discipline is valueless and wrong if it becomes an end in itself, or a means to anything which does not help the pupil's growth and development. External discipline may be imposed, for example, from the teacher's love of power, or from his personal fear of the consequences of indiscipline. The former is reprehensible, the latter may be excusable. But every thinking person would agree that this as a permanent state of affairs would be a confession of failure in education. A timid or inexperienced teacher, or any teacher at all in some schools, may be perfectly justified in insisting on rigid external discipline if this is the only immediate way of carrying out some of the legitimate purposes for which the school exists

—e.g. learning. Indeed, in any school some measure of imposed discipline is justified, since teachers are in natural authority, and the disorderly must not be allowed to interfere with the liberties and rights of others or even with their own. But all this assumes that there is something which justifies the discipline. This is that the pupils must be led, through the externally imposed conditions of discipline, to come to choose for themselves, and, one hopes, to choose to accept the 'laws' through which they may become emancipated in the third sense.

2. INCENTIVES OF DISCIPLINE: COMPETITION

This is all very general. But there are several special and important questions of the justification (or non-justification) of some of the particular incentives and sanctions which may be used in supporting externally imposed discipline. Extraneous motives may be evoked; the stimulus of competition, the hope of reward, the fear of punishment. Competition, rewards and punishments have always been part of the furniture of education. In the modern world some educationists reject the use of all such extraneous devices. It is worth while, therefore, examining these external 'sanctions'. The usual defence is that ordinary children tend to be careless or lazy, desultory in their attention, sometimes hostile to their work, to other people, to authority, sometimes anti-social. They need to be 'gingered up' or checked.

Competition can mean competing with oneself, competition between group and group (which implies co-operation within each group) and competition between individuals. Competition with oneself arouses little controversy. Provided it does not become an obsession, competition with oneself, attempting to improve and to beat one's own record, is natural and healthy. The conception of beating one's own record or improving oneself is perhaps an indication of naïvety in the person who holds it: at a maturer level the worker is more absorbed by the task in hand than concerned about his own progress in it. But competition with oneself is very innocent.

Competition between group and group is often advocated as against the alleged evils of competition between individuals. It is part of the very structure of team games, and as such can hardly be objected to. But as always it is a matter of emphasis, proportion, the values which dominate. The players themselves, if keen on playing the game well as a team, have little thought to spare on anything but good hard play, though desire to beat the opponent is an essential underlying drive. The same may be true vicariously of spectators, but it is perhaps easier there for rivalry to outdo good sportmanship.

Group competition in work is of more questionable value. The interest in games is so natural, and rivalry a healthy incident: if, on the other hand, group competition is an *inducement* to work, the proper end of education, interest in the work for its own sake, may be bypassed. In that it teaches group loyalty it may be good; as a stage it may do something. But, just as competing against oneself can be a distraction from proper absorption in what one is doing, so extraneous concentration on gaining marks, even for the group, can easily be a distraction from the attention to learning for its own sake. The theory behind the use of these extraneous appeals is that they should as it were insinuate children into a situation in which they will subsequently become interested in being orderly, or working hard, for its own sake. The danger is that in encouraging attention to these external interests, the transition to the internal essential and important ones may never take place. Preoccupied by counting scores, children may never come to see why they should learn unselfishness or history or mathematics. As we have repeatedly said, unless externally imposed discipline really in fact prepares the way for intrinsic self-discipline (say, in the study of a subject), it cannot be justified.

Competition between individuals can show all these dangers in an exaggerated form. This should not lead us to condemn this competition without thought. Competition between individuals happens, whether it is organized or not. It is impossible to avoid measuring ourselves up against other people, whether for better or worse. This in itself may be salutary if, for example, one's own inferiority is due to lack of effort or laziness. Even if it is due not to this but to lack of natural aptitude the recognition of this is not harmful in itself—although it can be if the measure of attainment is confused with and identified with personal worth.

It is not, I think, an argument for individual competition that it is a 'natural instinct'. Certainly it is natural. Boys and girls—not to speak of the heroes of the Nordic sagas—are fond of out-shouting and out-boasting, of showing off their prowess in strength and games and stunts. But because it is natural there is no reason why this should be deliberately used as an incentive in education. As has been said, it may divert the attention from things which matter, distorting growth, delaying maturity. Again, it is no argument in itself that because the adult world is highly competitive, competition between individuals is right in school. Much competition in adult society is artificial and degrading, for example the social competition which makes it necessary for the Smiths to emulate the Joneses in material possession. Education ought to develop the sense of intrinsic values which should in some measure leaven these shoddy and spurious values of contemporary society. Here the school can be in advance of society. But one may object to competition for wrong or sentimental reasons as well as for right ones. Recently a comment appeared in an educational newspaper on an attack by Dr Robin Pedley on grading children by marks, because it 'discourages those who most need encouragement and distorts the motives of the successful'. Dr Pedley criticized the *élite* of prefects 'with their caps, badges and colours, the trappings of the favoured few. . . . The selection of one person, . . . implies the rejection of others'. But 'Why camouflage the facts of life?' the paper asks. I am inclined to agree. It is all, of course, extremely debatable; these things can become a fetish and a distortion of sound values. On the other hand, it is true that human beings are *un*equal as well as 'equal',[1] some are abler, or work harder than others, some become leaders in this situation, others in that. Selection does imply rejection. Why not? Young people are realistic, and older people can miseducate them by over-protectiveness. What is wrong is not the recognition of differences and inequalities, but the dangerous and inveterate habit of valuing persons, human beings, in terms of their particular abilities, attainments or achievements. The clever child gets attention, the duller child is despised. Many of us teachers and other adults are confirmed snobs in one sense or another, and children readily absorb this. It is not the competition or the acknowledgment of inequality as such which is bad, but the making of these inequalities into a main standard of *human* assessment.

[1] See the Author's 'Equality and Inequality', *Brit. J. Ed. Studies*, Vol. VI, No. 1.

Ideally, we may say that if the use of competition is to be justified, at some stage it must lead to its own annihilation. Games are not a bad analogy. In a game the desire to win is not completely eliminable, but it can become a minor motive, and we know by experience that it is possible to educate people out of the merely competitive attitude. Competition in education is not an essential element as it is in games; it need not be deliberately employed as a motive. If competitiveness is used as a motive, perhaps the safe summing up is that it should move to its own subordination and be lost sight of in concern for things which are worth doing and enjoying in themselves—work, games, art, social and personal enterprises.

We come now to reward and punishment. I shall discuss punishment first, and afterwards mention reward briefly, since it can more easily be summed up in the light of the analysis of punishment.

3. PUNISHMENT

Punishment includes (*i*) the intentional and purposeful infliction of pain (of some kind), (*ii*) by a person or persons in authority. (*iii*) It is inflicted as a penalty for what the authority believes to be some wrong done (*iv*) by the offender.[1] This is, broadly, what 'punishment' *means*. We shall chiefly be concerned with the reasons which are claimed to justify its infliction.

We are dealing here in the main with punishment in school education, and not with legal punishment (a terribly complex problem), though it will be necessary now and again to refer to legal punishment. Sometimes punishment in school has a resemblance to legal punishment, as when a child is punished for a breach of written rules. But in school we are much more *directly* concerned with moral education and reform or regeneration than the law primarily is—though, as we know, reform and re-education of delinquents and criminals is being given increasing attention. But in the small community of family or school, personal and interpersonal moral influence is intimate and immediate, as it cannot be in the larger world of society.

It is not always quite easy to draw a line between what is and

---

[1] An exceptional case is where a group is punished vicariously for an offence committed by one of their members who is perhaps unknown.

what is not punishment. If I speak disapprovingly to someone, saying, 'You should not have done that' or, 'You can do a lot better than that if you try', is this punishment even in a small degree? It is difficult to answer with a simple 'yes' or 'no'. If the person to whom I am talking is painfully embarrassed or conscience-stricken by the reproof, the reproof might be called 'punishment'. It may be said of a teacher, 'his displeasure was punishment enough'. But on the whole it seems clearer not to call this punishment since there is no intentional infliction of a penalty by the reproving person.

A border-line illustration can be taken from school life. A child may be given extra work to do, as an unpleasant task the memory of which may perhaps deter him in future from being lazy or from again committing the offence. This is extra work given as a punishment. On the other hand he may be given extra work not as a punishment, but in order that he may gain the additional practice which he needs. He may dislike having to do it, but he is not being punished, since the extra work is not being given because of its unpleasantness; it is not a penalty for wrong-doing.

Several things may be noted here. (1) The person in authority inflicting punishment is normally another person, but might be oneself acting as an 'authority' over 'oneself'. I can deliberately make myself do unpleasant things in penance for what I have done wrong and to remind me not to do it again, though this is a strained use of 'authority' and 'punishment'. (2) Punishment must be a voluntary and purposeful act of an authority. It is not a mere natural effect. A person may get a thick head by eating or drinking too much, or venereal disease by sexual promiscuity. These are in no sense punishments, they are natural effects. If parents and teachers sometimes say that their punishments take the form of 'letting children suffer the natural ill-effects of their misdemeanours' this is doubtfully called 'punishment'. Authority is certainly present, but in so far as the effects are natural, they are not an intentional infliction of pain and so not punishment. If, on the other hand, a child after being warned not to touch a hot stove disobediently persists and is burnt, and if his parent watches, deliberately not interfering, and if the child recognizes that his parent is deliberately allowing him to suffer pain in order to teach him—then the parent

although not actually inflicting pain, is allowing it to be inflicted
and is in an indirect sense 'punishing'. This seems to be just
over the border-line. (3) The person(s) punishing must be in
authority and punishing must be done from that authority.
Mere vindictiveness or spite is not a motive of proper punishment. (Where there is no proper authority to inflict punishment
there may be a half-way stage. The old vendetta system was
partly a system of group revenge and partly an attempted substitute for legal authority.)

It is very important for the teacher to ask himself, '*Why* do
I reprove, scold, snub, give impositions, inflict pain and penalties?
How do I justify punishment?'

4. RETRIBUTION, DETERRENCE, REFORM

Three types of answer—which may overlap—can be given to
this question. Punishment may be imposed (*i*) as retribution,
(*ii*) in order to deter, (*iii*) in the hope that it may lead to reforma-
tion of the offender.

I begin with some preliminary remarks about all three.
Retributive punishment must not be confused, as it so often is,
with revenge—whether personal or socially authorized. Nor is it
to be simply identified with the infliction of so much pain for so
much wrong done—though it does contain, like all punishment,
a conception of some proportion between the two. The important
idea in retributive punishment is that wrong-doing is blameworthy, and that *some* forms of wrong-doing should not only be
blamed but the blame should be expressed through the infliction
of pain. This conviction may or may not be valid; but it claims
to be a *moral* conviction (which revenge is not). Negatively put,
it is thought to be *wrong* that some misdeeds should be ignored
and get off scot-free, without punishment. Violence and cruelty,
it is said, *deserve* punishment, deserve retribution.

The aim of *deterrent* punishment is to discourage the wrong-
doer, and others, from doing that wrong in future. It intends
to make the sequel to wrong-doing so unpleasant that potential
offenders will be warned off.

Reformative punishment is a confused term. The wish to reform
may be included as an ultimate aim in the minds of those who
punish, whatever their particular views. Deterrent punishment

may be used in the hope that the delinquent may refrain from wrong-doing in the future not only from fear of consequences if he does wrong, but because he sees the moral sense of going straight. The retributive punisher may hope that through suffering, and with time to reflect, the wrong-doer may of his own free will decide on new ways. Both parties may believe that their punishments may help the person to realize that he has done wrong and that he owes something to society. But the causal connection between punishment and reform is tenuous. Punishment *may* bring a person to the point of repentance for what he has done, and may be an occasion for making new personal decisions and new resolves. (This, if we are right, is free decision, and is not *caused*, without remainder, by punishment.) But punishment may make him resentful, obstinate and more set than ever in his ways. In legal punishment this unfortunate effect is well known, and that is one reason why the increasing emphasis today is upon understanding, sympathy, reform and re-education, with a minimum emphasis upon the punishment aspect. (The disturbing thing about this, most commendable, emphasis is that it underplays deterrence as a social agent. Violence is unquestionably held in check by fear of penalties—as was shown by the sudden outbursts in Liverpool during the police strike after the First World War.) In school situations, where the emphasis should always be upon education, and where, as we have said, personal influence is much more intimate, reform rather than mere deterrence or retribution must always be the end-idea influencing the whole philosophy of the use of punishment. But, quite clearly, when we have said 'reform' we have said something which *need* not contain the idea of punishment in every case, and which, positively, can be made to include all the good influences of total personal education.

5. EXAMINATION OF DETERRENT PUNISHMENT

Deterrent punishment aims at influencing people by some sort of fear, so that they will not do, or repeat, a wrong. Is it necessary? How does it work? What are its limits?

Legal deterrence I assume without argument to be self-evidently necessary, human nature being what it is. In school situations surely some measure of it is necessary too? Some school rules are necessary—to ensure tidiness, punctuality, order, ordinary social amenities, etc. Some children will always be untidy to the point of nuisance, or unpunctual or destructive or anti-social; they have, sometimes, to be stopped. But though to stop someone from doing the wrong thing is deterrence, it is not, as such, punishment. Nor will the stopping of an action now necessarily prevent its recurring in the future. In order to be punishment it has, as we have seen, to be painful, and to be inflicted with the intention of dissuading from repetition. It should be noticed that this is, to some extent, behaviouristic language. The theory is: inflict pain on or after the occasion of wrong-doing; this will tend to 'condition' towards avoidance in the future. In an animal, in order to produce the conditioned reflex, the pain would have to be repeated a number of times. In a human being, who reinforces painful experience with reflective self-consciousness, one occasion might be enough. Moreover, in human beings the imagination of pain, or the spectacle of others' pain, can be a deterrent. These things in themselves make deterrence in human beings more than just behavioural 'conditioning'.

Since deterrent punishment pure and simple is utilitarian, a means to an end, the justification of any particular form of it (corporal punishment, extra work, fines) is empirically based. It must be thought to be probably effective, or it would be useless and irrational to inflict it. This requires careful psychological study. Understanding of the techniques of conditioning may help, though it is highly dangerous to assume that because the conditioning of rats in a laboratory works in such and such a way, 'similar' treatment of human beings will work in the same way. The psychologists can, however, tell us that the effects of conditioning on human beings vary greatly with different 'types'. The infliction of pain in punishment has quite considerable effects on asthenics and introverts, much less on hysterics and extroverts, and little or no effect on psychopaths. We are told again that whilst punishment increases drive, making the person more active, it spoils skills. It may make a pupil anxious but stupid.

One could go on with this—though one must be keenly aware that the application of the analogy of animal conditioning to punishment is of worse than shaky validity. A rat may receive a painful shock and be conditioned accordingly; but an animal is never 'punished' in the sense in which we have been using the word here. There is use of the scientist's power and control, but no *authority* in the sense in which that means authority of persons over persons, and of course no recognition by an animal of 'punishment' or of moral wrong, or of the 'justice' of 'punishment'. But in the human situation itself it becomes a nice moral question how far the skilled manipulation and 'conditioning' of human beings for the teacher's (or the school's) purpose, can be a legitimate part of *human* education. We have said that deterrent punishment is certainly necessary in state and school that social order may be upheld. But though it is necessary, no good teacher would ever rate this training in conformity (or avoidance of disconformity) through fear, as much more than a necessary evil, or a condition of positive education for responsible maturity. Deterrent punishment may get nuisances out of the way; but this if it succeeds is only the preparation for development of the sense of personal responsibility. And, as before we saw that the encouragement of competitiveness tends to falsification of values, so here, if a person is treated (too much) as a mechanism for conditioning, he is apt to accept this to the damage of his capacities for being responsibly human. He becomes a skilful cynic, adept in avoiding detection, virtuous and 'smarmy' as long as the eye of authority is upon him, an undisciplined infant the moment the control is removed. In some so-called 'well disciplined' schools this stands out a mile.

6. The Idea of Retributive Punishment

Retributive punishment is a difficult and much misunderstood idea. It may be approached by recollecting the distinction between determinism and freedom.

If one punishes, what does one punish *for*? Something in the past, as a mark of disapproval of what a person has *done*: or in order to prevent wrong-doing in the future (as is the case with deterrent punishment)? In fact there is usually a bit of both. But it should be noted that it is only if one believes in some degree of real freedom and responsibility that one can rationally punish a person for what he *has* done. A radical determinist cannot rationally disapprove of him or logically hold him responsible or punish him for what he has done. For the 'wrong-doer' could not help it; he was 'ill' or 'unfortunate'. One doesn't blame ill or unfortunate people, though one may help them, or give them medicine or even operate on them in order to cure them. It is conditioning for the future which matters to the radical determinist. If it is true that the idea of punishment includes the idea of responsibility for acts freely done, then, although the determinist is certainly 'punishing' in one sense of the word it is (the retributionist would say) a 'thin sense'.

Most plain men do believe in some important degree of freedom and responsibility, and do believe that the idea of punishment must contain a reference to wrong responsibly done. When ordinary people read about cold-blooded cruelty to weak and helpless people, when they see a man 'let down' his friends, or break a promise without adequate cause, or encourage young people to become drug-addicts, they are *not* satisfied by saying merely: 'Poor things, they couldn't help it'. Thoughtful people are of course ready to admit that some haven't had much chance and that they need to be helped along. But it is quite possible to believe genuinely in this (since though there is freedom there is also conditioning) without denying responsibility. The ordinary man does not only feel angry when he hears of a harmless citizen being beaten up: he believes his anger is *justified*. A judge, addressing a criminal, may say: 'You disgracefully injured and then murdered a helpless person for his money . . . you will be punished with the utmost rigour of the law'. The judge is not *merely* thinking of protecting public safety. He is not *merely* sending him to prison to give him time to think, on the chance (perhaps a small one) that he will be reformed. He is not *merely* hoping to deter him and *others*. All these elements may certainly be included, but there is more behind his address than all of them put together. It is a *retributive* statement expressing *moral* disapproval.

Just as it can be said that the plain man's anger is revenge or a sublimation of it, so it can be alleged that the judge is a public official expressing social revenge, the vengeful feelings of society. But whilst it is admitted that feelings of plain revenge may get mixed up with properly moral feelings, it is quite wrong (as we said) to identify retribution with revenge. Revenge is making one who has injured me or my group, 'pay' for it, suffer in kind. It springs from a primitive desire to hurt another person who has hurt oneself or one's group, in order to balance things up, to compensate one's individual or social ego. The vendetta is the social crystallization of this where there is as yet no law to deal with it. Retribution, then, is not revenge, though a person or group desiring retribution may entertain feelings of revenge— which is a dangerous state of affairs. Desire for retribution springs, as we have said, from the belief that wrong-doing is blameworthy and should be condemned, that it is morally wrong to ignore it, pass it over lightly with an exclusive emphasis on future deterrence. And it develops into the idea that sentiments of blame and condemnation should (in extreme, though not in all cases of wrong-doing) be expressed and conveyed to the wrong-doer by inflicting a 'proportional' punishing pain upon him. He should not, retributionists believe, 'get off' when he has done some abominable thing, without being made to feel in his person, through his suffering, society's vehement condemnation of his responsible act. In addition, as I have already said, the retributionist may hope that *through* this realization the wrong-doer may not only feel condemned by society, but feel that the condemnation is just, may accept it, condemn himself in sorrow, repent, and start on a new voluntary enterprise of self-reform. This hope may well be present, and ought to be present. Without it, the 'moral' attitude of the retributionist would be very one-sided. But it goes beyond the idea of retribution as such.

This is an interpretation of retribution as a *moral* idea. Retribution has been (we have said) too much associated with revenge. It is also too easily reduced to the attempted impersonal equation of 'so much pain for so much wrong done'. The justification of the moral idea can perhaps best be understood if one thinks of some personal experience of legitimate moral anger when one is confronted with, say, two bigger boys cruelly bullying a smaller boy who is ill and miserable. One might deal with them with considerable punitive—and retributive—violence on the spot. This *might* not be the wisest course; [1] yet (I should say in defence of the retributionist) one would be wrong if one felt no moral indignation and (further) no impulse to make the bullies *feel* (i) the moral indignation through its most direct expression in a strong-armed act, and (ii) some considerably violent pain of something of the same kind as they had been inflicting. This is certainly not just revenge nor a cold calculation of pain for pain. It is an attempt

[1] See below, p. 145.

(wise or not) at bodily personal communication of authoritative indignant moral condemnation. It is done (we are supposing) in the heat of the moment, and is no doubt tainted with some of the impure motives to which frail human nature is heir. But can anyone say that the feeling of retribution is in itself reprehensible, or indeed that the absence of any such feeling would not show feebleness and moral irresponsibility? Is not retributive desire in this sense at least *part* of moral responsibility? And in larger society, do not our feelings, that violence or cold-blooded calculating fraud committed against the helpless should be condemned and retributively punished, spring from our essential moral convictions?

7. THE DANGERS OF APPLYING RETRIBUTIVE PUNISHMENT: REFORM

This is a defence of the *idea* of retributive punishment. But it is one thing to say that the idea has a serious moral foundation, and quite another to suppose that this in itself gives a rule telling us that retributive punishment is 'right' and that we ought to administer it. Right decisions, as we have seen, have to be made in the light of circumstances as well as of principle, and the concrete circumstances in which retributive punishment would have to be applied may often make it unwise or wrong to apply it. To take an extreme example: to have retributive feelings about some trifling misdemeanour which can hardly be called 'moral' or 'immoral', would be silly. A library fine for keeping a book too long, or a penalty for a parking offence, is deterrent simply; retribution in any important sense does not enter in.

But even when the offence is a morally more serious one, and the judgment of deserved retribution is justifiable, it does not at all follow that to express that judgment in retributive punishment is right. It can be argued [1] that it might be: where punisher and punished know one another, and their relations are generally sound, the shock of retributive punishment may (it is said) clear the air for a new start. The delinquent, let us suppose, understands why he is being punished, accepts its justice, and having taken his medicine may be better for it. This is a healthy state of affairs in so far as the delinquent is being accepted as responsible, and so accepts himself—which is in sharp contrast to being

[1] The language here is cautious; see below, p. 146.

thought of as a poor *thing* to be manipulated for the better. Retributive punishment responsibly given *and* responsibly received can be, with some human beings, a necessary catharsis. But very often it is not so. Retributive punishment may fail of its purpose for two connected reasons (*i*) that the moral meaning of retribution is not *communicated* from the punisher to the punished, and (*ii*) that partly because of this, he reacts against it in a way which makes him worse rather than better.

(*i*) Communication may break down. The symbolism of retributive punishment is rough and its analogies poor. In the case of dealing retributively with the bully on the spot, the punishment may fail of its object for various reasons, but the bully at least feels directly—in the communication of bodies— the resentment of superior authority, and (if it is punishment) something of pain coming directly from the punisher. But even here, the moral mentor's resentment may be misinterpreted as a mere personal attack by a bigger man; its moral significance may be missed: and the pain felt may not be taken at all as an expressive symbol of the pain the bully has himself inflicted. If the bully entirely fails to understand, not only may the whole efficacy of retributive punishment be lost, but the way may even sometimes be blocked for real reform.

If communication can fail so easily in direct face-to-face encounter, how much more may it do so when the personal relationships are remote! The idea of 'proportioning' the suffering of punishment to the wrong done is obscure in the extreme. How can 'suffering', relative to a person, be objectively measured? How can the suffering of the injured party be 'given back' (retributed) to the injurer? The suffering is often quite different in kind. The robber of the widow and the fatherless cannot be *made*, by imprisonment or any other punishment, to suffer what he has made others suffer. He might be compelled to make reparation,[1] but that is another story. If one woman blinds another by throwing vitriol in her face, she is not nowadays made to suffer in kind; we have abandoned the 'eye for an eye' policy. Again, although the suffering imposed retributively is intended as an *expression* of moral indignation, in itself it need not, as we have seen, convey anything of that to the guilty person.

---

[1] Which could be called 'retribution'—but of course in an entirely different sense from that which we have been discussing.

Only by a sensitive and fairly intelligent person can the indirect symbolism of the pain of punishment be translated back to its moral intention: and if this does not happen the punishment has served little purpose except the limited and aborted one of expressing the moral sentiments of the punisher.

(*ii*) The failure of retributive punishment to convey its meaning to the punished is not only a failure of communication but can do deadly harm. The misunderstandings of its meaning can set up attitudes of mind in the wrong-doer which makes deterrent punishment less effective and reform far more difficult. He takes just condemnation and moral indignation to be injustice and personal dislike; instead of condemning himself, he is resentful of others. Where he is supposed to be feeling sorrow and repentance he only feels angry and rebellious. Instead of starting on the road to reform he is on the way to becoming an 'old lag'. Influenced by popular deterministic assumptions he may think of himself as the victim of an unkind social fate.

All this is true, with different emphases, of legal punishment and of punishment in school. I should say that, broadly speaking, the retributive motive of punishment (though in itself morally considerable) is so dangerous when expressed that it is hardly ever justifiable in practice. Even some of the conditions—e.g. understanding between punisher and punished—which may seem to make the meaning of retribution communicable, are the very conditions which make retribution less necessary. If, for example, this child is likely to understand the justice of his punishment as retributive, and to repent and to reform through it, is it not probable that the understanding teacher can get his point accepted without punishment with its attendant risks and tensions? It need not be so: occasionally the thunderstorm may be necessary to clear the air.

But in education it is *always* a clearing of the air, the freshening of atmosphere for positive free self-disciplined growth which is the ultimate aim of any external discipline. Impersonal deterrent punishment at the less mature stages occasionally, more personal retributive punishment possibly once in a blue moon, may play their part. But, as the *forming* of mind, character, personal and interpersonal life are the chief ends of all education, so *reform* is the aim of punitive discipline which finally makes punitive discipline unnecessary.

8. REWARDS

The ethic of reward is clear in the light of our discussion of punishment. For what has been said about retribution, deterrence and reform can almost all be said in reverse about reward. Rewards can be given retributively for meritorious action—expressing authority's approval of that action, hoping that the child will enjoy this approval and come to value for its own sake this kind of action, and that perhaps others will take note and learn. But here again the symbolism has its weakness. Virtue ought to be its own reward; the offered reward is extrinsic to the virtuous action; the pleasures of reward are different in kind from the pleasures of virtue. Reward, although it is intended to lead to virtue for its own sake, may have exactly the opposite effect; virtue for reward is no virtue. All this is supported empirically—or so some would argue. Retributive rewards have not come under such fierce criticism as have retributive punishments, perhaps, but many teachers are doubtful of their efficacy and believe that they tend to produce a false sense of values.

In the second place, as punishment is a deterrent, so reward is used as an incentive in conditioning. All that has been said about competition and about conditioning in deterrent punishment applies, with suitable modifications, here. If justified occasionally at the earlier stages, we should aim at its elimination as children mature. Retributive reward and reward as incentive to better efforts may, as before, to some extent prepare the way for growth and reform. In so far as they do, they progressively fall away until they disappear.

One word ought to be added here about something which may easily be confused with reward, but which should be distinguished from it. I mean *recognition*. Approval of what a child has done may easily be given, and received, as a 're ward'. But it need not be so. Approval is an entirely rational complement of what is rightly done, and to express approval is to do no more than justice. This *recognition* is, as just, *due* to the person. To learn to receive it reasonably is an intrinsic part of education. Not to receive it when it is due is not only to be reasonably disappointed and discouraged but to be deprived, so to speak, of a growing point. A teacher may be cautious about offering rewards; he should have no hesitation in offering recognition.

CHAPTER X

Teaching

1. The Grammar of 'Teaching': the Interplay between Teacher and Pupil

It may be helpful to begin our examination of 'teaching' by looking at the implications of the grammar of ordinary talk about teaching.

(*i*) In grammar, 'teaching' is an active verb and a transitive one, suggesting that teaching is an active process, which it is, and that something is being taught. Sir John Adams, as is well known, extended and illuminated this by pointing out that the verb 'to teach' has a double accusative. In his example, you not only teach Latin, you teach John: you teach John Latin.

This is all right as far as it goes. But ordinary grammatical use can, we know, conceal philosophical conceptions or misconceptions; ordinary speech expresses ordinary common-sense ideas which may require investigation: so it is here. Ordinary language about teaching says one thing simply, and for practical purposes; a teacher does teach subjects, and he teaches children. But if we are too much dominated by ordinary grammatical use, a wrong idea may become fixed which is difficult to unfix. The picture here is of the teacher doing something active *to* children, or even *at* them, talking actively and pointing at them. He is not only doing this, but in his teaching of a subject is *presenting* them— on a plate as it were, in a parcel of samples, on a blackboard, in books, with a 'subject', knowledge, 'facts'. . . . If one were to draw a picture of this simple-minded grammatical idea of teaching, it might show the pupil sitting receptively at his desk, and the teacher standing on a platform (a *raised* platform, for he is the important person), one hand pointing, in the other a plate extended to the pupil.

(*ii*) Against this view there has been, as everyone knows, a strong reaction. It may be helpful to think, to begin with, of the development of the idea of teaching in a rough dialectical way— thesis, antithesis, synthesis (which becomes a thesis with a further antithesis, and so on). This formal technique is crude and over-simple, but it may serve to elicit at the outset contrasting views clearly and to show how, dialectically, they build up into a complex picture—soon too complex by far to be expressed in dry logical terms. Let us therefore use the form for what it is worth, dropping it quietly overboard when it becomes too awkward. This will happen very soon—and the reasons for this will be quite illuminating.

The first thesis then (crudely) is: TEACHER DOES, AND GIVES, ALL TO THE PUPIL, WHO ONLY RECEIVES. The formal antithesis is a very extreme imaginary caricature of 'activity' theory, in which the children's activity is all and the teacher's nothing. In the first picture the child *looks* attentive and receptive. But of course his mind may be wandering, or he may be simply copying the words of the teacher or of a book. The teacher may be 'teaching' in the grammatical sense and yet be doing very little teaching in a more important sense, for a child may not be learning, or if he is, may be learning only pre-digested material which may fail to develop his growing organism. As against this, it is said that education and learning can only take place through the pupil's self-activity. St Thomas Aquinas (who is *not* an extremist) says that it is the pupil's own intellectual self-activity which is the 'efficient cause' of the pupil's learning, of his being educated. St Thomas (I repeat) was not an extremist; but there have occasionally been extremists—few and far between, and usually only at moments—who have in effect preached the abdication of the teacher. It is only through his own activity that a child learns, so, they say, leave him alone and let him learn in his own way. This extreme view—the antithesis—might be pictured as LEARNING SPRINGING SPONTANEOUSLY, as the jack-in-the-box seems to be the sole initiator of his own springing up.

(*iii*) But no one has affirmed this for long, or consistently. There is, I think, little trace of it in John Dewey, though some of his extremist disciples have gone in that direction. Every sober educationist has taken the part of the teacher seriously. (In dialectical terms, they have wanted a *synthesis* of functions of teacher and children.) Admitting that the pupil's self-activity is that without which no learning can take place, the teacher is always admitted as having much to do with the induction of the activity and generally with its direction. Although for St Thomas it is the pupil's own intellectual self-activity which is the efficient cause of his learning, the teacher has a function, which is that of an 'extrinsic proximate agent'. The active intellect of the child is helped by the external ministrations of the teacher rather as the return to health is helped by the doctor and in a different way by drugs. The child possesses the 'potency'; the teacher is one factor in the change from 'potency' to 'fulfilment'. In a more up-to-date analogy, the teacher is sometimes called a 'catalyst'.

But these views, although they correct the one-sidedness of their extreme opposites, do not provide an adequate image of teaching. The term 'extrinsic proximate agent', which is based on Aristotle, needs to be interpreted in the light of the Aristotelian assumption that (in the words of the late A. E. Taylor [1]) 'the efficient cause and that on which it exercises its efficiency are *en rapport*'. The idea of *rapport* introduces a new idea. Learning does not take place just through the 'external ministrations of the teacher'. There has to be *rapport* too. Indeed, learning takes place through complicated interactions in relation to a teacher, to a subject matter and to oneself, the learner.

The teacher may be an 'extrinsic proximate agent', but he does not *merely* set going processes which unfold from within. This terminology does no justice to the internal relations between teacher and pupil or to the complexity of the teacher's function. The term 'catalyst' is likewise inadequate for something like the same reasons. One small part of the teacher's function may be 'catalytic' but in itself the analogy is inadequate and misleading. (Formally, this synthesis, TEACHER-PUPIL IN EXTERNAL RELATION, is again a one-sided thesis needing to be complemented by an antithesis which affirms a unique sort of internality of relationship of teacher and pupil. Here formal dialectic becomes too, too artificial, and is now dropped overboard. The dialectic, which works up to a point with things or logical ideas, breaks down in the human situation, where the relations are personal and inter-personal rather than material or logical. 'Dialectic' has to give place to Dialogue, and much more.)

[1] *Aristotle*, A. E. Taylor, p. 47 (T. C. and E. C. Jack, 'The People's Books').

2. MATERIAL AND SELECTION OF MATERIAL

The account so far has mainly discussed the teacher's function with little reference to the part played by the subject matter or material (though in the first imaginary picture there is a filled plate). The presence of material in itself is a stimulus to learning. In the case of young children it may be enough to give them sand, water, tins, etc., and leave them to it. Earlier still, the baby is continuously learning in his waking hours by his own unaided experimentation with himself and the world around him. In other words, play with materials is the earliest kind of education; and it is an education which can go on for a considerable time without any teacher. (Here the half-drowned Dialectic bobs up gasping, 'MATERIALS WITHOUT TEACHER'.)

(*i*) But this is only true of the early stages. After the early beginnings the teacher is urgently needed to select appropriate 'materials' as well as to present them in a suitable way. She selects stories for reading, she perhaps tells them. She selects the problems to be solved, prepares lessons in history, biology, poetry. . . . The teacher does not simply leave the children with unarranged materials, saying, 'Do what you like with that'. She (or he) shows them selected material in a certain way for their attention and for learning in certain directions. (With the last drowning gasp the cry comes, 'TEACHER SELECTS MATERIAL'.)

(*ii*) *Why* does the teacher select and arrange as he does? The answer to this to be adequate would have to be long. Briefly, he selects in the light of slowly acquired knowledge of his subject matter. He selects it, too, in the light of his knowledge of the children he is teaching, some of it scientific knowledge, some of it personal. From his knowledge of the psychology of development, he is helped to choose what is appropriate to his particular age-group. From his knowledge of social conditions and the children's background he is able to adapt to their interests and abilities. But behind all this (and much more) he chooses, in so far as he is a free agent, because he is making 'philosophical' assumptions of different kinds. As we have amply seen, his sense of values determines at every point what he teaches and the emphasis he lays on this or that. His decisions express them.

The teacher's assumptions about the nature of knowledge and learning are involved too. The old-fashioned teacher may still unwittingly assume a *tabula rasa* view of the mind as a tablet to be written upon, or alternatively as a kind of mirror. The disciple of Dewey will regard ideas as essentially activities, and learning as taking place through active participation, experimental enterprise. The teacher's metaphysical assumptions, we have seen, also affect what he does and the way he does it. Is he acting under the authority of God, or only under human authority? Is he preparing his children finally for the life of society in this world, or for this world and a world to come? What are his assumptions about the person? Is the pupil something to be conditioned by the teacher? What does he assume about the relation of symbols to experience? In teaching biology, for instance, does he use symbols in place of, or before experience, insisting on the learning of names of plants or animals or their parts before seeing and handling actual specimens in their colour and three-dimensional vividness, and with all their æsthetic impact? Does the name and the concept, instead of arising out of a total experience and abstracted from it, become a dry substitute merely to be one more item stored in an over-burdened memory, reproduced correctly in the examination?

3. Involvement of Teacher and Pupil in Teaching and Learning

(*i*) But the teacher does not only teach selected material in a particular way. The 'material' he offers is not really separable from *him*. It is not just objective 'stuff'; it is material mixed with the teacher's mind, and not with his intellect only, but with his will and character. Geography, History, English, Mathematics, Physics . . . they are, no doubt, 'subjects', carefully planned and chosen, selectively presented. This is an intellectual conception. But there is so much more than that; what is offered by the good teacher is offered with his personality. We talk about the 'discipline of the subject'. This is, in part at least, what happens to character through a tussle with the subject; the intellect submits itself to the subject's demands, and the person through this dialogue grows in integrity. When a teacher teaches his subject in a living way, these effects upon *him* can be seen and felt by the pupils, who themselves come to participate in it through contact with him. His love for the subject, his excitement in it, is directly conveyed, and this is not a mere emotional infection but an intellectual passion which is the pupils' very active education. In the earlier stages of education, his pupils are very dependent on the personality of the teacher; 'Tommy likes nature study because he likes Mr Smith who teaches him'. Later on it is still through the teacher's personality that Tommy is learning the subject-discipline: but he is coming to be skilfully weaned from the teacher to the strong meat of the 'subject'; he has now learned to take the responsibility of its discipline upon himself. He now knows how to use libraries and how to read books or organize his own expeditions.

What we have been saying has emphasized the teacher's influence, even to the point of weaning from that influence. But the natures of the children taught, and the teacher's knowledge of this, is a potent factor in the growth of their learning. 'Knowledge' of his children is of several kinds. He must know something about children in general and about children of that age and intelligence range in particular. He must, in other words, have some objective psychological knowledge. He must also have some objective knowledge of them as individuals, something a little like what would be called in medicine their 'case histories'. He comes to know their background difficulties, their temperamental 'blocks' and facilities, their dominant interests. All of this knowledge has to be acquired, and it can, in a sense, be pigeon-holed. But the effective use of such knowledge would not (as we saw in Chapter VI) be adequately described as taking the ideas 'out of the pigeon-holes'. Acquired objective knowledge has not only to be 'pigeon-holed' but assimilated, and the assimilated knowledge can be used relevantly only in the vital act of the teacher. His knowledge will help him to help them in the way they need, to teach them better. It will help him too to temper his own enthusiasm to their needs. Without this, he can easily become a bore.

But even more is required than this skilled one-way knowledge and intuitive perception. So far, we have been speaking of the children as *objects* of his knowledge, and of his teaching. This is almost true of the more formal types of teaching. But where there is freedom and activity (using the word 'activity' in a wide sense), the children's freedom and initiative is continually changing the teaching-learning situation, so that the teacher, although he has a general plan of campaign, must adapt himself continually to a dialogue, actual or implicit. And this is not an intellectual adaptation only, but a total one; and the relationship to the pupils is, when everything is going well, one between person and persons. The whole now fairly familiar philosophy of the I-Thou can be applied here. In an atmosphere of freedom the child and the teacher are open to each other. The teacher has authority and greater experience. He has much to give. But he has much to receive too. Where the relationships are what they should be, he is learning and experiencing in a fresh way through his encounter with the free inquiring minds of his pupils. It is not too much to say that not only is he educating his pupils, but 'becoming educated' is taking place here and now in the persons of the children and teacher alike in the small free community of the happy classroom. The children are learning something for the first time, and the teacher is rediscovering, and discovering new significance through the eyes of his pupils. This is one of the delights of 'teaching', through sympathetic understanding dialogue to enjoy the discovery of other younger minds and to recover, perhaps, the springtime of learning.

Because of the subtlety and complexity of this relationship, a teacher never knows the results of his work—for good or ill. The odd word or look or gesture, in or out of the classroom (not only within the four walls of the school), may spark off something significant which remains all the pupil's life. Conversely, what the teacher thought he was doing, and thought so good, may have had little influence upon the children's characters, development and real education.

4. AUTHORITY: THE QUALITIES OF THE GOOD TEACHER

All these things require many qualities, of intellect, sensibility, character and will in the teacher. When things go well, their success is in part the fruit of these qualities—though in success the qualities are simply taken for granted and hardly noticed. But things do not, of course, always go well, and then the need for the qualities becomes more apparent. The tidy-minded teacher who likes a clear plan and likes things to go according to plan, might be a good enough lecturer, but may be an indifferently successful teacher. (I say 'good enough' lecturer, for the good lecturer ought to be aware imaginatively of the general temper of his hearers.) He is very easily tempted to resist and perhaps to resent the untidiness of interruption, the raising of irrelevancies—or what, in the neat plan, seem to him to be irrelevancies—the loose ends which may seem to lead away from the central point. Things become more difficult still for him if questions asked, or new lines of investigation suggested, seem to show up his own inadequacies of preparation or understanding. The young teacher especially is apt at such a point to exercise his authority, not liking to acknowledge his own puzzlement or confusion. The experienced good teacher, on the other hand, one who is both master of his subject and at the same time continually learning more of it, may use such occasions as growing points for new discovery and fresh illumination. But this needs confidence; and it is confidence which in part springs from humility, humility in face of the subject and in face of the pupils, the sort of humility which in fact earns the pupils' respect rather than their contempt. In this way, it is character, shown by the way of the teacher's whole approach and attitude, which 'teaches' more effectively than anything else. It is intellectual and moral education at the same time.

The qualities of character needed by the teacher are, of course, seen in a more obvious way when the situation is in a plain sense a 'moral' one. Rebellion, indiscipline, open or covert, is a challenge to the teacher's status. It is very tempting for him to regard it as a personal challenge and to act in an authoritarian way, teacher *versus* pupil. (Sometimes this reaction is necessary.) But, as the good teacher of a 'subject' submits himself to the 'authority' of the subject, and to the 'cause' of teaching, so the teacher in his moral capacity regards himself and his pupils as under the 'authority' of moral principles. It is the teacher's duty as a more experienced and mature person, to lead his pupils to moral as to intellectual responsibility, and he is much more likely to be successful if, in his dealings with younger people, he does not yield to the temptation of playing the rôle of an absolute. If, by understanding the problem of the rebellious at the point where it hurts most (and perhaps hurts both the pupil and his teacher), he can help his pupil to understand himself and to seek after his own solution, the 'cure' is likely to be most effective. Learning here, as in intellectual learning, is best when it can be a co-operation between persons. Of course it is often far more difficult than this. But always, it requires as much sympathy, objectivity, humility, firmness, as one can muster.

If the above, very sketchy, account of teaching and the demands upon the teacher is sound as far as it goes, it sets a programme for the professional education and training of teachers.[1]

What, in review, are its main *desiderata*? Any stress on this or that aspect will of course depend upon the kind and range of teaching which we have in view. For the *infant* teacher, sympathy with and understanding of children, their growth and their needs, are of paramount importance. In the *junior school*, understanding of the basic skills and of the best ways of teaching them, of 'fields' of knowledge gradually emerging out of concrete experience, will be essential. The *secondary modern* school teacher will be concerned with the development of the same thing, but with an eye on the life interests of the pupils as they approach the time when they will leave school, take up jobs, organize their own leisure, marry, become citizens. The *grammar school* teacher is expected to have a greater 'subject' expertise, but in the walled protection of the 'subject' he has, somehow, to cope with the danger of fragmentation which can arise out of high specialization, and to see his teaching as relevant to the lives of his pupils. The *technical school* teacher has *his* expertise; but it is particularly important for him to understand the meaning of 'liberal' education; he too is faced with the problem of fragmentation though in a different form. These are some obvious emphases. It should be hardly necessary to say that they are only emphases, are not exclusive of one another, and that many other qualities and attitudes are needed. The grammar school teacher, for example, ought not to assume that life begins at eleven plus or that its function can ever be a solely 'academic' one; the teacher of young children, in her essential concern for the understanding of and attention to children *now*, has to learn the pattern of later growth, and has to realize that one's idea of children's growth can never be adequate without study of what human nature in its maturity *should* be. 'The end is in the beginning.' It is sometimes too easily assumed that the *whole* programme for teacher education can be summed up in the word 'child-study'.

[1] Discussed in Chapter XIII more fully.

CHAPTER XI

The Need for 'Roots': the Humanities and the Sciences

1. MASS CONFORMITY AND PERSONAL EMPTINESS

We suffer today from a complex social disease. Many books have been written about it, and I shall begin by mere reference to some of its familiar symptoms.

One is the loss of a sound sense of personal individuality in face of the tremendous drive to social conformity. The Americans have it worse than we; as an American writer puts it [1]:—'The crisis of modern public education is one of finding ways in which the demand of social conformity may be reconciled with the intrinsic natural diversity in human beings'. Much so-called 'progress' is in the wrong direction—towards a mass conformity, a stereotyping and machine-making of taste and opinion, a conditioning of response by psychological techniques. This is not only applied to advertising of goods for sale but increasingly to politics itself. In America and here politicians have their advertising experts, interested in making the irrational appeal. Public opinion polls are openly used in the attempt to determine what people *ought* to think, like, vote for. What the majority think to be right, *is* right. Children will not have the breakfast food which is not advertised on T.V. There is the tyranny of fashion in motor cars and clothes, an almost fanatical conformity to type in adolescent dress and behaviour.

All this goes along with a kind of emptiness, and a fear of realizing it, so that a person becomes incapable of being alone, quiet, with himself or herself. The scramble to conform seems a kind of safety device, an attempt to escape from internal disruption by continually increasing the pace. The very resources of

[1] George F. Kneller, *Existentialism and Education*, p. 32 (Philosophical Library, Inc., New York, 1958).

oneself, the roots of being from which spring personal growth and all the potentialities of healthy social living, are choked up. The art of leisure is lost; the drugs of sensation must be continually increased.

This is well shown in many parts of Richard Hoggart's *The Uses of Literacy*.[1] He illustrates the 'pervasive emptiness' from typical gangster-novelettes. In one of them, the death of a girl is described as follows. 'When I saw that Fan was dead and cold, I just turned away. Spikey was saying something over and over, but I only knew there was a great hollow inside of me. I left the joint and started walking. I walked a mighty long way in the cold night. In the end, Spikey overtook me, "Come on, pal," he said, "there's a gang of us going on to Mike's place. The girls'll be glad to see you." I didn't answer. Maybe I didn't really hear. I only knew I wanted to go on walking, walking alone in the night.' Mr Hoggart remarks, 'In both books that final emptiness, though it is in each case specifically related to a death, symbolizes also a much wider and more pervasive emptiness. Indeed, the girls can only mean so much because they have seemed the only meaningful things in a whole disillusioning world. . . . In the world of gangster-fiction there can be no happy endings, nor any endings which are really beginnings, attempts to restart life by staying in the same spot and doing what you can to build the city. You either end in the flat emptiness just illustrated, or induce the temporary impression of a new start by getting into a fast machine and roaring away down a concrete highway (the characters are usually rootless, without homes or permanent work). The tyres scud on the surface, the demands of the city are left behind; the demands on the personality are—you continue to hope—left with it; you are heading West, to a world where there may still be the childhood dream. Not that you really think so, but you go on—progressivism translated into an endless and hopeless tail-chasing evasion of the personality. This is the usual manner: "So we quit that city and headed down the turnpike for the next. I was dead sick of that joint and the countryside sure looked good to me with the sun on it. I let the old Chev. full out and she roared down the concrete at a steady eighty. I kept on like that for I don't know how many hours—biting off the miles—heading for I don't

[1] Chatto and Windus, 1957, pp. 222–223.

know what. . . ." ' This rings of despair. The following newspaper
extract illustrates another sentiment for space-filling: 'More
than 15,000 people crammed the three-mile sea-front at Southsea
yesterday. Every inch of car parking space was taken, and the
roads over a wide area leading from the sea-front were also
jammed with cars. Mr Alex. Kinnear, the town's publicity
official, said: "I have never seen anything like it. This is easily
one of the best August Sundays ever." '

2. 'ACEDIA'

Josef Pieper describes the kind of boredom through which a
person is unable to live his own life, as an incapacity for *leisure*.
It has its source in a deiect which in the Middle Ages was called
the sin of *Acedia*. This is a fundamental restlessness which must
escape through activity of some kind—which is sometimes ex-
cessive work. Fundamentally, Acedia or 'idleness' or 'sloth'
'means that a man prefers to forgo the rights, or if you prefer,
the claims that belong to his nature. In a word, he does not
want to be as God wants him to be, and that ultimately means
that he does not wish to be what he really, fundamentally, *is*.
Acedia is the "despair from weakness" which Kierkegaard analysed as the "despairing refusal to be oneself". Metaphysically and
theologically, the notion of *Acedia* means that a man does not, in
the last resort, give the consent of his will to his own being. . . .'[1]
In another passage, speaking of the sense of wonder and mystery,[2]
he contrasts the person who has the sense of mystery with what
he calls the 'bourgeois mind'. 'Yet wonder really is unbourgeois.
For what do we mean by saying in a spiritual sense that something is bourgeois? Above all, in the first place, that a man accepts
his environment defined as it is by the immediate needs of life,
so completely finally, that things happening cannot any longer
become transparent; the great, wide, not to say deep, world
which is at first sight invisible, the world of senses and universals,
is not even suspected; nothing wonderful ever happens in this
world, and wonder itself is unknown or lost. The narrow insensitive mind, that has become narrow through being insensitive,
takes everything for granted. And what, in truth, is to be taken

[1] Joseph Pieper: *Leisure the Basis of Culture*, p. 49 (Faber, 1952).
[2] See below, pp. 174 sq.

for granted? Is the existence of "sight" or "perception" to be taken for granted? No one imprisoned in everyday life *can* ask such questions because, in the first place, he is unable to forget his immediate needs . . . whereas that is precisely what characterizes the man capable of wonder.' [1] Another part of this same defect is the inability to put the question to oneself what one *ought* to do or be. Either the answer is given in terms of obvious matter-of-fact wants and needs immediately at hand, or else in terms of the mass-given values of which we have spoken. The capacity for originality in posing and answering the question, What ought I to do? How ought I to dispose of my life? is lost.

Teachers ought to address themselves to these questions with the utmost seriousness. In so far as education is *not* turning out persons who have at least begun to learn—at home, in school, in their own conversations with themselves and others, to come to terms with themselves and the world, to enjoy what is worth enjoying, to wonder, and to grow through these contacts, education which has not developed personal values in which the genuine is distinguished from the spurious—such education has failed.

3. Educational 'Materialisms' and the 'Educated Person'

How far education actually succeeds or fails in these things it is of course impossible to estimate with scientific precision. It partly depends on where one looks. But it is certainly far too easy, in a utilitarian world, to forget the deeper human aims of education in preoccupation with the immediate ones. In an article in *The (Manchester) Guardian* a reporter wrote: 'The secondary modern is all things to all men. . . . But the main rôle of secondary moderns is to staff the lower echelons of Britain's vast industrial machine—particularly with unskilled and semi-skilled workers.' This in itself certainly contains part of the truth. But the following passage of the same article sets it in a rather different light. 'These C stream girls do not try a lot. Many of them giggle, and confess they are looking forward to marriage more than anything else. . . . On one of the visits the school organized to local factories the girls looked and listened with well-behaved attention, but remotely, not really like people

[1] Pages 130–131 *op. cit.*

contemplating possible futures.' [1] In a scorching reply to this article, Mr David Holbrook writes: 'The C stream girls *confess* that "they are looking forward to marriage more than anything else." How shocking of these girls to be more preoccupied with life rather than with earning a living! . . . Perhaps we should ask where does all the "go" of the vast industrial machine go to, if not to potentialities of living, at the centre of which are love, marriage, a family. And ought not the "main rôle of the schools" which educates three-quarters of the population to be teaching children to seek out life's possibilities rather than provide "skilled and semi-skilled workers"? Do they need to be educated to work at the assembly line? Or rather, do not anyone's capacities as an adult, at the assembly line, or at the executive's desk, or as a father or citizen depend upon his having something of balance and security? And it is this which must needs be given by the school, largely, in a world elsewhere so unthinkingly preoccupied with making that "vast industrial machine" "go", merely because it *is* "vast".' The writer adds that the conception of ' "staffing the industrial machine" will be called "realistic", yet the "realists" will be heard in the same breath criticizing the young for their lack of aims . . . and for their instability. Aims and stability can be given only by an education which does not abrogate its function and take the easy way of merely training towards "earning a living".'

This 'realism', which is a sort of materialism, is paralleled on the more academic side by what can be called a 'materialism of the curriculum'. We have got into the habit of thinking of the curriculum too exclusively in terms of subjects to be collected, and as though 'subjects' were fixed by independent nature, to be learned and reproduced, whereas they are (in part) artifacts expressive of and revealing vital human interests and activities. As learnt, we know, they are only educative in so far as they become integrated into the mind, the vital interests and activities of the pupil. He must, it is true, possess some 'objective' knowledge of history, science and the rest in order to become an educated person. But he does not really possess it unless it 'possesses' him. This inwardness is very easy to overlook because it is much less easily accessible to cursory inspection than the chunks or gobbets which can be readily itemized, checked,

[1] *Manchester Guardian*, 28th July 1959.

added up. The 'materialism' of the curriculum is shown in the obsession for carefully recording how *much* 'knowledge' you have. We have 'done' this bit of history or mathematics. We have, as we say, 'covered the ground'. 'That's over', we say, 'another on the list', and being over is done with—perhaps gone and dead. Professor Walsh has some penetrating things to say about all this. He speaks of the temptation of the teacher to allow subject matter to engage the largest share of his attention. But 'if we judge by the standard of permanence, subject matter discloses itself as of much slighter importance. Some simple learning and skill aside, few of us, unless professionally required to do so, could or would wish to recover ,rom the discard into which our minds have thrust it much of the truck on which we and our teachers spend effort, energy and patience at school.' [1] And he adds that it can be doubted how much has been forgotten *because* it has modified the mind and its perception so that 'it is no longer an object of thought but a means of insight. For it is not the permanence of memory but the permanence of being and power which is the criterion most relevant here. And what lasts, what enters into our being as a result of school and college is a blend of value, attitude and assumption, a certain moral tone, a special quality of imagination, a particular flavor of sensibility—the things that constituted the soul of our education.' [2]

The radical mistake of over-emphasis upon data to be learned is encouraged by the current passion for measurement and exact assessment, by the influence of the examination. Counting, valuation in terms of amount is a symbol of the 'materialism'. There is an assumption that nothing which cannot be formulated in a way which can be set down in examination answers is much worth considering: it is dismissed as 'vague and nebulous'. (This would seldom be explicitly said; but actions speak louder than words. The machine-marking, applied in America even to higher studies such as philosophy, is an example of this assumption at work.) Some forms of examination can assess the impact of education much better than others. But in the end the assessment of an 'education' is the assessment of a person, of a person

---

[1] These, and other quotations in this and the next chapter, are taken from William Walsh, 'Coleridge's Self-unravelling Clue: its Meaning for Education'. Reprinted from *The Western Humanities Review*, Vol. IX, No. 3, pp. 209–216.   [2] *Op. cit.*

whose mind has been formed by study, experience and decision, who has come to approach questions in a certain way, who can express himself, in whose outlook there is a certain proportion and perspective. An educated person will no doubt 'know' many different things. But the education of his mind will certainly not be measured by the amount he knows, even when it is well set out and organized. It is often assumed, says Professor Walsh, 'that there is some necessary relation between the educated mind and a wide range of scholarship, a notion to which university teachers are especially prone'.[1] Once again this is 'materialism' in a subtler form.

Knowledge is never identical with propositions although it often must use them, and it is never identical with areas of any subject matter. As we acquire it, we are living actively; as we assimilate it, it becomes part of the substance and structure of ourselves. This, I suppose, is what is meant by the common saying that 'education is what is left over when you have forgotten all you have learnt'—at school or elsewhere. It is by being himself an educated person in these senses that the teacher can, perhaps for the most part unconsciously, help his pupils at least to feel what being 'educated' means. This applies both to the educative teaching of a single subject, and to the sense of relation with other subjects in the whole of education.

The same kind of thing can be said not only of the relation of 'subject matter' to the self, but also of the relation between feeling and understanding within the self. Feeling is not only a condition of certain kinds of moral, æsthetic and religious awareness, but of any total awareness in which (as at some points of scientific inquiry) it is not deliberately excluded. In an essay on Walter Pater, Lord David Cecil says of Pater, 'He was that rare hybrid, the scholar-artist. We can easily see why it is rare. The scholarly spirit is intellectual and impersonal, and refers its judgments to standards of reason and fact; the artistic is sensuous and personal, and refers its judgments to standards of feeling and imagination. It is unlikely that the two strains should appear in the same man.' [2]

I do not know how far Lord David Cecil is right in speaking of the scholar-artist as a 'rare thing', or in saying that it is 'unlikely that the two strains should appear in the same man'. If it is so,

[1] *Op. cit.*
[2] *Walter Pater, The Scholar-Artist*, p. 4 (Rede Lecture, Cambridge, 1955).

perhaps it is for the very reason that our education has been so divisive of feeling and intellect. But however this may may be, it is certain that we should *not* in education acquiesce in the separation of the two strains.

4. THE HUMANITIES AND THE SCIENCES

The idea of the 'educated person' and of the need to develop thinking and feeling together is closely bound up with the increasingly pressing problem of 'all-round education' in a world of increasing division between the 'arts' and the 'sciences'. The 'two cultures' and how they can be bridged, or how the arts man should have more science and the scientist a more 'humane' education—are constantly discussed. I shall now say some quite general things about the 'sciences' and the 'humanities' without attempting here to deal with the practical problems of a 'balanced' education at school or university. But it must be remembered that the problem of 'arts and sciences' is only a manifestation of a much deeper one—to which I shall refer later.[1]

Let us, then, start by some broad observations on the contrasts and relationships between what are broadly called 'the arts' and the 'sciences'. It must be emphasized that this approach is *only* a broad and relatively superficial one; to be accurate, it would have to be greatly refined and modified.

The 'humanities' or 'liberal arts' include literature and language of all periods and places and also history. Very generally speaking, a differentiating criterion of education in the humanities is that it teaches discriminating appreciation of *values*. 'Humanities' and 'values' go together. (This is an ideal: we know it often fails.) We learn, by living imaginatively in them, about the whole *gamut* of human values, of good and evil. This is obviously true of literature, and in a different way of history, which is not merely a story of events, but of events mixed with human feelings and motives—hopes, fears, ambitions, courage, power-seeking, cruelty, love ... The emphasis of the empirical sciences, on the other hand, is upon clear understanding and statement (often, but not always, in mathematical symbols) of fact. Whereas in the study of drama or history we are often challenged to ask 'What did these people care about or (perhaps) what in those circumstances *ought* to have

---

[1] Pp. 174 sq.

been done?', to raise questions of human motives, of ethics or even æsthetics, in the sciences we are in the end concerned to understand aspects of things as they are. Another way of expressing the same thing is to say that in the humanities, feeling and will, more of the whole person, is involved, whilst in science we are aiming as far as possible at detached objective statement. If emotion is in *some* ways relevant to the understanding of drama or history, it is equally in *some* ways irrelevant to the understanding of the formula expressing a natural law. This is not to say that the scientist is a man without emotions about science. There is a 'feel' and a joy about science and technology (e.g. engineering) but their primary aim is clear abstract knowledge or efficient making or doing rather than feeling or joy.

Again, whereas in the humanities we try to appreciate *whole* situations in their concreteness (including voluntary and feeling elements)—a religious outlook, the situation for a moral decision, a whole lyric, an historical event in its setting—in a great deal of science we are naturally and rightly thinking of the highest abstractions, e.g., of formal mathematical relationships abstracted and extracted from their concrete context.

Still another mode of expressing the same thing is to say that the humanities study the *individual*, whilst science studies the *general*. The formula of the law of gravitation is purely general $(F = kM_1M_2/d^2)$ and does not require immediate attention to any single instance. Or (to put it another way) when we are talking of instances of a general concept, the individuality of the instance is not ordinarily [1] taken into account. The demonstration of the relation between the volume and the pressure of a gas at a constant temperature $(PV = \text{constant})$ can be simply shown in a thousand different laboratories and sets of apparatus, and it does not matter. But an individual historical event is unique; the time and circumstances are themselves and no other, and are not repeatable. Likewise each sonnet and drama is utterly individual and must be known in itself and not merely as an instance of 'sonnet' or 'drama'. In the humanities these 'individuals' are of *central* importance. And, it should be strongly emphasized, extensive and intensive *education* is needed in the

[1] I do not mean that it *never* is—sometimes it may be in a living organism or even in non-living material structure. But this raises different problems: and one would then not be thinking of mere logical *instances*.

appreciation and understanding of these individuals. Deliberate 'arts' education is essential for full human development. It cannot be properly relegated to the time left over from other things. Deprived of it, a human being is, so far, starved and underdeveloped.

The contrast and relationship of the humanities and the sciences can be expressed in different ways. In a number of essays in *Science and the Creative Spirit* [1] the relationship is well put. Harcourt Brown writes: 'Old and respectable tradition associates the humanities with the study of the record man's mind has set down in books, the information available concerning man himself, his taste in morals, his manners and thoughts, his social relations, his beliefs, his arts of peace and war, his relation with the world within himself, as well as with nature and the elements.' From these are derived modern disciplines—history, geography, natural philosophy, political and social science, æsthetics, psychology, history of art, etc. In the first essay of this book Carl W. Deutsch argues that whereas the humanities are concerned with the emphasis upon the whole man, on the interrelation of all his ways of thinking, feeling, acting, science sets out to isolate a small number of aspects of individuals or situations, as well as to isolate events or situations from their context. Even when the poets or the painters are conveying only particular moods, their concern is with integrity and wholeness, whereas the isolated aspects which are the concern of science are investigated with the utmost thoroughness, and a few of their implications pursued with single-minded persistence. Specific propositions and predictions are derived, and these can be verified by equally specific observations. Creative art, and generally humanistic knowledge, cannot be tested in this kind of way. They can be validated only if they ring true as a whole.

Again (Harcourt Brown writes), the humanist is not concerned with use, with tools, with the ulterior purposes, nor with power. He is concerned with things for their own sake, for their values as expressions of the human spirit.

On the other hand (Deutsch) there is continuity between the sciences and the humanities. Science cannot exclude relative uniqueness and individual perception. And no humanistic knowledge is entirely free from the problems of repetitive con-

[1] (Ed.) Harcourt Brown, University of Toronto Press, 1958.

sistency. (We have already ourselves seen examples of this over-lap in clinical medicine and in the psychology of personality.) The humanities and the sciences can indeed be regarded as lying along a continuous spectrum, in which at one extreme end are the pure arts and at the other pure sciences. At intermediate points come history and philosophy. In history and philosophy there is need for both emotional and æsthetic satisfaction,[1] as well as for objectivity and impersonality. History is the history of the writer, and of the reader. Philosophy, on the other hand, whilst it seeks to be as objective as it can, includes all the time the data of individual and unique experience. In the latter respect philosophy is humanistic. But both history and philosophy can lean to either extreme. When the historian explains and organizes his material in terms of numerical formulation, com-piling statistics and economics to account for events in historical sequence, he is approaching the scientific outlook. On the other hand, if he is interpreting human actions and motives, if he writes with elegance, if he introduces elements of impressionism to fill out the picture extending beyond the data, if he introduces drama and art—he approaches the humanities. Likewise the philosopher as concerned with the freedom of man—in ethics, the arts, ordinary living—is a true humanist, in that he uses intuition and imagination to produce results beyond those justified by cold operational reason. But as a symbolic logician, or when he is referring to objective cumulative knowledge, to repeatable experiments, to impersonal structures of thought, the philosopher leans towards science rather than the humanities.

The view of science expounded so far is, I hope, a fair short statement of an ordinary, sound, conventional view. It can be summed up as follows. The scientist in putting questions to concrete nature must, in formulating them and in formulating tentative hypothetical answers, select, simplify, abstract. On the theoretic side he constructs formulæ, very general hypothetical statements, often but by no means always mathematical, and on the empirical side arranges to make observations to check them. These abstractions both theoretical and empirical are common and 'public' (it is said) to any competent scientific thinker and observer. Clear communication is possible between experts. In this sense science is impersonal—in contrast to, say, the personally

---

[1] This is true of the sciences also.

involved and individual experience of moral value or religion or poetry.

5. SCIENCE AND 'PERSONAL KNOWLEDGE'

But these statements are over-simple; and they are not undisputed. In his important book *Personal Knowledge* [1] Professor Polanyi contends that although scientific knowledge is continually striving after objectivity (and in a sense after impersonality), science is not nearly so impersonal as is commonly supposed. The great discoveries of science have been made through a sense of intellectual 'beauty', by a kind of æsthetic intuition. Pythagoras, Copernicus, Kepler, Newton, Einstein, all worked in this way. Professor Polanyi shows how Einstein discovered the Special Theory of Relativity by speculative intuition. In Einstein's own words, 'the Michelson-Morley experiment had a negligible effect on the discovery of relativity'.[2] Scientific 'passion' is not merely a psychological by-product of scientific discovery, but has a guiding function indispensable to science. As an artist feels his way to what is æsthetically important, so the sense of intellectual beauty directs the scientific discoverer towards what (out of a limitless mass of material) is of real scientific interest and *importance*.[3]

Again, the pursuit of science is a skill, an *art*; it has to be learned, as the master teaches the apprentice. 'Articulate content to science can be taught in new over-seas universities' but the 'unspecifiable art of scientific research' requires the direct teaching of traditional connoisseurship. Furthermore, the full scientific experience contains a *contemplative*, sometimes almost mystical, aspect. And in some branches of science the involvement of the personality is very great. Biology, he tells us, is life thinking itself; one requires to project imaginatively one's own life-experience in the understanding of life. Still more so is it with the knowledge of man. To know man, one has to *be* a man.

Polanyi develops the idea of personal involvement in scientific knowledge in many ways which it is impossible to go into here. It is a liberal interpretation of the nature of science which, whilst not denying the abstractness and the objective aims of science,

[1] Routledge, 1958. [2] *Op. cit.*, p. 10.
[3] Dr J. Bronowski, in *Science and Human Values* (Hutchinson, 1961), especially in the first of these three essays, develops a similar theme.

affirms that science is a more full-blooded human activity than it is sometimes supposed to be.

But the question is worth posing at a deeper level still. The scientist, we agree, must in his full development of science draw upon many human capacities which are not commonly recognized as 'scientific'—upon intellectual passion, imagination, the sense of beauty, the moral and sometimes even the religious sense. How far are we to distinguish between saying that the *scientific* enterprise must draw upon resources *beyond* the enterprise itself, and saying that the æsthetic, moral and religious life are an intrinsic part of scientific enterprise itself? If we adopt the latter course, we are apt to blur the distinction between science and other forms of human activity or knowledge; we are apt to make 'science' into *everything*, thus destroying the conception of science as an important but essentially self-limited enterprise. If we adopt the former alternative, we are in effect saying that the pursuit of science as a body of techniques and abstract knowledge is not *ultimately* a self-sustaining enterprise, and that there is a wide life of experience strictly outside science which claims to be cultivated. But this is an obscure statement; it needs to be analysed.

CHAPTER XII

Intellect, Depth and 'Dialogue'

1. SCIENCE AND THE SCIENTIST'S LIFE

Is science self-justifying? [1] This question is put by Mr G. R. G.
Mure in his book *Retreat from Truth*.[2] He states his own answer
in no uncertain terms. Science (and mathematics) is *not* a self-
justifying activity, but a practical one (or after Croce) an
'economic' activity. Mr Mure is well aware how outrageous
this statement sounds. He writes: 'I have none the less, by
treating science and mathematics as no more than a part of
man's practical adventure, committed myself to a position likely
to excite in orthodox circles the nearest present-day equivalent
to horror at blasphemy against the Holy Ghost.' [3] He attempts
to answer the objection that his views are a confusion of science
and mathematics with technology, and that they fail to notice the
obvious passion of great scientists and mathematicians for the
pursuit of truth for its own sake. He contends that 'since the
geocentric celestial mechanism of Aristotle dissolved before
Galileo's telescope, and since science rejected the idea of creation
as "a diapason ending full in man", the inorganic universe in
yielding its secrets to ever more subtilized scientific observation
has revealed no *raison d'être* whatsoever of its own. The starry
heavens, save to the æsthetic eye, have grown duller and duller,
progressively more pointless.' [4] And, save where knowledge is
power, why should any man desire passionately to study that
in which nothing is intrinsically better or worse than anything
else? Positively speaking, it is only in so far as science and
mathematics, in synthesis with other knowledge, contribute to a
philosophical view that they become justified. He quotes
Schroedinger: 'The isolated knowledge obtained by a group of

---

[1] Better expressed as, 'Is the pursuit of science self-justifying?'.
[2] Blackwell, 1958. [3] Pp. 34, 35, *op. cit.* [4] *Op. cit.*, p. 35.

specialists in a narrow field has in itself no value whatsoever, but only in its synthesis with all the rest of knowledge, and inasmuch as it really contributes in this synthesis towards answering the demand τινες δὲ ἡμεῖς; Who are we?' [1]

These statements need careful scrutiny; in the form in which they are put, they are, I think, profoundly misleading.

In the first place, let us be clear about the genuine importance of science even as an 'economic' activity, even as the basis of a technology which is applied to 'useful' human ends. The 'improvement of man's estate' is certainly a justification for the pursuit of science.

It *is* a justification, however wisely or unwisely the benefits or technological application are employed. It is *better* that human beings should be fed and clothed and warmed, have all the benefits of transport, manufacture, healing drugs, modern midwifery, medicine and surgery, the reproduction of sight and sound than that they should go without them. It is *better* that they should have increased knowledge and control of nature—in the air, or the earth, under the sea, of microcosm or macrocosm, even if they use them for selfish indulgence or for destroying one another. This is an important point; we often confusedly argue that because benefits are misused, they are not benefits. But benefits they are; we should be morally wrong if we did not seek and accept them. Their use for the *true* welfare of mankind—whatever that may be—or their abuse, is a further question.

But although all this is true, it is obvious both that the values of the extrinsic usefulness of science are not normally present in the mind of the pure scientist, and that he would want to say a great deal more about the *intrinsic* values of the pursuit of science. Science, it is claimed, has its own ethic, its own æsthetic, its own autonomy, its categorical imperatives and its peculiar self-justifying joys. There is some intrinsic value, is there not, in coming to know or understand anything better, in solving problems, in increasing the range of our mental grasp? This can be good fun, but it goes deeper than that, satisfying a fundamental need of human nature. There is, again, the æsthetic joy of science and mathematics, which is intrinsic in the sense that it does not need to be 'justified' by anything outside itself. And there is a whole range of imaginative and moral qualities

[1] *Science and Humanism* (Allen & Unwin, 1957).

trained and called out daily. Added to these there are values which are of a more personal instrumental sort—as distinct from the external benefits to humanity already mentioned. In oneself, even a little increased knowledge increases self-esteem, sense of intellectual mastery. This is greatly enhanced when particular bits of knowledge get connected together in wider systems: the sense of intellectual power and self-esteem of the scholar with a wide grasp of things is familiar.

But there is more to it than that; these personal 'justifications' have a slightly subjective ring about them—perhaps even a hint of intellectual and æsthetic self-indulgence? Is it not possible to maintain in a broader way that the devotion of a life committed to science is self-justifying, needing no apology or defence? I believe it is, but that the nature of the devotion needs to be stated rather carefully.

There is, I think, something to be said for Mure's findings, supported by Schroedinger. But the form of the statements is wrong. In order to get a fair conclusion, it is quite unnecessary to denigrate or to misrepresent 'science'. Why should science be regarded as concerned only with 'the inorganic universe', and why should the supporting quotation speak only of 'the isolated knowledge obtained by a group of specialists, in a narrow field'? These are departments, or bits, within science, but not 'science'.

I spoke in the last chapter of the 'sciences' and the 'humanities', and of what 'science' does and does not do. This is allowable language in certain contexts, but it is dangerous if the legitimately defined activities of 'science' become identified with the life work of 'the scientist', as though the scientist in doing science ceased to be a man and became a highly complex sort of electronic brain designed for one set of exercises only. Sometimes, admittedly, the single-minded pursuit of science does produce a human effect that looks like this, and we know that every highly specialized work has its dangers in distorting and limiting human beings. But there is no inevitability about it, and it is indeed one of the responsibilities of education in a wide sense to see that it does not happen.

The trouble is the personification of 'science'. Some of the procedures of science (e.g., the deductive and empirical) become identified with the characteristics of 'the scientist', whilst in fact scientific procedures are procedures adopted—at certain places and times—by a *man* whose nature includes more, perhaps infinitely more. The false identification becomes more pointed when an abstraction such as the 'inorganic universe' is assumed (by Mure) to be *all* that 'the scientist' is apprehending in his approach to inorganic nature. *If* he is merely this human (or half-human) electronic brain, then of *course* there will be no *raison d'être* in anything, and of course the starry heavens will be completely dull—because the electronic brain is not designed to respond to their beauty. For the same reason, obviously nothing will seem intrinsically better or worse than anything else. Again, if the 'narrow specialist' is defined as narrow, then he will not be broad.

We all know the dangers; but they are not inevitable. They are not in the least inevitable if it is kept firmly in mind on the one hand that it is a *man* who is carrying out highly specialized (sometimes highly imaginative) activities, and on the other hand that 'nature' or 'the world' is not identical with the construction of this or that part of science—e.g. 'the inorganic universe'—or even with all of them put together. (Incidentally, this simple statement, if fully grasped and accepted, could make all the difference to the teaching of science as part of a liberal education.)

Einstein wrote in 1918: 'Man tries to form a simplified and clear conception of the world in a manner somehow adequate to himself, and to conquer the world of reality by replacing it to a certain extent by this picture. The painter, the poet, the speculative philosopher, and the naturalist do it, each of them, in his own way. He places in this picture the centre of gravity of his emotional life in order to find the tranquillity and constancy which he cannot find within the narrow limits of turbulent personal experience.' And J. R. Oppenheimer, in his Reith Lectures, said, 'For most of us, in most of those moments when we are most free of corruption, it has been the beauty of the world of nature, and the strange and compelling harmony of its order that has sustained, inspirited and led us'.[1]

These writers are speaking as *men*, whose chief love and expertise is in science. They speak as men with a faith and the sense of a great 'vocation'. They are thinking, as I believe we should think, of scientific work as a form of the engagement of a

[1] Both quotations are taken from C. A. Coulson's Rede Lecture, *Science and Religion* (Cambridge, 1954).

person with the world. On both sides, the subjective and the objective, there is a continuity with the rest of things which can easily be forgotten. The person, *qua* scientist, is carrying out a highly specialized task, but if he remains a whole person the moving experiences within the scientific enterprise will have personal repercussions which take him far outside science. On the objective side it is a world which he is exploring in one specialized way. If he approaches the world in humility and natural piety, he finds overtones and undertones which as pure scientist he cannot comprehend. If he remains whole, he will not dismiss them as unimportant, but conserve them for the time when he can attend to them in the way and with the methods they rightfully demand. If he does do this he will naturally turn for help to those who are expert in the overtones and undertones, expert in the humanities—in philosophy, poetry, the arts, religion. . . . The life work and selfless devotion of the man who is a scientist is, surely, if it is interpreted in this way, an integral part of a kind of life which is self-justifying, and needs no further justification.

Some of the under- and overtones of the scientific life raise questions which are philosophical. Mure and Schroedinger are perfectly right in suggesting this—although the word 'philosophical' is a little limiting. To say that it is *only* 'in so far as science and mathematics, in synthesis with other knowledge, contribute to a *philosophical* view that they become justified', is to speak with too exclusive intellectual emphasis. There can be strongly *experiential* sides of the devoted scientist's life, experience through feeling of depth and mystery. I should like to look at some of these, first saying something about philosophy.

Whether the further questions which may arise out of scientific inquiry are 'philosophical' or not will depend of course on what one means by 'philosophy'.

2. PHILOSOPHY, CLARIFICATION AND MYSTERY

One of the important emphases in contemporary philosophy is, we know, upon 'clarification'. Clarification is the resolving of what are called *puzzles*, and this is distinguished on the one hand from the solving of *problems* and on the other (very sharply) from any dealings with *mystery*.

A large range of *problems* fall within the purview of science, and the scientist solves them as far as he can in his own way. Michael Foster,[1] expounding Mascall, explains the distinction between problem and puzzle as follows. 'A puzzle is like a problem in that it looks mysterious but is not. The apparent mystery is dispelled in this case, not by acquiring further knowledge, but by clarification of what we know already. An example of a puzzle is the apparent mystery that when we face ourselves in a mirror our left and right sides are transposed in the mirror-image, but there is no similar transposition on the other plane, of our head and our feet. We resolve the mystery, not by acquiring any knowledge of physics or optics which we had not before, but simply by clarifying to ourselves what is involved in our use of the words "above" and "below" and "left" and "right". . . . We could describe the relations of the sides of the body in similar terms, if we talked about the "east" and the "west" sides.' [2]

It is right that philosophy should include this clarification, but of course more than questionable whether clarification of puzzles should be the whole or even the main task of philosophy. There are those who have thought, like M. Schlick, that questions are of two kinds only, empirical and logical, that the former, though often unsolved, are not in principle—with the limitless increase of scientific empirical knowledge—insoluble; and that the latter, if *clearly* stated, are always soluble. There is therefore 'no unfathomable mystery in the world'. But the neatness of this statement gives rise to uneasiness. The total impact of human experience with the world—æsthetic, moral, religious, inter-personal—is not so neat, and seems to give to the word 'mystery' a meaning quite different from 'problem' potentially capable of solution. And if, as one great traditional interpretation of philosophy assumes, all aspects of human experience are data for philosophy, the philosopher, to be aware of the data, has to be open in feeling and sympathy and imagination to receive the impact of often baffling experience. His style will be very artificially and arbitrarily restricted if he is told that he must confine his investigations to quasi-science or logic. Indeed, if the function of the philosopher is pre-determined by an *a priori*

[1] In *Mystery and Philosophy* (S.C.M. Press, London, 1957).
[2] *Op. cit.*, p. 19.

definition of the methods he must use, the paralytic effect upon the person of the philosopher and his thought will be disastrous. Coleridge has some words which although written a long time ago are apt. 'I have known some who have been rationally educated as it is styled. They were marked by a microscopic acuteness but when they looked at great things, all became a blank and they saw nothing, and denied (very illogically) that anything could be seen, and uniformly put the negation of a power for the possession of a power and called the want of imagination judgment and the never being moved to rapture philosophy.' [1]

This is one extreme view of philosophy. It not only worships clarity but denies 'mystery'. At the other extreme end of the scale there is the view of Plato that science and philosophy are revelations of mystery. But for Plato philosophy not only begins in wonder but goes on in wonder. Problems may be to some extent solved, but mystery remains and is revealed, not dispelled.

3. WONDER, *Ratio* AND *Intellectus*

According to Josef Pieper, we should distinguish between doubt and wonder. Wonder was the beginning of philosophy in ancient times but in modern philosophy it is doubt which is the beginning of philosophy. The true sense of wonder does not lie in uprooting the mind and plunging it in doubt. It lies in making it possible and even necessary to strike deeper roots. 'The sense of wonder certainly deprives the mind of those penultimate certainties that we had up till then taken for granted—and to that extent wonder is a form of disillusionment, though even that has its positive aspect, since it means being freed from an illusion; and it becomes clear that what we had taken for granted was not ultimately self-evident. But further than that, wonder signifies that the world is profounder, more all-embracing and mysterious than the logic of everyday reason had taught us to believe. The innermost meaning of wonder is fulfilled in a deepened sense of mystery. It does not end in doubt, but is the awakening of the knowledge that being, *qua* being, is mysterious and inconceivable, and that it is a mystery in the full sense of the word: neither a

[1] From Walsh, *op. cit.*

dead end, nor a contradiction, nor even something impenetrable and dark; mystery really means that a reality, the singular existing thing, is inconceivable because it is an inexhaustible source of light, and for ever unfathomable. And that is the fact which is experienced in wonder.'[1] Pieper also emphasizes that wonder is not simply the starting-point to philosophy but its lasting source. The philosopher does not cease 'wondering' at a certain point in his philosophizing. He does not cease to wonder unless he ceases to philosophize. Philosophy in this sense has a markedly contemplative aspect. We are apt to think of science and philosophy as hard active work—and so in a sense it is. But there is in knowledge a passive element. If one looks at a rose contemplatively, one opens one's eyes receptively to whatever offers itself; the things seen enter into us, so to speak, without calling for any effort or strain on our part to possess them. The same is true, at least in ancient philosophy, of intellectual contemplation. Contemplation involves the reception of something which is given or revealed. In a sense it is the acceptance of a grace, something given freely. Pieper points out the mediaeval distinction (which follows the ancient phrase of Heraclitus, 'listening to the essence of things') between the understanding as *Ratio* and the understanding as *Intellectus*. '*Ratio* is the power of discursive, logical thought, of searching and of examination, of abstraction, of definition and drawing conclusions. *Intellectus*, on the other hand, is the name for the understanding in so far as it is the capacity of *simplex intuitus*, of that simple vision to which truth offers itself like a landscape to the eye. The faculty of mind, man's knowledge, is both these things in one, according to antiquity and the Middle Ages, simultaneously *ratio* and *intellectus*; and the process of knowing is the action of the two together. The mode of discursive thought is accompanied and impregnated by an effortless awareness, the contemplative vision of the *intellectus*, which is not active but passive, or rather receptive, the activity of the soul in which it conceives that which it sees.'[2] The *ratio*, the ancients held, 'is distinctively human; the *intellectus* they regarded as being already beyond the sphere allotted to man. And yet it belonged to man, though in

---

[1] Josef Pieper: *Leisure the Basis of Culture*, trans. Alexander Dru, pp. 134–135 (Faber and Faber, 1952).

[2] Josef Pieper, *op. cit.*, pp. 33–34.

one sense "super-human"; the "purely human" by itself could not satiate man's powers of comprehension, for man, of his very nature, reaches out beyond the sphere of the "human". . . .' [1]

This, as I have said, is the other extreme from contemporary analysis, for which it would be philosophically irrelevant. But does it not go too far in the opposite direction? If we distinguish between the man who is the scientist and his strictly scientific techniques, should we not stress that 'philosophy' is in the main an exercise of *ratio* whilst the cultivation of the inseparable *intellectus* penetrates into the whole life of the man who is the philosopher, and thus includes much more than strictly philosophic activity? Whilst certainly agreeing that philosophy is the action of *ratio* and *intellectus* together, is it not better, whilst including in philosophy all that is essential to full philosophical thinking, to insist that philosophy is mainly thinking (in the sense of *ratio*) and not in itself having the sense of mystery or worshipping or anything of that kind? If we make 'philosophy' (or 'science') into the whole of man's spiritual life, it loses its distinctive character as an essential part of that life. One need not wish that the philosopher should *never* break into poetry, nor that he should not sometimes write with feeling, even religious feeling. But the main emphasis in philosophy, though it is both *ratio* and *intellectus*, is upon the activity of *ratio*. And thinking in this sense is but one great function of the human mind, however inseparable it may be from the other functions.

4. BUBER AND 'DIALOGUE'

Science and philosophy, which are intellectual, are ways by which the more-than-intellectual total self-justifying life may be realized. Science and philosophy, however, are ways of life available only to a minority of people. But there is something else which, though it is involved in the total human life of the scientist or philosopher, is distinct from it, and does not require men to be either scientists or philosophers. This is described by Martin Buber as 'encounter'. Buber, in his strange, often irritatingly obscure, oracular and challenging way, has made encounter, or 'dialogue', the centre of his thought.

A typical form of 'dialogue' is, of course, that between human

[1] *Op. cit.*, p. 34.

beings who meet and know each other. But 'dialogue' is conceived by Buber in a much wider way. He speaks, for example, of an occasion 'when in a receptive hour of my personal life a man meets me about whom there is something, which I cannot grasp in any objective way at all, that "says something" to me. . . . It means, says something *to me*, addresses something to me, speaks something that enters my own life. It can be something about this man, for instance that he needs me. But it can also be something about myself. The man himself in his relation to me has nothing to do with what is said. He has no relation to me, he has indeed not noticed me at all. It is not he who says it to me, . . . but *it* says it'.[1]

It is always dangerous to try to express in one's own words exactly what Buber is saying: but this seems to me to be a convenient transition case between the complete dialogue of two human beings in an 'I and Thou' situation, and what he seems to call the 'dialogue' between non-human nature and a human person. He speaks somewhere of the 'I-Thou' relationship between a man and a tree; and in what follows the above quotation he writes: 'It by no means needs to be a man of whom I become aware. It can be an animal, a plant, a stone. No kind of appearance or event is fundamentally excluded from the series of the things through which from time to time something is said to me. Nothing can refuse to be the vessel for the Word. The limits of the possibility of dialogue are the limits of awareness.' [2] He develops at length the idea of 'the World' 'addressing' us. 'What occurs to me addresses me. In what occurs to me the world-happening addresses me. Only by sterilizing it, removing the seed of address from it, can I take what occurs to me as a part of the world-happening which does not refer to me'.[3] Buber speaks of the 'armour' which encases us, whose task is to ward off this 'address'. 'All our knowledge assures us, Be calm, everything happens as it must happen, but nothing is directed at you, you are not meant; it is just 'the World', you can experience it as you like, but whatever you make of it in yourself proceeds from you alone, nothing is required of you, you are not addressed, all is quiet.' [4]

The world 'addresses' us. The question arises, Who speaks? The question suggests a religious answer: but Buber has many

[1] *Between Man and Man*, p. 9 (Routledge, 1947). (Reprinted 1954.)
[2] *Op. cit.*, p. 10.   [3] Page 11.   [4] *Op. cit.*, p. 10.

comments to make upon the claim that it is God who speaks. His general view, if I understand it, is that it *is* God, but on the one hand mystically and not theologically conceived, and on the other hand existentially known and not the reproduction of an historical pattern of thought. 'It would not avail us to give for reply the word "God", if we do not give it out of that decisive hour of personal existence when we had to forget everything we imagined we knew of God, when we dared to keep nothing handed down or learned or self-contrived, no shred of knowledge, and were plunged into the night'. We can know only of 'him who gives us' the signs, through 'what we experience from time to time from the signs themselves'. 'If we name the speaker of this speech God, then it is always the God of a moment, a moment God'.[1] As, in understanding a poem, what we know of the poet is what we learn of him in the poem—his biography is of no value here—so 'out of the moment Gods there arises for us with a single identity the Lord of the voice, the One.'[2] This is the religion not of 'theophanies' but of 'conversations.' And as existential, it is a religion of risk. 'Religion as risk, which is ready to give itself up, is the nourishing stream of the arteries; as system, possessing, assured and assuring, religion which believes in religion is the veins' blood, which ceases to circulate. And if there is nothing that can so hide the face of our fellow-man as morality can, religion can hide from us as nothing else can the face of God. Principle there, dogma here, I appreciate the 'objective' compactness of dogma, but behind both there lies in wait the—profane or holy—war against the situation's power of dialogue, there lies in wait the 'once-for-all' which resists the unforeseeable moment. Dogma, even when its claim of origin remains uncontested, has become the most exalted form of invulnerability against revelation. Revelation will tolerate no perfect tense, but man with the arts of his craze for security props it up to perfectedness.'[3]

Both Plato and Pieper seem to stop somewhere short of the 'dialogue' of Buber. Philosophy and science in both the ancient and modern worlds are seeking to contemplate *objects*, not to achieve the dialogue of I and Thou. What the late Professor A. E. Taylor once called 'the initiative of the Eternal' has little or no place in the Hellenic outlook, as it certainly has in the

[1] *Op. cit.*, p. 15.   [2] *Op. it.*   [3] *Op. cit.*, p. 18.

Jewish-Christian outlook (and Buber is a Jew). The thought of Pieper, the Christian, is necessarily influenced by the Jewish-Christian conception of the revealing agency of God in history, and by a strong suggestion of the reception by human beings of the Divine Grace. But it is a Christian view very strongly tinctured with Hellenic *Theoria*. It never reaches the robust, if strange, sense of *dialogue*, mutual encounter, which is so strongly marked in Buber. Buber is the Jewish mystic who thinks existentially, emphasizing the dynamism of dialogue in a way which is unique. I have quoted from him at some length because his contribution seems to be a very necessary component in the total picture of what may be called the human being's 'coming to terms' with the world.

5. BEARINGS UPON RELIGION AND EDUCATION

The 'humanities' (including philosophy) in one way, science in other ways, the acceptance of encounter and dialogue with the world, all are modes of coming to terms with a mysterious existence. I hold that the growing power of coming to terms is just what being educated *is*. And it is one of the chief tasks of the teacher so to bring these things, as far as he can, to fruition in himself, that something of what he has come to learn may be communicated to those whom he teaches.

How far does all this imply a religious interpretation of life? It is impossible to answer this question adequately without spending a great deal of time in explaining what is meant by religion.[1]

All I can therefore say on the matter in hand must be confined to a few sentences.

I have been arguing that all our main educating enterprises should lead to a deeper sense of the mystery of being, sometimes dark, sometimes bright. What is taught and studied and learned must not only in itself come alive in the person, but must light up

[1] I have written elsewhere upon religion (e.g. in *Ways of Knowledge and Experience, op. cit.*, Part II), and may do so again; I do not propose in this limited volume either to discuss religion in detail or religious education. It would be unfair for a writer who believes without reservation in the importance of religion and who yet has the most radical doubts about what is called Christian orthodoxy and orthodox Christian education, to treat fairly this immensely important subject in other than a full way.

the sense of wonder and sense of mystery which is beyond it. Is this religious language? Not necessarily: it depends upon who speaks it. For myself, the sense of the ultimate through the immediate is religious in intent, and if expressed more fully would require religious language to convey it. For one whose sympathies are (as mine are) for the mystical and 'existential' interpretation of God, something after the manner of Buber, it is difficult if not impossible to imagine how the flooding sense of mystery can stop short of Otto's *mysterium tremendum et fascinans* [1] which for that writer is the essence of religion. That is all I can say here. It could not be said at all in the language of a purely secular humanism. That is, however, in no sense a denial of the right of the secular humanist to use *his* language.

What are these two chapters all about? We seem to have strayed a long way from the opening paragraphs, which spoke of mass conformity, the sense of futility, boredom, *acedia*, the dead-pan faces of young people who seem to have died before sixteen, the commercially exploited drugs of excitement. It seems an infinitely long way from this to the sense of wonder and mystery. It is and it is not. It is, because there often seems to be no trace of it in their lives. It is not, because again and again teachers with compassion and understanding have been able to discover by their insight the sparks of interest—in films, plays, books, history, in honest talk about love—which, gently fanned, grew to central fires. But teachers who can do this must be alive themselves. The 'elders and betters' of these young people have often failed because they themselves are dead or half-dead, or have never really been alive.

There is no pre-determination in all this. Buber says somewhere: 'In every hour the human race begins'. My plea in these chapters has been in effect that teachers, and educators of teachers, should above all set themselves to discover for themselves a sense of the depth of living, which is the attaining of education. In so doing they may be able to open up the way for others to life, in place of the living death, or the half-sleep of death, which seems at present the awful prospect for some of them.

[1] Otto, *The Idea of the Holy*, trans. J. W. Harvey (Oxford, 1924).

CHAPTER XIII

The Professional Education of Teachers

1. THE CENTRAL PURPOSE OF TEACHER EDUCATION; DESIDERATA AND LIMITATIONS

This chapter might be called, a little pedantically, 'Some principles of the practice of the professional education of school teachers'. It will deal mainly with the fundamental elements which (in my view) ought to be included in this professional education, with some of the ways in which these may be developed, and with some of the practical limitations under which teacher-educators must work. Most of what I have to say applies to the professional education of all teachers—whether graduates 'training' for one year after taking their degrees, or taking a four-year course concurrently with the degree (as at the University College of North Staffordshire), or non-graduates participating in the new three-year courses in Training Colleges. But the limitations of time in the one-year course for graduates obviously create their special problems; from time to time I shall refer to those specifically.

Everything that follows is to be read in intrinsic relation to the philosophy of education developed in this book. I have stressed, for instance, that the 'application of principles to practice' takes place always through the transforming medium of personality and personal action. From this it follows that the quality and vitality of the teachers of teachers will more than anything else determine the quality of the professional education which their students will receive. I shall not bore my readers by keeping on repeating this. But though a truism and even a platitude, it is indispensable to keep it in mind; it is all too easy to think of a topic like the present one merely in terms of syllabus, curriculum, timetable, organization. . . .

A dominating belief of this book, again, is that educative

teaching arises in a situation of interpersonal relations, in which the educated character and personality of the teacher is a major influencing force. Educative teaching takes place *within* this interpersonal situation; that does not mean that this gives the whole story; of course it does not. Teaching is a highly differentiated and complex function, requiring special knowledge of different kinds and many 'techniques'. On the other hand, unless all this knowledge and these techniques are (in the sense in which we may now be assumed to understand it) assimilated into the creative and individual hour to hour decisions of personal teaching, they have no meaning and may do more harm than good.

We have, then, to take the personal development of the student in certain directions as the centre and core of teacher education. 'Personal development' here does not imply any overwhelming concentration on the internal life of the student with constant emphasis on introspection—though introspection has its place. Personal development, reasonably conceived, takes place through interchange and dialogue with the world of things and people and ideas. This process can be conveniently itemized under a number of headings—so long as it is remembered that the process of growth, though very complex, is single, continuous and organic, so that—when it is healthy—every part of it affects every other part. When things go wrong in teacher education it is usually because some of the parts of it get unduly emphasized, or become separated from the others. At one time, for instance, the aim of teacher education is thought to be chiefly the training in skills and techniques of teaching, or in 'classroom management'; at another it is 'efficient subject teaching'; at another, understanding child psychology. . . . It would be equally a mistake to think that 'personality development' is the one and only thing that matters, or that this can take place in a vigorous way unless all the other important things are happening too. With these provisos, we may safely proceed to list some of the most important emphases. I shall give the headings first, later dealing with each in turn, some briefly, some more fully.

(*i*) We have argued throughout that the teacher must experience and come to terms with *values* at a deep level. (*ii*) He must, to the best of his ability, think philosophically about the nature of education and its setting. (*iii*) He must pay a new kind of attention to the subjects or areas of his teaching, trying to understand on the one hand 'the philosophy of the subject' and on the other hand to understand, both theoretically and practically, the methods and techniques of teaching it. (*iv*) He has to learn to meet and to understand children; in so doing he may learn a great deal about himself. (*v*) He must develop and enlarge his mind by beginning to explore new fields of knowledge, some of which contain information which he should have if he is to be properly equipped as a teacher. These include the history, system and organization of education, some understanding of the social background of the children he will teach, some knowledge of the psychology of children, their development, their physical and mental health. (This is, or should be, inseparably related to his contact with children, and his own increasing self-knowledge.) (*vi*) Over and above the 'techniques' of teaching—or interspersed with them—he has to learn, by experience, discussion and reflection, what the living personal situation of teaching can and should be. (*vii*) A part of this is learned in actual teaching practice—but this practical experience bears its best fruit only when it is integrally related to the whole of the rest of his professional education.

Looked at from one point of view, this is quite an impossible programme to carry out for the graduate who has only one year to spend. (In one respect at least graduates in England or elsewhere who spread their study of education over a number of years are more fortunate than those who have to get what they can out of a year.) It is 'impossible', that is to say, if one thinks of this year as a year of academic *achievement* in any way comparable to the academic achievement of a degree course, in which intensive study is possible over a number of years. Because it is often—by those of rigid 'academic' habits of mind—misconceived in this way, the 'training' year is frequently unfairly criticized as an academic 'let-down', as a superficial smattering to which it is beneath the dignity of university graduates to give serious attention. No doubt, if so conceived, it can be so. But in my view the assumption is a sheer blunder. What such a year can do, and ought to do, is to introduce and open up new fields of thought and experience and practice; everything should be planned and done with this in view. This is a 're-orientation' year. The graduate student comes to it with his specialized academic knowledge. He is confronted with the new practical challenge of becoming a teacher, for which his orthodox academic education has prepared him little; it may even have bent him in *wrong* directions. He has to make a new adjustment, with the whole of himself—not with his intellect only. He cannot possibly complete this adjustment in the short time of what is in fact much less than one year. In truth it is an adjustment which goes on taking place during a lifetime. Everything he receives and learns during the year, therefore, should as far as possible be a stimulating introduction to new ways of feeling and thinking and acting and to new fields of relevant knowledge, given and taken in such a way that the student will be intrigued and interested. Stirred up to have some idea of the 'size'—the depth and height and extent and implications—of his job, he should be moved to go on from where, in his 'education' years, he makes a mere beginning. The student who is given, and is willing to receive, this kind of an introductory professional educa- tion, will say (and does say) that his 'training' year is, in an important sense, a new beginning of his education. (If this does *not* happen, we shall hear the usual conventional—and complacent —clap-trap about a 'waste of time'). He quickly learns that the aim is not to turn him out as an 'efficient' teacher (for good teaching is only learned after considerable experience), but to prepare him to become an intelligent and perspicacious learner of a job seen in its magnitude and proportions.

There is an important corollary to all this. If a year's course for the graduate is only the beginning of an introduction to professional education, it ought to be recognized routine that teachers should receive 'in-service' leave from time to time to reflect upon and consider their job in the light of their riper experience. This at present is badly lacking. It is common knowledge that experienced teachers can gain enormously by the proper kind of 'refresher' courses.

With these ideas of re-orientation and adjustment in mind, how may the main aims of teacher education be implemented?

2. Learning Values

(*i*) The student must realize *values* in his own experience at as deep a level as he can. Values are learnt through experiencing them. It is without doubt helpful to hear about the important values in talks and lectures, before and after experience of them. But as values they can only be realized in personal lived experience. Much of this experience is, or should be, gained through the student's education before he arrives, and part of his new duty is to take stock of what he already has. But at this stage he also needs to experience freshly. He can do so in all sorts of ways— by exploring some new art or craft (alone or along with others in a group), by taking part in drama or music or poetry reading, by critical discussion of these (or of films, broadcasts, television programmes), by excursions or visits (including school visits), by club work. . . . He may learn much through contact with a tutor whose view of his teaching field is fresh to the student, or perhaps by informal contacts in the tutor's home. He may learn a lot by taking the chance to go off by himself to think.

But specially in this year new values can often be discovered through students' contacts with one another over their teaching experience in schools. Discussing perhaps a problem of discipline which has arisen during teaching practice ('What would *you* have done in the circumstances?'), different, perhaps sharply opposed, opinions will be expressed; individual personalities react in various ways; some are mortified by indiscipline, others are angry, others comparatively unruffled. These reactions, seen in one's contemporaries, bring out, modify and educate one's own; students can learn from each other as they may be unable to learn from someone in 'authority', and they learn quite as much through their own emotional—maybe strongly emotional—reactions as through their intellects. Or perhaps a student who has given an unsuccessful lesson tends to camouflage it before his tutor, or even himself. In a group, however, one of the members happens to be not so inhibited, and acknowledges or even proclaims publicly his failure. This to the others is impressive and important. They may then be emboldened to admit their own mistakes; and nothing is more educative than free honest discussion of the reasons for what went wrong. The weaker are encouraged to think (and feel) again. The sharing of failures, learning to be objective instead of covering up, can be the most rewarding of experiences. Students may learn entirely new and much more genuine values from sharing their experiences, either among themselves privately or under the guidance of a tutor who keeps his own authority in the background—and, it should be added, is equally ready to admit and to discuss his own mistakes in his dealings with them.

3. PHILOSOPHICAL THINKING

(*ii*) Not a great deal more needs to be said about this. Since most students (graduate or non-graduate) in England very unfortunately know no philosophy, a guiding course of lectures is indispensable, their purpose being to illustrate by example the ways of philosophical thinking, and to bring out the main questions relevant to education. But formal lectures, although necessary, are in themselves only a guide and a stimulus to thought, reading and discussion. Discussion, indeed, is the life-blood of philosophy; it can be stimulated and directed if necessary by pre-planned topics culled from contemporary writings in the press and elsewhere which have a general bearing on questions of education and which are in a broad way related to the lectures. Or it may be helped by the discussion of carefully chosen books. There are many different ways of achieving the same result, the guiding principles being that the students should feel the issues to be alive and relevant, that they should be encouraged to discuss them at a fundamental level, and that they should find their own personal answers (or, if questions cannot be answered easily, that they should be clearly put). The difficult task of assuring students that philosophy is not just one more 'subject' to be mugged up, that it is genuine thinking which is asked for, with questioning as important as answering, can to some extent be helped by ensuring that the examination questions are such as to encourage students to tackle them in their own individual independent ways. If an introduction to philosophy of education does no more than encourage a care for the use of language, and a watchful eye to scrutinize the tags and catchwords which so beset educational journalism and talk, it will at least have done some good—though, as we have seen, there is much more to it than that.

4. TECHNIQUES: GENERAL KNOWLEDGE: PROPER PROPORTIONS

(*iii*) I have already said something on the importance of thinking freshly about 'the philosophy of the subject'.[1] In addition

[1] Above, pp. 30–33.

to this there is much to be learnt about the methods and techniques of teaching a subject or area of study. The two things, of course, go together; one cannot, as I have suggested, teach mathematics or history in the right way if one does not understand the nature of what one is teaching; 'techniques' arise out of the structure of the subject; and its place in the curriculum is well judged only if one understands its nature. But techniques also depend on other things too, for example upon psychological understanding. Piaget and others have helped us to understand how important it is to relate, for instance, the teaching of mathematics to the image- and concept-forming stage of the child's development. Psychological knowledge of children's interests, or the ways in which they learn a foreign language, or to read, or to imagine a poem, knowledge which apprises the teacher of individual differences in children, which enlightens him about the ways in which emotional attitudes affect the capacity to learn . . . all this and much more is inseparably part of the knowledge of techniques and methods of teaching. As always, teaching experience is a challenge to questioning, questions are tentatively and in a general way answered by 'theory', which in turn modifies the teacher's discriminative apprehension, and in that way his practice. The gradual acquisition of teaching skills is contributed to by all sorts of factors; good tutorial work makes the student-teacher aware of them in a way which makes teaching an intelligent art.

(*iv*) The need to meet and understand children is implied in most of what has been already said. It will be referred to again under heading (*vi*) below.

(*v*) The 'educated teacher' does not deserve the name if he is not sufficiently well informed of the background knowledge of his profession or does not know where to find out more when and where needed. He must have, as has already been said, a foundation of psychological knowledge. This must, to some extent, be a systematic knowledge; the particular areas of information required for, say, the techniques of teaching English cannot be intelligently understood except in a context of general relevant psychological knowledge. The children who are being observed or taught are beings with a past and a future. They are now at a certain stage of development, and the teacher who is competent must know as much as is necessary of the stages of child development. They are growing: how do they grow healthily—in body and mind? What will help their growth without over-stimulating them? What do their capacities and interests generally tend to be at such-and-such age ranges? How does their intelligence and temperament and interest affect their learning? What do the psychologists mean by 'intelligence', 'temperament' and 'interest'? What does 'learning' mean, and what are the conditions of its happening in the best way? Again, children in school are under 'authority' and under 'discipline'. What are the psychological phenomena of being under authority? What are psychologically the best forms of authority? What are the psychological phenomena of being in authority? All these things (and many others like them) can be understood in two quite different ways, ways which are always and necessarily complementary. One way is the way of experiencing events of the classroom as they happen, and then ruminating upon them as experienced. The other way is the conceptual way, study of the books, hearing the scientific experts on child-development, learning, emotional structure, intelligence; . . . In both these ways, too, the teacher should have some knowledge of the social context and background of the children he teaches. Much of the particular knowledge can of course only be acquired through considerable experience of the group of children with which he is concerned. But the teacher should receive, during his professional course, some general foundational knowledge on which to build.

Some basic knowledge of the history of education and of educational ideas, and of the contemporary administrative structure of education, is obviously required. All this can be classed as 'information', but if it seems less immediately and obviously relevant to the work of teaching and educating than the other studies mentioned, it is still necessary for the teacher. It is hardly possible to conceive a responsible English teacher, for example, completely ignorant of the administrative system in which he works; he would be working blindly; he would not know what he was doing. He undoubtedly requires some general systematic knowledge of the structure of his own educational set-up. The same is true, in a rather less direct way, of the history of education. History is not, directly, of 'use'. But if we try to imagine an extreme case (which had an actual parallel in Nazi Germany) of a teacher who has simply no knowledge at all of the past history of education, who lives only in the present without background, we shall be bound to say that he too is equally blind and directionless.

Having acknowledged all this, however, it is important to remember the central aim and proportions of the course—particularly if we have the graduate one-year period in mind. There is, in fact, no time, in a 'year' of some eighteen academic weeks [1] to study everything equally. There has got to be selection and emphasis, and a principle of selection. I have argued that the central and fundamental purpose of professional education is what some would call an 'existential' one—a *personal* re-orientation of the student, a fresh assessment of himself and of his beliefs, of his relation to other people, a rethinking of the meaning of his subject, and the techniques of teaching it, the new beginnings of an approach to the understanding of children and to the immediate and more remote aims of education. It is an 'existential' approach in the sense that the emphasis is upon the student's discoveries through his own personal experiential life, his 'existence', through his thinking, feeling, deciding, acting, His discoveries are achieved in part, no doubt, by his learning *about* many things; but during this brief formative period it is that information and thinking which can be brought most directly to bear upon his personal orientation to the teaching and educating of children which is of the *first* importance.

If this principle is accepted (in addition to all the other important things mentioned), it will follow that the informative background knowledge of history and administrative structure should be regarded as subsidiary to the rest. Students should receive enough of it to realize its importance, to have a general idea of its proportions, and to be able to find their way about so that they can explore it at greater leisure (possibly in a later advanced course).

(*vi*) and (*vii*) I have left to the last—in this 'list'—the learning 'by experience, discussion and reflection, what the living personal situation of teaching can and should be'. It is absurd, of course, to divide things in this way; only the limitations of having to say things *seriatim* makes it necessary. For this personal learning of what teaching and education can be is necessarily integral with everything else that has been said. The remarks which follow

[1] In London, three terms of ten five-day weeks, less about twelve weeks' teaching practice.

are only glosses, or arbitrarily chosen illustrations of ways in which students may gain more intimate insight into what educative teaching and learning really are.

5. The Problem of Overcoming Stereotypes; Teaching and Art

One of the things which has to be overcome is domination of the 'stereotype' idea of the teacher. It is very difficult for the student beginning to teach not to think of himself as playing a rôle, or cutting a figure, or otherwise conforming himself to his idea of what a 'teacher' should look like and how a 'teacher' should act. This is not always made better by observing demonstration lessons (though of course a lot can be learned here). The student may watch, with justified admiration, the ways in which a master of the art deals with children and the teaching of a topic. Next time when he is on his own he tries to emulate the admired teacher. If he is a good actor he may be successful up to a point—and again I am not arguing that there is no value in observation and even some imitation. But it does not take him far; he is an insecure immature copyist. The teacher is himself, not another, and if playing the 'sedulous ape' teaches the beginner something, it is something which also has to be unlearned as he discovers his own 'style'. But it is just as likely that his attempts to copy the figure which he admires will break down; 'X can do it so easily; I can't'. When the principle of watching a good teacher at work is carried to the extreme of attempting to 'train' a teacher by regarding him as a sort of apprentice exclusively to one master (as is frequently advocated in current journalism and elsewhere), the very worst results can follow.

The domination of the stereotype-image is bad for a number of reasons. The student teacher is focusing his attention on the wrong thing—*himself* as acting a part worked out for him (at least to a considerable extent) by another. He should be thinking of the job, of what he is teaching, of the children as learning, of what is happening to and in them, rather than of his own success. Again, what he needs is *principled* understanding of the task in hand as it now presents itself, not a formula to be applied. If he can cast his mind back to the philosophy of teaching, he will realize that it is not himself-doing (or performing a rôle) which chiefly matters, but the imaginative understanding of the children's learning. The analogy of art is helpful here. 'Form' in art is not the application of a previously prepared ready-made pattern to something else, the matter or material. True æsthetic form is something which is unique and utterly individual to *this* work of art (e.g., this poem), which is discovered in its embodied reality and nowhere else. So a teacher errs if he thinks that a 'lesson' is something the shape of which can be finally fixed beforehand, and which is then 'taught' to the children who 'learn' it. Of course the teacher has to prepare his lessons (as the artist may ruminate long on what he is going to do), and of course he knows generally the sort of children he is going to teach and the conditions under which he will teach them (as the artist knows the material he is going to work with). Nevertheless what the good teacher is really doing by *his* imaginative art is to bring to birth new discovery in the children's minds and imaginations, and this never happens till the actual event in which they with their independence participate. This is what matters—not the teacher's successful carrying out of an act or even 'getting across' what *he* had in his mind before he started— important as that plan may be in its own place and time. Good teaching is the midwife of discovery.

The domination of another stereotype—of teaching as a *technique*—is also a danger. There are, of course, 'techniques', as we have said. But if techniques are conceived as practical formulæ to be put into operation, prescribed modes of procedure providing the answer beforehand as it were, there will be applied science but not genuine teaching. The same analogy can be applied as before. The artist possesses high technical skill, and has to learn it. But the artist best learns his techniques as and when he requires it, on the job, and in the service of his art. In his practice of art, his techniques are being used all the time, but they are servants and not master, subsidiary and not principal. They have to be learned and assimilated till they become second nature, subservient to the central artistic purpose. So with the good teacher.

It is, of course, easy to say all these things, and very difficult to do them. Saying them is of some value; but as always they have to be learnt in experience and action.

6. Developing Imaginative Sympathy for Children's Learning

The experience of the student teacher as a teacher is only beginning, and can ripen only with time. Nevertheless some things can be done during a year of professional education to increase the capacity for intelligent learning from experience and to help the imaginative understanding of the dynamics of teaching-learning: some have been mentioned. One great advantage of practice in art or craft, for example, is that it develops the sense of the importance of discovering the right thing to do *as one goes along*. This can be 'transferred' to the experience of teaching. Another advantage of beginning to learn a *new* art or craft during a professional course is that in coping with hitherto unexperienced difficulties one is in much the same position as the children being taught, who are learning new things. Experience and analysis of one's own difficulties, related to theirs, helps through actual experience the understanding of their learning. If the student's learning takes place within a group, he may learn, in many ways, through sharing and discussing the difficulties of others. If he has a marked preference for working alone, an examination of his own reactions may well help him to understand the child who appears solitary and who prefers to do things alone. (If he prefers to work in a group he may better help the children who have to do things in 'bunches'.) Another, more theoretical, way of helping the student to understand what 'being educated' means is to ask him to write a critical essay on his own education—and mis-education.

With much the same ends in view, a number of my colleagues in London have tried in various forms an experiment described by one of them [1] as follows:

'To bring home the reality of self observation I find it is useful to ask the students to make some detailed introspection in structured present situations. Throughout, the function of this is continually linked with the understanding of the child's problems, or predicament, and written descriptions can remain anonymous should the student wish. For example, when discussing intelligence I set them a problem such as the following to solve,

[1] Edna M. Oakeshott in the *Sociological Review Monograph*, No. 1, p. 56, 1958

which is designed to be sufficiently difficult to tax them to their extreme limits. 'There are twelve pennies, one of which is different in weight from the others. You are required to find which is the different penny and whether it is heavier or lighter than the others. You have scales available but you are allowed only three weighings.' I assure them that a solution is possible and that there is no trick in the question. I ask them to write an account of their thought processes, their feelings, tensions, etc. while tackling it. The insight gained is used to further the understanding of the experiences and possible effects on the child, of setting work that is too difficult for him—different effects on different children, attitudes to failure, frustration, and success, resultant self picture, etc. This leads on to the student's own early childhood memories, fears, anxieties, achievement of moral standards, winning and losing, the basis of character development.'

It can be seen that experiments of this kind, although they are concentrated on a moment of educational experience, go far beyond the moment, and raise many important questions of psychology and philosophy.

7. 'TEACHING PRACTICE'

It is for this reason that 'teaching practice' must be seen as an integral part of the whole professional course. This may seem obvious enough in the light of all that has been said; nevertheless it is easily possible to misconceive the function of teaching practice. It is easy to assume that it means nothing more than some practice in teaching, an initiation into the real thing, in which as far as possible the conditions of professional life are reproduced, but for a short period. Of course teaching practice *includes* this, with the reservation that this temporary experience can never exactly reproduce professional life—any more than 'trial marriage' could possibly reproduce the full conditions of married life. But 'teaching practice' is a great deal more than practice in teaching, much more, for example, than the practice a student may have before he starts his course. Teaching practice is indeed a practical experiment carried out in the light of a theory—or better, carried out in the light of everything else that goes on during the professional course. Not just practice, but a first attempt at personal embodiment in teaching of all that is being assimilated through the teacher's education.

It is for this reason that the main control and direction of it ought, so far as is practicable, to be in the hands of the tutor (or tutors) in charge of the student throughout the course. To say this is in no way to under-estimate the hospitality of the schools, nor to belittle the important part which the teacher in the school can play in helping the student to teach better. This is indeed an essential contribution—and for more than the reason that the tutor can only be in school for part of the time. But the teacher's part here is one of co-operation rather than of main direction. For this reason it is very important that there should be coming and going between the school and the Department or College as far as time will permit—the tutor being familiar with the school, its staff and its aims, and the teacher having a fair general idea of the dominating ideas of the professional year. But the teacher has, of course, his full job in school; his time and energy are limited; he has to guide the student as best he can, sometimes under difficult circumstances. The tutor, on the other hand, lives and works within the professional department, he has had to learn, slowly and perhaps painfully, the complex implications of his own unique function. He learns it mainly by absorption, by daily contact with his colleagues who are making their own, and varying, contributions to the same single end. It is by this kind of living together in a community that 'theory' and 'practice' become a part of single organism—and something of this unity can be realized in turn by the students.

(If these things are true, it will follow that the suggestion, sometimes made, that the 'prac..cal training' of the student should be left entirely to the teacher in school, must be rejected outright. If one wanted effectively to divide 'theory' from 'practice', this would be the way to do it.[1])

8. 'THE MATERIALISM OF THE CURRICULUM' AND EDUCATIVE LEARNING: CONCLUSION

I spoke earlier of what I called 'the materialism of the curriculum'—the deadening tendency to count up subjects 'done', to measure a teacher's success in terms of the amount of the syllabus covered for the examination. (To give an actual ver-

[1] There is, on the other hand, a possible case for some half-and-half (half school, half professional department) appointments.

batim quotation: 'In this school we don't teach what's not in the syllabus'.) In some schools there is a hard inertia of materialistic counting against which it is difficult for an intelligent young teacher to make headway, and which may dangerously discourage and perhaps disillusion him. It is all made worse by the vicious habit of second- and third-hand learning—memorizing answers ready worked out for the pupil in diagrams and textbooks, with no real mental enjoyment of anything real—whether it be science, or poetry, or history. This is a deep-seated evil; many of the students are victims of it themselves; all of them have been through the examination mill.

The evil is not only deep but widespread; obviously it cannot be cured easily or quickly—even if we optimistically assume that it is not a chronic disease. But some things may be done, even in a short professional year, to provide a little yeast which may in slow time help to leaven the lump.

Something may be gained if students are encouraged to reflect upon their own preparation for examinations and on the reasons for their own comparative success (or comparative failure). Did they succeed by officially approved meritriciousness, and if so, what do they now think of its effects on their own true education? Or did they fall short of success because this kind of cramming simply did not work for them? What was wrong? Or were they fortunate in receiving a more liberal education, but a bit disillusioned because it did not seem to fit the procrustean examination bed? Or did they find that their more liberal education made it easy to take examinations almost in their stride? Again, has this or that student discovered sadly that he was slower than other people, had to work laboriously for perhaps very moderate results? Whatever the case, the analysis of the reasons, particularly if carried out under the guidance of a good tutor, in company and in discussion with others, can prove not only to illuminate the individual experience, but to develop better understanding of bad and good education and the difficulties of children.

In these ways students may be led to think constructively and positively about the educative (as opposed to the 'materialistic') teaching of their own field and its relation to examination. Each discipline has its own order, and it is dangerous to generalize, unless after an extensive survey. But might it not be said that in a course of study leading to the G.C.E. at 'O' level the first two or three years might well be spent in free and enjoyable (though guided) exploration of the basic principles of a subject, leaving the details to be learned—perhaps with a good deal of hard grinding—which could at that later stage be cheerfully accepted? This, I am told, works well in Biology. Might it not be expected to apply, *mutatis mutandis*, in other fields? Is it not educationally self-evident that it is better for children to learn the 'discipline' of a subject through direct and genuine engagement with it rather than, as so often happens, being warned to conform to what they do not yet understand (and taught in this way may never come to understand at all), and to memorize it? To be able to repeat the 'correct' opinions about literature, to be able to reproduce the scientific textbook definitions and diagrams, to remember and to apply the mathematical formulæ and procedures—what does it profit a child if he gains all this and loses his soul—his native power of enthralled absorption in drama or poetry, in the ways in which nature, living and animate, 'works', in the fascinating logic of mathematics? The slavish way is not only depressive of natural intellectual and emotional vitality; it is a sin against children's integrity. Most of us would fiercely condemn the introduction of children to noxious drug-taking which in time destroys their human capacities. We do not always see that by certain ways of teaching we are forcing in children the deadly habit of what Plato calls 'the lie in the soul', and so maiming a natural capacity for integrity. Too often from the beginning of their secondary education they are taught to pretend to what they do not possess; if they can produce the right appearance of conformity to what is expected they can romp through.

The complex causes of this evil it would be impossible—and irrelevant—to discuss here. The question which is relevant for the teacher is whether bad methods—which seem to get children through their examinations—are necessary, or even expedient, to attain this result? Among other reasons, it is fear and insecurity which drives teachers to cling to the abstractions of syllabus-headings and textbooks. These have 'authority', and to conform to authority—and to the powerful authority of the examiners—seems to be the way of earning the title of 'efficient'. But is the way of fear the only way? There are good teachers, large numbers of them, who teach educatively, and whose 'results' are excellent.

Since even keen young teachers after first appointment easily fall prey to the cynicism of their elders, it is of great importance for students during their professional education to have a chance of looking into the relation between educative teaching and examination success.

I have tried in this concluding chapter to view the several parts of teacher education—theory of various kinds, practical teaching, knowledge of children, the development of the students' own experiences individual and social, the learning of techniques . . . in relation to one another and to the one central aim of that vital educative experience which is the other side of educative teaching. Once again (and for the last time) the imaginative and co-operative understanding of this complex aim—and not merely its intellectual formulation—is that which gives life to every part of the professional training period.

Index